Hawk's Ascension

S.J. Garl[...]

MAPLE KAKAPO PUBLISHING
Napier, New Zealand

Hawk's Ascension

Copyright 2016 by S.J GARLAND

All rights reserved. This book or any portion thereof may not be reproduced or used in any way whatsoever without written permission of the publisher except for brief quotations used in a book review.

All characters appearing in this work are fictitious.
Any resemblance to real persons, living or dead, is purely coincidental.

First Printing, 2016

ISBN 978-0-473-36046-7

Maple Kakapo
2069 Pakowhai Road,
Napier, New Zealand
4183

Candy Jane Jane, I still like the sound of that.

Chapter 1
Nathaniel

A handful of knaves. Looking down at my hand, I tried to subtly catch the eye of my whist partner across the table. Unfortunately, my young companion was trying to concentrate on the cards held tightly in his hand while still casting glances at a young courtesan walking toward the table. To add to his temptation, she was running a blue silk scarf through her fingers. With a groan, he slapped his cards on the table and used the back of his hand to wipe the sweat from his face. The stump of his right arm twitched for a couple of seconds before he let out a long breath.

"Control yourself, Master Hindly," the man, with glowing eyes and a knowing smile, to my right said to the young man. He jerked his head in my direction, "You're supposed to help the groom win a trick or two this evening."

Hindly swallowed hard making his Adam's apple bob in what looked like a painful manner. "Certainly, Master Lockheart." The boy's eyes focused on picking up his cards with one hand and spreading them out.

"We have all the time in the world," I murmured giving Lockheart and his partner on my left a long, hard look before reaching for my glass of Scotch. Hindly had done well in the past few months to regain his confidence after losing most of his arm, but he still had a long way to go before his nerves settled. "This is my evening to enjoy playing cards in Singapore's most lavish brothel."

Lockheart dismissed the comment with a smirk. Usually, I would partner a more experienced player and quickly divest my warehouse manager of some of his weekly wages. This evening, it looked as though he might regain some of those losses.

"You're right." I held up my glass and saluted. "To me and the future happiness of my bride." Just thinking of Charlotte Carstairs caused a burn in my lower belly that I had a hard time keeping under control. She was all wanton curves under her prim gowns, and the few embraces we had shared since our engagement became public were feverish and terribly unfulfilling.

The other men at the table saluted me with their glasses, and I cleared my throat by taking another drink.

"Where is Thistlewaite this evening? I thought he might be joining us," Lockheart asked as his partner set down a card to begin playing for the next trick.

"He's busy," I replied roughly and played my card.

"Is he coming to the ceremony tomorrow?" Lockheart asked as he played his card.

"I have no idea." I said, while studying Hindly's face as he concentrated so hard on the cards in his hand I thought they might catch fire. "He is my best man. One would think he might have the decency to show his face." I let out a long breath in surprise as Hindly laid down his card. The angels rejoice, we might win this hand. "Stop trying to distract me, Lockheart."

A slow grin appeared on the other man's face, and I frowned back in return. The rest of the hand finished in a frenzy of cards with Hindly slapping the table, letting out a loud whoop as he celebrated finally winning a trick.

Lockheart gave him a stern look. "You are not supposed to celebrate in whist."

Hindly grabbed his full glass of rum and tipped it toward Lockheart in a mock salute. "I don't care for the rules of your toffee-nosed game." He took a couple of large gulps before setting the glass back down on the table.

The courtesan used the break in the game to sit down on the arm of my chair. The woman continued to run the silk scarf through her fingers. Playing the game, I wrapped an arm around her waist and pulled her close, letting her jasmine perfume float around my senses. She was beautiful and young with large almond-shaped dark eyes, artfully lined in kohl. A loud squeak had me glancing across the table at Hindly as his face burned bright red.

The other two men at the table watched the rise and fall of the woman's breasts straining against the see-through fabric of her light gown.

Catching her eye as she looked down, I lightly traced my fingers through the scarf she was holding. "What is this for, love?"

It was the opening I knew she wanted. Licking her lips deliberately she lowered her voice enough to be sultry but not unheard by the rest of the men at the table. "I can use this to tie up your cock and balls and make you come without even touching your skin."

I felt my balls tighten at the thought of the erotic pleasure the courtesan offered. Smiling, I took the scarf and used one end to trace the top of the courtesan's gown where her breasts strained to be free. A choking sound from the far side of the table tore my attention away from the woman. Hindly looked as if he might have a fit.

I reached down and selected a couple of chips and pressed them into the woman's hand. I felt her breasts press into my shoulder, but I caught her hand before the woman could grab my lengthening cock through my linen trousers.

"Not me." I gave her a look of regret as I shook my head. "My young friend over there." She gazed toward Hindly who appeared as though all the blood had drained from his face. Knowing exactly where it had gone made me chuckle.

The courtesan stood and sauntered around the table and took an unresisting Hindly by his arm. She winked at me before steering the boy away.

"Damned generous of you," the man to my left remarked.

"I only want to see his face tomorrow morning." "I think it's time I let the cards fold for the night, gentlemen. See you in the morning." I pushed the chair away from the table. I ignored Lockheart's frown.

"We can find you another partner, Mr. Hawk or a game of faro?" He nodded toward the green felt-covered tables.

Scooping up the rest of my chips I said, "I cannot let you divest me of the remainder of these." I smiled pleasantly.

"You act as though you're already married." Lockheart shook his head and waved a couple of men to the table who had been watching the exchange.

I let the smile fall back into a grimace the moment I turned around. A cashier exchanged my markers for coins, and I left a tip for the young waitress at our table. With a final glance around the gaming hall, watching the rest of the sinners dressed as saints fondle the women and play cards, I turned and headed for the door.

Safely out on the step, I reached for my pipe and filled it with tobacco, lighting it as I strode through the Chinese Campong quarter of Singapore. The rainy season had ended, and the air was humid and stale without the trade winds to carry away the fetid climate of the swamp surrounding Singapore. It had been only a few months since the defeat of Captain Collaart, and his absurd quest for revenge against my father ended. Pulling a long breath through the pipe and letting the smoke fill my mouth I wanted nothing more than to forget everything except my wedding to Charlotte Carstairs tomorrow.

In the months since spotting my father on the deck of the ghost pirate ship, I had searched for any trace of the ship or my father. Hindly helped me send out dozens of letters to shipyards from Europe to the Americas requesting information on any ship built to the specifications I had seen. Blowing out another puff of smoke, I reached the drawbridge over the Singapore River, the gateway between the world of the Chinese merchants and the rest of Singapore. I took a moment to look out over the harbor.

Not many ships lingered this late in the season. The end of March saw most of the profitable shipping companies and trading houses counting their spoils. I tapped my pipe on the rail and let the ashes fall into the swirling current below.

The few replies I had received for information regarding the construction of the ghost ship had come back. No one had seen or built anything like the double hull construction and two tiers of gun decks I described.

Turning away from the view, I continued to the European Quarter on the far side of the river. Either there was a wall of silence going up around these particular builders, or they had no information. It was still my best idea for finding my father. What I was going to do with the information was another matter entirely.

The streets were mainly empty this time of the night with only a few men dressed in the military red of the British army patrolling the darkened streets. Raffles had requested more military aid and received it after the fallout of the ghost ship and Collaart threats, even though no one had spotted the mysterious pirate ship since Collaart's demise, which confirmed my dark secret: My father was the captain of the nefarious ghost.

I squeezed my eyes shut and recalled the memory from only a few months ago. The acrid smell of gunpowder faintly assaulted my nose as I conjured the image of the man saluting me through the spyglass. He was the very image of my father, and yet there was something in his manner that screamed doubts.

The gate to the front of the house pushed back easily, and I tried to bury the shadow of my father. More than anything I wanted to put the matter of the ghost ship and my father to rest before I started the rest of my life with Charlotte, and I'd be damned if I would wait any longer before making her mine.

Using my key, I unlocked the door and stepped through, making sure to remain quiet. Dutta, my houseboy, slept in the rear of the kitchen, and I didn't want to disturb him. Trudging up the stairs in the dark, I began to pull my cravat apart, happy to have the silk folds peel away from my sweaty skin. The house had felt curiously empty after Hindly had healed enough to take quarters down at the warehouse with the rest of the clerks.

Charlotte would be here by tomorrow evening. She was a force of nature, and I smiled in anticipation of her disrupting my life and especially invading my bed.

Throwing the cravat on the floor, I began to unbutton my shirt and felt some thing. I whirled around to face the threat behind me. The catch of a flint came from the corner of my room near a worn leather chair, and I watched the spark bring a candlewick to life. The glow illuminated the face of a woman around the same age as myself with large blue eyes and hair so blond it was almost white.

"Had I known I would be greeted with such a magnificent display, I would have undressed accordingly," Sarah Buck's voice purred from her perch, and she licked her lips salaciously.

"Christ's bones, woman, what are you doing here?" I fought the urge to rebutton the front of my shirt.

"Is that any way to greet your lover?" she asked, leaning forward to display her ample bosom.

"One afternoon in my bed does not make us lovers," I said with a frown. "I told you months ago I wasn't interested." With a critical eye, I examined her face and breasts, knowing she was not without charms underneath her muslin gown.

"Are you finished?" she asked testily and sat back in her chair.

"Are you?" I inquired while finishing with the buttons on my shirt. "I ask again, what are you doing here?"

She frowned, and Sarah Buck looked up at me from beneath thick lashes. Had she ever a need for money she might do well on the stage, I thought dispassionately.

"I am with child." Sarah Buck said the words with a determined note in her voice.

"What does that have to do with me?" I asked while turning to the pitcher of water Dutta had left for me. Splashing some water on my face, I washed away the worst of the sweat.

"The child is yours, Nathaniel," Sarah whispered.

I rubbed my face a towel before turning toward her. "I find that very hard to believe and very convenient for you, especially since several men have bragged about their enjoyment between your thighs recently." I made my words as crude as possible.

The blood drained from Sarah's face, and a small part of me wanted to sympathize with her.

"I will admit that when you didn't want to continue our relationship, I was forced to seek comfort in other men's arms," Sarah said in a steady voice. I admired her for at least being honest. "However, I am several months gone now, and you are the only man who could be the father."

"You seem to be forgetting you were married to Buck." I reminded her of my friend and her late husband.

She hesitated and waved a hand in the air in front of her face before answering. "Yes, well, Buck was never very constant with his affections." Sarah sat up straight and looked me in the eye. "The child is yours; will you do the right thing by me?"

My eyebrows shot up into my forehead, and I could feel astonishment welling up inside my guts as my jaw wanted to drop. "What exactly are you suggesting?"

"Marry me instead of Miss Carstairs." Sarah Buck's request met utter silence for a few moments.

Laughter bubbled up from deep in my chest, and I watched as Sarah Buck's face fell. After a minute, I was able to control my response. "I think we both know the answer to your request. Now, I suggest you leave and forget how you ever got in here in the first place."

"You cannot dismiss me." Sarah stood up and faced me. "I will tell Charlotte the truth."

"Your truth maybe, but you forget she already knows we shared a bed once." I put extra emphasis on the last word. For a minute, the darkness I kept under the surface of my civilized façade rose up, and I sneered at her. Pushed to a place I could never escape, I leaned over her until I knew my breath washed over her face and dared the fates to bring my life crumbling down. "Why don't you march over to her house right now and tell her."

For the first time since our discussion began, she looked uncertain and pulled away from me. "You would like it if I did. I can see it in your eyes."

I wrestled with my darker emotions and tried to appear collected. "Tell her or not, at this point I only seek the comfort of my bed. I have a long day ahead of me no matter what you choose." I waved a hand in dismissal.

"You two deserve each other." Sarah Buck walked to the door but paused for a moment on the threshold. "She might play the virgin with you, but she is no better than me. I have heard rumors of the many men she has had between her legs, and she is no saint."

"Get out." I snarled and watched with satisfaction as Sarah Buck took an alarmed step out of the room.

"I thought you ought to know the kind of woman you're taking to wife. At least, I'm honest about my little indiscretions and do not play you for a fool." She held her quivering chin high.

"No, you at least admitted your lovers to me before you proposed marriage. I wonder if Buck ever knew of the many men you had while you were married. I wonder if the marital yoke bound your tongue but lifted your skirts." I watched the insult hit home and didn't bother to hide my smile.

"You are a bastard," Sarah spat.

"Most days I wish I were." I shrugged and shook my head at her gasp of anger. She turned on her heel and stormed down the hall and into the darkness. I listened for the front door to open and close, but it never came. Instead, her slippers pattered on the floor to the back of the house. I would have to reprimand Dutta for not noticing Sarah Buck's invasion of my home.

Stripping out of my trousers and leaving them on the floor, I blew out the candle lit by Sarah earlier and crawled into bed naked. It did not take long for the sheets to become sticky with sweat as I stared up at the ceiling waiting for my eyes to adjust to the gloom.

Sarah Buck did not worry me much. Charlotte would not be pleased if Sarah Buck made her claims public, but there was nothing to be gained by it except condemnation for her actions. As a man, I was above such things. I would feel guilty about hurting Charlotte, however, and I wished I had not let my demons push the volatile woman into publicly revealing her supposed secret.

The rumors circulating about Charlotte were another matter. When I first set my eyes on her, I knew she had a history with my boyhood friend Bishop. The connection ended when Bishop suffered horrific injuries in a battle at sea with the Dutch. His extensive injuries led him to turn away from Charlotte, much to her grief.

I never asked Charlotte how intimate her relationship was with the other man. It was not unusual for couples who were committed to one another to give in to their physical needs before the man went out to sea. Hell, I had seen too many women pregnant while their lovers were away, not to know the truth.

Sighing and closing my eyes, I pushed the image of Bishop and Charlotte engaged in an erotic clinch out of my head. Instead, I replaced it with one of myself looking down into her bright eyes, lips swollen from my kisses. She was my light, the only thing keeping the darkness of all my secrets from pulling me down into hell. Without knowing it, her devotion during the past few months, despite her family problems, had shown me how to escape the mundane worries that now filled my days.

My work at the newly renamed Thistlewaite and Hawk Enterprises was going smoothly enough, and we profited from the Chinese Junk season. I tried to settle into life as a gentleman trader, but I still found London calling to me with greater frequency. My dark side called out to the hellish brothels of the British Empire's capital. My former life as a rakehell was the reason I dared Sarah Buck to tell Charlotte of her suspicions regarding the child's paternity.

Swallowing hard, I rubbed a hand over my eyes. Whatever happened, I knew I needed Charlotte to keep me from falling into a place I knew existed but did not want to venture. Bishop had died there, unable to wrest his soul from the demons haunting him. I had to do better for her.

Chapter 2
Charlotte

"Are you sure the second glass is wise, Miss?" The diminutive maid gave me a sideways glance over her shoulder as she straightened from inspecting the hem of my wedding gown.

"Penny, it's my wedding day, and if I want to sip champagne all morning, I shall do so," I replied before taking another gulp and setting the glass aside. I was relieved to see the clouds had burned away for the most part. Weddings needed sunny days.

"You're so lucky." Penny smiled brightly at me. "Mr. Hawk is such a gentleman."

"Yes, he is, thank you," I said, trying to keep my smile under control. The last few months had been a trial, and Nathaniel was my only saving grace. I had managed to put my father's trading company, Carstairs and Son, in the green and wrangled it back from the brink of collapse. Now, however, I could step back and be a wife. Enjoy all the carnal things Nathaniel's kisses had promised over the past few months.

A crash from below the stairs and raised masculine voices caught my attention. I pulled my silk robe tighter across the front of my chest and walked quickly to the door.

"Oh, Miss, what do you suppose is happening?" Penny gave me a nervous look and winced as something heavy fell to the floor shaking the windows in my room.

"I'm sure it's only a commotion for the wedding. Some workers must have mistakenly come here instead of setting up at Government House. I will go and speak to them." I tried to give her a reassuring smile before yanking open my door and rushing down the hall to the landing. Several coolies stood around in the front foyer. Addressing one, using my best voice of command, I asked. "You there, what is your business here? The reception is at Government House."

The man frowned up at me as if I had grown a second head. Thinking he did not speak English well, I repeated my question as I came down the stairs. He only shrugged and pointed to the back of the house. I could hear my father bellowing at someone in his office, and my heart sank.

Trying to preserve my modesty, I cinched my robe around my body again and ignored the rest of the dockworkers as I made my way to the back of the house. The door to my father's study was open, and I could hear a voice speaking in a cultured English accent.

"Mr. Carstairs, those who have accrued debts to us must pay them or suffer the consequences," the man said in an earnest tone meant to chastise small children.

"It's my daughter's wedding day; could you not come tomorrow?" My father sounded harassed as his voice cracked. "I do not understand."

"You're not the only one," I announced as I sailed confidently into the office. I tried to give my father a reassuring smile before turning my attention to his tormentor.

"To what debt are you referring, sir?" I asked as I halted beside my father's desk.

"The one Carstairs and Son owe to my conglomerate." The Chinese man answered succinctly diverting his attention from my sputtering father to me. "It should have been paid last night at midnight."

"Mr. Zheng Jing, I have not had the pleasure." I held out my hand and waited.

Zheng Jing rudely inspected the proffered greeting for longer than necessary before finally reaching out. He shook my hand with confidence before releasing the digits. "Miss Carstairs, the pleasure is mine. I do apologize for disturbing you this morning. However, debt waits for no man."

"I confess to being confused since I sent the pay packet to you two days ago." My mind went back two mornings previous when I handed the money to our man of business, Mr. Bigham. We were both jubilant over finishing the season with the skin on our backs.

Shaking his head as his eyes narrowed on my face, no doubt searching for any hint of a lie. "I am afraid the money never made it to me."

"There must be a mistake," I said confidently. Bigham had been running the warehouses for my father for years, both here and in Calcutta. There was no way he would neglect to deliver the money.

"Do you have the debt receipts?" Zheng Jing asked quietly.

"I'm sure my man of business has them filed away at the office," I said with a growing sense of unease. Why hadn't I asked to see them? Because I had been busy with the wedding, and I trusted Bigham implicitly.

Zheng Jing sighed. "There has been an error in communication, I think."

I nodded, hoping he would give me time to sort this mess out. Trying to glean the way of Zheng Jing's thoughts, I was momentarily distracted by my brother Freddie peering through the door to the study.

"As your father has reminded me, it is your wedding day. I will give you until noon tomorrow to sort out this wrinkle in your debt." He reached into an inside pocket of his gray morning suit and plucked out a card. "You will find me here." I took the card from his hand while he watched with an eagle eye. "Good luck today, Miss Carstairs."

I frowned at the neatly printed card and looked up at the last minute. "Thank you, Mr. Zheng Jing."

He merely nodded back at me before passing Freddie as he went out the door. I listened as his footsteps rang on the polished wooden floorboards. The front door shutting behind him made me exhale with relief.

My father slumped forward in his chair looking as if he had aged ten years in the space of a morning. "I thought we were out of debt," he whined.

"We are," I said with force. "The payment was sent two mornings ago." I glanced at the clock on the mantle. "I have to go and find Bigham. He can fix this mess."

Freddie cleared his throat, and I looked up at him. Staring past my face at the wall behind me, a feeling of dread inched up my spine.

"Do you have something to say, little brother?" I reminded him of his place in a way I knew he hated the most.

Swallowing hard, he let out a long breath. "You must let me explain before you get angry."

I shook my head and began advancing upon Freddie before I consciously realized I had moved away from my father's desk. I scanned the room for a weapon I could use to bludgeon information from my brother. I raised a finger and pointed it under his nose. "What have you done?" I demanded in a menacing voice. I was a foot shorter than Freddie, but he shrank back in horror.

"There was a card game, you see." His eyes flickered between father and me. "They cheated; Lavroche and I had the whole thing figured."

"What scheme has that spineless Frenchman got you involved in this time?" Unable to keep my control, my voice rang out shrilly, and I watched as Freddie winced.

"It was a sure thing," Freddie said lamely.

"For all that's holy, Freddie." I cursed and pushed on my brother's chest, losing the grip I had on my control. "There is never a sure thing; how many times have Father and I tried to explain this to you. How much did you lose?" I hoped the damage might not be as bad as I thought.

Freddie licked his lips. "I was doing well at first. I thought I could double our money and get the Monarch back. I know we need her."

"How much did you lose?" I asked again, not bothering to explain the Monarch was lost to us and if we wanted another ship, we would have to buy one.

"It's all gone." He shook his head and looked at the ground.

The breath left my body, and I sagged to the floor. Only minutes before I had been enjoying my first taste of success, looking forward to marrying a man I loved after years of heartbreak.

In a small voice I hardly recognized as my own I asked, "Why did Bigham give you the money?"

"He didn't want to at first." Freddie was silent for a minute. "I told him I wanted to prove I was ready to come back to work. He trusted me. I thought if I won more money you would see I was capable of running the company, and I would be a hero."

Bigham was a marvelous businessman, but he had a soft heart when it came to our family. He thought he was doing Freddie a favor by giving him some confidence.

"We can fix this, right?" Freddie said as I looked up at him.

"How do you suppose we get 20,000?" I asked as I gathered up the folds of my dressing gown and stood on shaking legs.

"There must be money in the bank somewhere?" Freddie asked hesitantly. I only shook my head. "We could sell another ship?" he asked hopefully.

"Freddie, even if we sold every last thing we owned down to the silver candlesticks, we couldn't pay Zheng Jing and his Chinese consortium, not to mention the debt we still owe to Thurlestone's in Calcutta."

"What of Mr. Hawk?" Freddie asked tentatively.

I looked at Freddie critically before wiping a hand over my brow. "What about Mr. Hawk?" I repeated his question.

"He has shares in Thistlewaite and Hawk as well as an inheritance from his father. Surely, he can spare some coin to help his bride's family?" Freddie looked as if he had come upon our salvation.

I unstopped the brandy bottle and took an unladylike swig from the decanter. "His shares are only worth something if he chooses to sell them, and I know for a fact he will not. As for any money his father may have left in his last will and testament, the details are outstanding; his father's creditors have finalized nothing."

"We are utterly ruined." My father lurched forward in his seat and cradled his head in his hands.

"Yes," I said as a calmness settled over me. Everything appeared clear now. All the clawing and fighting, late nights, Maggie Thistlewaite's death, it had all been for nothing. This was the way it was supposed to be, and nothing I could have done would have prevented this catastrophe. "I will meet with Zheng Jing tomorrow and try to negotiate through our debt. Once it becomes apparent to Thurlestone's, we cannot pay them, it's highly likely they will seek both your incarcerations in debtor's prison."

Freddie burst into tears while my father's shoulder shook with silent sobs. There was nothing further I could do for either of them. My brother had set them on this path, and now it was time for me to step away, begin my life. I only hoped to spare Bigham. Perhaps Nathaniel could take him on at Thistlewaite and Hawk.

"I hope the two of you can pull yourselves together for the rest of the day," I said with as much dignity as I could muster. "My wedding will probably be the last event this family celebrates together."

Walking past my brother, I suppressed the urge to slap his wet face until I saw my handprints appear on his cheeks. Rigid with fury, I caught sight of Penny, standing in the hallway, no doubt eavesdropping on our woes. She wore a shocked and frightened expression.

"Come, Penny, the morning grows late, and I have a wedding to attend." I swept by her and down the hall trying my best to wrap a calmness around my shoulders that I did not feel.

Chapter 3
Nathaniel

"Are you sure this is what you want?" My friend and mentor Cornelius Thistlewaite asked, for what I hoped would be the last time.

"I believe we have had this conversation," I coolly replied while straightening my cravat in front of a small mirror in the church vestry. My father's ruby cravat pin shone through the light silk folds and gave me some reassurance.

Cornelius shook his grizzled head like a frustrated lion and sat back in a chair while he watched me. "It has been such a trying time for you; first your father's death, then the fiasco with Collaart. I would hate to see you jump into something for the wrong reasons."

"Maggie's death sits heavily on all of us." I looked at Cornelius and dropped my hands. "She might have been your wife, but she was my cousin and the only family worth knowing, besides my father. I know I'm selfish by not waiting out the year of mourning for her…" I let my voice trail away.

"Have you heard from Masters recently?" Cornelius studied his hands lying loose in his lap.

I knew how hard it must be for Cornelius to ask after my best friend and Maggie's lover. "He sent a few letters back even before his arrival in Portsmouth," I said slowly, wishing him to hell and back. "Masters speaks of resigning his captaincy of the Valkyrie and taking a job on land."

"Her death has touched us all," Cornelius replied then looked away.

My cousin's death had plunged her husband and my best friend into the depths of grief. I tried not to think of her selfishness, but when I did, it did not bring anguish, only anger and resentment. I was determined to marry Charlotte. She was nothing like my cousin, despite Sarah Buck's insinuations. We would have a marriage different from the rest of the people I knew. One based on loyalty to one another. The darkness of the secret I held in regard to my father's supposed death called to me, but I thought of Charlotte and kept it at bay.

"What do you think your father would say today?" Cornelius looked up at me through dull blue eyes. "I have tried my best not to replace him." He shook his head. "No one could replace Sebastian Hawk, but I can at least guide you in the same manner."

A grim laugh forced its way past my pursed lips. "You have only to start an argument over nothing, and I will rise to the bait. You know I loved my father." I almost choked on my words as I thought of the man standing on the quarterdeck of the ghost ship. "But especially in later years, we never did anything so well as argue."

"He wanted what was best for you, Nathaniel." Cornelius forced a smile to his lips. "Old Seb spoke of you often, expressing his disappointment when you quit the sea."

Shrugging off thoughts of my father and my demons, I walked to the door leading out to the front of the church. "An old argument and one we need not indulge in today. I'm getting married, by hook or by crook." I pulled the church door open with more force than necessary and scanned the gathered crowd. People had already taken their places in the pews. Most sat and chatted with their neighbors while the ladies waved delicate fans in an attempt to stir a breeze.

I smiled and nodded to Sir Stamford Raffles who, along with his wife Sophia and their surviving daughter Ella, had taken seats in the front pew of the groom's side. It was only appropriate since they volunteered to hold the reception at Government House; Raffles claimed the planning of the wedding had brought out some of Sophia's old spirit.

Cornelius followed me out of the room, and we made our way to the front of the church. The priest was busy at the back of the church, speaking to several guests. I took several long deep breaths and did my best to remain calm. The flutter I felt in my stomach was incomprehensible. I had sailed most of the sea with my father, battled pirates and the Empire's enemies, played cards against some of the most nefarious individuals to frequent gaming hells, and then slept with their wives and mistresses. Waiting for my bride should have been easy. Unfortunately, as the seconds ticked away, I found it increasingly harder to keep control over my spiraling nerves.

Guests began to rush to their seats, and a hush descended on the church. I stopped breathing when I spied Charlotte, walking slowly down the middle of the aisle, on the arm of her father. A long veil, weighted down with shining seed pearls, draped across her head, obscuring her face. Her white dress was the latest fashion, edged with lace and more seed pearls. Knowing this vision was all for me, I grinned. I would never admit to anyone how nervous I had become.

As father and daughter stood in front of me, I waited as Mr. Carstairs lifted the veil from his daughter's face. He kissed both of her cheeks and placed her warm hand on mine. She looked up at me with so much warmth I wanted to believe it was love. I vowed I would believe it was love as we both turned to the priest waiting for the ceremony to begin.

I hardly knew what to say as the priest had us repeat our vows, and I placed a gold ring upon her finger. We turned as one toward one another, and the priest gave his permission for us to kiss. In a daze, I captured Charlotte's face in my hands and leaned down, never closing my eyes once. I pressed my lips to hers and felt the quiver of anticipation on her lips.

She tasted of honey and spring rain, salvation, and hope. Vaguely aware of the guests clapping and cheering behind me, I lifted my lips and smiled at my new bride before clasping one of her hands. We faced our guests, and triumph soared through me. There were so many things that became tarnished in my life. I would never let Charlotte be one of them. To me, she would always be pure and perfect.

I grasped Charlotte's hand and pulled her down the aisle, barely nodding at the guests who stood to watch. We exited the church, and I swept Charlotte through the gardens to the road where an open landau carriage awaited us, decorated with ribbons and furbelows.

Charlotte gasped. "Where in the world did you find this?" The driver opened the door, and I helped her to the front seat.

"I didn't," I replied with a grin as I settled my coattails on the seat facing her. "Raffles dug it out from somewhere." The heat from the unrelenting sun was already burning through my morning suit.

"He and Sophia have been good to us." Sadness tinged Charlotte's words. "You have been good to me," she added a weak smile on her face and a tear slipping from the corner of her eye.

Leaning forward, I cupped Charlotte's face in my hands and brushed the lingering tear away with my lips. "No tears: Today is for our happiness."

"I wanted this day to be perfect." Her voice trailed off as her eyes closed. The driver cracked the whip over the horse's rumps, and we jolted into motion. The movement unsettled Charlotte, and we bumped heads. She looked at me for a second before bursting into laughter.

"You see, it can still be perfect with a few bumps along the way." I released her face and sat back. "Tell me what's bothering you; after all, your problems are now my problems."

Charlotte stared out at the passing landscape as we turned up Government Hill, the horses straining against the leather straps as we climbed. She stared back at me. "I cannot tell you." When I made a move in protest, she held out her hand and took mine. The silk and lace of her gloves burned into my skin, and I wanted nothing more than to pull them off with my teeth. "I will, but I want us to have this moment, we are starting a lifetime together."

Shifting, to make room for her on my bench, I carefully lifted her and placed her at my side. I kissed her eyes, nose, and finally, her mouth. "I will give you this wedding present, but tonight you will give me your worries. From now on, you must share everything that goes on inside that beautiful mind of yours."

Charlotte burrowed further into my side. "I was rather hoping we wouldn't be doing much talking this evening."

"Minx," I said under my breath as we passed the military barracks. The sentinels on guard duty watched, and I gave them a wave.

I looked on as Charlotte tried to gain control of her feelings. Whatever was bothering her must have happened in the interval since I visited with her yesterday afternoon. Frowning, I let several possibilities run through my mind and discarded them. There was no point in dwelling on what was bothering her since she had put it from her mind.

Minutes later, I helped Charlotte out of the carriage, and Raffles' servants approached to serve us champagne and refreshments while we waited for the rest of the guests to make their way up the hill.

The garden around the bungalow was a work of art. I knew Raffles spent hours out here in the heat and humidity, planting newly discovered species of flowers and making records for the Royal Geographic Society. As I watched, servers prepared to serve the arriving guests; it looked as if Sophia and Charlotte had thought of everything.

Taking Charlotte's hand, I led her over to the edge of the hill, and we stood in silence for a moment, gazing at Singapore below. It had grown in the last few months since I'd been here, and a year from now it might be unrecognizable. Raffles and his nemesis, Major General Farquhar, had definite plans for the newly acquired East India Company port.

"Will we always live here?" Charlotte asked, squinting against the sun. I looked down and watched a bead of sweat disappear down the back of her gown. How I longed to be that trailing moisture as it ventured down the slide of her shoulders and down the curve of her spine.

"I don't know," I said lifting a tendril of her hair to rub between my thumb and forefinger. "Where would you like to live?"

She turned to me. "We could go home," she said, watching my expression.

"Calcutta?" I asked with a bit more force than needed. I was surprised by her suggestion; I hated the city I had grown up in before my father took me aboard his ship to learn the trade of sailing.

Charlotte's brow wrinkled, and she laughed at my response. "Not Calcutta." She sighed and looked at me as if I should know better. "I mean London. I would like to go home, to our country."

"You have never been there, and I am not sure the weather would suit you at all, my dear. One rainy, cold summer would have you flat on your back sick with an ague," I said in a matter-of-fact tone. She already knew I loved London and had not been prepared for my sojourn in Singapore to last any longer than a few months.

"Beast," she said and stood up on her toes to press a kiss to my mouth.

Our lips fused. The arrival of our first guests distracted me.

"Duty calls, my dear, but don't worry. I will finish this later tonight," I said holding my arm out for her hand.

"I will hold you to it," she said as she turned and smiled for the new arrivals.

"Sophia," Charlotte called as she released my sleeve and reached out for the other woman's hands. The use of her Christian name spoke of the intimacy between them. "We cannot thank you enough. It's even better than I imagined."

I turned to greet Raffles as his wife's face lit up in delight. "Sir, thank you for letting us use your house."

"Anything for you, my boy." Raffles beamed with delight and gave me a cuff on the shoulder. "I only wish your father were here to say a few words." His brow wrinkled. "For a man who toiled as a ship captain, he often knew just the right thing to say."

"It's from all the time he spent alone in his cabin, sailing the seas. I expect he had gathered up treatises on many different subjects to keep himself occupied." I watched Raffles mull over my comment.

"You're right, of course. Sailing for the East India Company is a lonely business." He opened his mouth to say more but quickly closed it with a click.

Sophia grabbed her husband's arm and pulled him away. "We need to let them greet the other guests. Besides, I think Ella should lie down for a bit; she looks rather peaky."

Raffles grumbled at his wife as she led him away. Mr. Carstairs and Charlotte's brother, Frederick, took the place of Raffles and his wife. The latter glanced at me several times and looked as if he was ready to run from the devil. I knew there was little love between the siblings; Frederick's constant drug use and shirking of his duties at Carstairs and Son had made Charlotte's life much more complicated than it should have been for a girl of her station.

"Congratulations." Mr. Carstairs' mouth formed a smile, but it did not reach his eyes as he stuck a hand out. "May you have many happy years ahead of you." He choked on the last words.

Ignoring the other man's distress, I had not realized he would be so upset by his daughter's marriage.

I took the other man's hand in a firm grip, "I will take good care of her, sir, and she will only be a few streets away." I tried to reassure the other man, but my words appeared to make him more agitated.

"Of course, Mr. Hawk." Mr. Carstairs gave me a penetrating look before turning his attention to Charlotte.

There was no time to consider the other man's actions, as Frederick Carstairs stepped into his place. He held out his shaky hand. Annoyance roiled up inside me, and I wondered how high on opium Frederick Carstairs was. I also wondered, with some irritation, why he couldn't have sobered up for just one morning.

With a nod, I accepted the other man's hand. "We are brothers now," I said firmly.

Frederick Carstairs swallowed hard. "I always wanted a brother." He glanced at Charlotte for a second before turning his attention back to me. "Not that, as a boy, I did not enjoy tormenting my sister."

I did my best to refrain from commenting on how his current behavior affected his sister and how she worried about his health.

Redcoats caught my eye, and I watched as Major General Farquhar made his way through the crowd with two armed guards at his back. The regimental honors on his chest reflected sunlight while whispers from others broke out. He walked with singular determination toward me.

Frederick Carstairs strained his neck to discover what had riveted my interest. Out of the corner of my eye, I noticed the color had drained from his face. His jaw worked silently. Beside me, I felt Charlotte stiffen, and I reached for her hand, giving it a reassuring squeeze.

"Major General Farquhar," I said, addressing the other man by his formal title. "A pleasure to see you this morning. Have you come to congratulate us on our wedding?" I asked as pleasantly as possible.

"Congratulations," the other man said perfunctorily. "Though I hardly think my presence is a pleasure." He looked over his shoulder, and I wondered if Raffles was standing there. "We both know you are a Raffles man, as was your father."

"We might have still been friendly had you not tried to have me kidnapped and handed over to His Majesty's enemies," I said curtly, trying not to betray my contempt. "There are some things even a gentleman cannot forgive."

Major General Farquhar raked me with an appraising gaze. "Are you a gentleman now?" He turned his attention to Frederick and Mr. Carstairs while reaching into an inner pocket.

"This is my wedding day," I said tightly, trying to rein in my temper. Charlotte lightly pressed her fingers into mine, and I decided to focus on the small movement. "State your business and leave."

Farquhar held out a sheaf of papers. Frederick Carstairs let out a little moan. Glancing at his face, I worried he might collapse. Mr. Carstairs grabbed his son's arm in a grip hard enough for his knuckles to turn white. Farquhar cleared his throat.

"You have been summoned to Calcutta by Lord Hastings." Farquhar held out the thick sheets of paper.

Reluctantly, I held out my hand to receive them.

"What is the meaning of this?" Raffles barreled to my side blustering with anger. "Are you up to something, you scoundrel?"

"Not at all," Farquhar replied determinedly. "I have merely carried out my orders. It appears there are some serious questions over Sebastian Hawk's behavior."

Ignoring the papers in my hand, I addressed Farquhar. "Too bad my father is dead. I do not see how I can answer any questions in regard to my father. As you and everyone else knows, we were hardly on speaking terms." The image of the man standing on the ghost ship floated before my eyes, and I blinked several times to focus on Farquhar.

"There are some at the East India Company who believe the apple might not have fallen far from the tree." Farquhar sighed in mock despair.

"This whole episode is unconscionable." Raffles blustered and planted himself in front of Farquhar. "You cannot simply come into a private event and accost the groom on his wedding day. What do you have planned in Calcutta?"

"We are standing at Government House. It might be your private residence, but it is still East India Company property." Farquhar glared at his nemesis. "Enjoy the rest of your day." He nodded at me and turned on his heel.

My eyes narrowed as I watched the other man ignore the silent crowd as he left the reception, his two guards at his back.

Chapter 4
Charlotte

Raffles continued to sputter and call out to Farquhar long after the other man had disappeared through the crowd. Guests shifted their gaze with questioning eyes toward us, and I held my chin up. After the events of this morning, I felt like the whole world was falling apart, but I would not give into my fears.

I watched as Nathaniel unfolded the slightly crushed packet of papers in his hand. His eyes read over the scripted text quickly. My gaze shifted to my father who appeared as though he had received a stay of execution. There was no need for us to speak. We both erroneously believed Zheng Jing had somehow managed to gain the patronage of Farquhar and not get arrested.

Placing a hand lightly on Nathaniel's arm I cleared my throat. "What does it say?"

Nathaniel waited a moment before answering. Staring directly into my eyes, I felt the full weight of his punishing blue gaze. "It is as Farquhar has said. I am to depart as soon as convenient for Calcutta, where a panel will ask questions concerning my father's loyalty." As he said the words, I thought I saw a flicker of fear in his eyes. It was gone before it had a chance to take hold.

"The company has no right to ask for your presence." Raffles drew up to his full height, which was not much more than my own. "You are a private citizen."

Shaking his head and refolding the packet, Nathaniel replied, "I am a private citizen who lives and works in an exclusive East India Company port. There is no way I can deny the summons without putting Thistlewaite and Hawk in jeopardy. Everyone knows how much power they have."

Cornelius Thistlewaite joined our small gathering, and I watched as the two men exchanged a silent communication.

"We have only just married." I tried to smile as I said the next words. "Surely, they will not expect you to leave right away?" If Nathaniel left, I might have a chance to sort out the debt problem with Zheng Jing. He might never need to know about the Chinese syndicate's threats.

Turning his attention back to me, Nathaniel shoved the packet back into his coat. "None of this has to do with my father or me. It is simply a way for Farquhar to prod Raffles where he knows it hurts. There is no danger in my going to Calcutta. We will have the rest of our lives together." He swooped down and gave me a spine-tingling kiss. My breath came in sharp, heavy gasps as he lifted his head to smile. For once I thought one lifetime with this man might not be enough.

He gave me a lopsided smile. "Why don't you go and mingle with our guests. It would be a blasted shame if Farquhar knew he ruined the day for us."

"You're right, of course." I sighed and stepped away from him.

"I hope you will say that often in the future." Nathaniel let a grin spread across his face before resuming his expressionless mask and facing Raffles and Cornelius Thistlewaite.

"Come, Father." I grabbed his arm and forcefully led him away from the other men watching as Freddie trailed behind us. "Let us reassure the rabble there has been no blood spilled this afternoon."

Reaching out a shaking hand, my father snatched a glass of dark liquid from a passing server dressed in a white uniform and turban. He clumsily brought it to his lips and drank it down in one gulp.

"When I saw the guards with Farquhar," he breathed rapidly as he stared at me with unseeing eyes, "I thought the bastard had come for us." He choked on the last words.

"There is no need to worry." I tightened my smile, knowing the words were meaningless. "Farquhar has business with Nathaniel." I couldn't think of anything else to say. "Come, we must speak with the rest of the guests and do the pretty for them."

Father jerked his arm out of my grip and spun around. He raised a thick finger and pointed the digit under Freddie's nose and said, "This is your doing. You have ruined me, and I will never forgive you." Heaving at the emotional turmoil swirling inside him, Father tugged on the jacket of his blue morning suit and stalked away. As he approached an older group of men, I watched for a minute as they took their turns congratulating my father on my good fortune.

"I do not see why this is all my fault," Freddie whined.

Staring at him, my mouth worked, but no words formed on my tongue.

"He is the one who did not insure the Navarch. Had she been insured properly, we never would have lost all that money." Freddie petulantly let his bottom lip stick out.

"Grow up." I finally found something to say. My brother stared at me in astonishment. "Father made a choice. One that might have paid off very well had the ghost pirate ship not chosen one of our vessels to raid and sink." I pulled on Freddie's arm until he moved with me farther away from a group of ladies I knew to be terrible gossips. "You gambled away our salvation with the roll of the damned dice. There is no comparison."

"I could have saved us." Freddie pointed out stubbornly.

"I saved us, and if you cannot see it, then I do not have time for this argument or you." Sniffing, I stepped around him, only to be halted by his hand on my arm.

"Your new husband can still pay the debt," Freddie said with hope in his voice.

"How do you suppose he will pay the debt?" I asked, stepping up to Freddie, crowding his space. "As you heard, he is off to Calcutta to meet with Lord Hastings. He hasn't time to sort out his new bride's family affairs." Rage built inside me, and I had to blink back scalding tears. "You believe everyone else can solve your problems for you, Freddie, but you have ruined us this time." Swallowing past the lump in my throat, I said, "Do not meddle in business affairs again. Do not put one foot in the offices of Carstairs and Son."

Spotting our man of business, Mr. Bigham, speaking with another gentleman, I ignored my brother's gaping expression and walked away. I thought perhaps I might forgive him in time, but the enormity of what he had done rested on my shoulders now that the wedding was over.

"Mr. Bigham." I greeted the man who had tirelessly worked with me over the past several months. He smiled as he acknowledged me and disengaged from the man he was conversing with. His mannerisms revealed he had no idea of the catastrophe that had befallen my family and the business.

"Congratulations on your wedding." Bigham's gaze traveled over my features, and I knew he saw the strain I had been trying to hide from everyone all morning. Misinterpreting its cause, he continued, "Do not worry about the Major General and the East India Company. They have chosen an opponent with claws if they seek to bring Mr. Hawk down."

"As you say." I took a place on one side of Bigham and surveyed the rest of the guests. People were mingling and enjoying the food and drink the servers brought around. The day was becoming uncomfortably warm in the sun, and some of the ladies rested in lawn chairs under an awning. "Why did you let my brother talk you into giving him the money?" I decided it was best to get to the heart of the matter. Bigham would appreciate it in the end.

Lifting his eyes from my face, I watched as Bigham found the target of his growing annoyance. Freddie stood off to one side speaking to a familiar woman wearing a lilac dress. A brief feeling of irritation swept through me as I watched Sarah Buck laugh up into my brother's face. I wondered if they knew each other from previous social gatherings. Impossible, my brother was hardly fit company for the coolies and tars working the docks most days.

"He told you," Bigham said without any attempt at subterfuge. "I thought it would be a real responsibility for him. Get him back to his old self." He continued to frown at my brother as though thinking of something important.

"He hasn't given you the debt receipts," I stated, knowing what was going through Bigham's head.

Bigham swung his face toward mine and his intelligent brown eyes pierced mine. "How did you know?"

"Zheng Jing came by early this morning with his thugs to tell us there was no payment." I couldn't look Bigham in the eye as I said the rest. "Frederick admitted later he had lost the money on a gamble, trying to double it."

Silence greeted my announcement, but I could feel the rage and anger coming from the man next to me. Finally, Bigham spoke. "I will snap his damned head off."

"Not here, not now," I said, trying to keep my emotions under control. "The gossips do not need any more grist for the mill."

"They will soon have it." Bigham shook his head. "Do not trifle with Zheng Jing. He is dangerous. I told your father that when he went to beg for the loan. He will give no quarter."

"He has asked to see me tomorrow afternoon." I nodded as two older ladies paraded in front of us. "He will want something from me." I finally admitted the thought plaguing me since his departure this morning. "I know he's dangerous, but I may have no choice."

"You cannot possibly think to go there alone." Bigham faced me, his larger frame blocking out the sun. "Zheng Jing is a bloody pirate for all his business airs. They say he's the leader of the Brotherhood."

"I listen to the gossip, too," I said with exasperation, thinking of the Chinese secret society half of Singapore revered and the other half feared. "Debts once accrued must be paid, even if a foolish boy lost the money."

"Send Frederick for pity's sake. Let Zheng Jing take it out of his unworthy hide." Bigham's hand clenched, and I wondered if he was thinking of throttling my younger brother.

"What would that serve? I'm the only one who can deal with this mess." I shook my head.

"Mr. Hawk could shoulder the burden. He's your husband, now" Bigham said, as I looked over to where Nathaniel was speaking fervently with Cornelius Thistlewaite.

"He has enough to deal with." Taking a deep breath, I tried to feel like a fresh, new bride. "Besides, he must leave for Calcutta immediately. Once he is away from Singapore, there will be nothing he can do but worry about what's happening. I would not do that to him."

"I will go with you." Bigham rubbed a hand over his face before pushing the sweat from his forehead into his thick dark hair. "No matter the outcome, we will face this together. It's my fault."

Before I could respond, Sophia Raffles came forward with her arms outstretched. There would be a time of reckoning, but for now, I had a role to play.

Chapter 5
Nathaniel

"I will be on the packet tomorrow morning." I watched my companions carefully as I said the next words. "Hindly, I will need you to fetch the necessary travel documents from my office and meet me at the wharf." Turning to Cornelius, I raised one eyebrow. "Since you did very well running the business before I wormed my way in, I assume you're more than capable for the next few weeks."

"You did not worm your way in, as you say it," Cornelius said reassuringly. "Shares were bought fair and square. Besides, over the last few months, you have shown your worth many times over."

"Not to worry sir, I will have everything you need organized," Hindly interrupted.

"Do not think to spend any more time at Rejā. No Josei. No matter how beautiful the ladies are with their scarves, I shall hear of it," I snickered.

"Yes, sir." Hindly bobbed his head, and I could see a dark stain growing on his cheeks before he hurried away. I knew he had been frequenting the brothel we visited on the night before my wedding.

"You took the lad to Rejā? No Josei?" Cornelius watched Hindly's retreat. "I'm surprised the boy can still blush."

"For drinks and cards last night. You should have come along." I turned my attention to my best man. "It would have been good for you to get out of the house."

Cornelius lowered his voice. "I heard there is a special menu at Rejā No Josei. There is a particular shipowner of the aristocracy who enjoys number 51." Cornelius tilted his head slightly, and I caught his subtle glance toward Lord Meacham, who was currently speaking to an older woman who was not his wife while spilling his drink liberally down his sleeve.

"I have never indulged in the special menu," I said stiffly.

Cornelius studied my expression and sighed. "You had a sense of humor before you married."

"Perhaps being summoned by the mighty East India Company has changed my temperament for the moment," I spit out. The last rays of sun started to fade. It was time for me to collect my bride and make the best of our night together. "Would you watch out for Charlotte? I know you have a problem with her. One you will not speak to me about, but it would be a relief to know someone with half a brain was watching over her." Frederick Carstairs had left much earlier. Scanning the crowd, I could not find Mr. Carstairs, but I was sure he was doing his best to drink the port dry.

Cornelius said, "I will make sure she doesn't get into any trouble while you're in Calcutta."

"Thank you." I slapped him on the back as I saw Charlotte trying to disengage from a conversation with Lady Meacham. "You will excuse me? I have a few things I need to take care of before I leave Singapore tomorrow."

"Be my guest." Cornelius reached out with his big paw and tugged on my sleeve. "Be wary of the East India Company's motives while you're in Calcutta. They may only be glorified administrative clerks, but they will stab you in the back with their quills and feel no remorse."

"You've been listening to Raffles," I said trying to keep the mood light.

"Lord Hastings may be on the way out if we believe rumors, but like a drowning sailor, he will take others with him. Use caution." Cornelius let go of my sleeve.

"Duly noted. As I said before, I will send updates, but I want to be back for the little trading season. I have some ideas on how to boost the profits from the Bugis traders." I looked back to where Charlotte still stood speaking with Lady Meacham.

Cornelius said nothing as I stepped away, clearing a path in the crowd toward my new wife. My few acquaintances tried to catch my attention, but I focused on a singular purpose: Escape with Charlotte and have her writhing, naked underneath me as soon as possible.

Laying a hand on Charlotte's neck, I felt her stiffen under my touch until she recognized my voice. "Lady Meacham, thank you again for spending the afternoon with us. The hour grows late, however, and I think it is time for me to take my wife to her new home."

"Mr. Hawk, Lord Meacham and I are delighted you decided to settle down here in Singapore. We were speaking of your father recently. He and Lord Meacham were close once. The East India Company is demanding your presence in Calcutta! Well, how will you bear it?"

"I assure you, my lady. Those are my sentiments exactly." With my free hand, I reached out and took the woman's pudgy, sweaty fingers and gave the ends a firm kiss before releasing her. "A good evening to you, Lady Meacham."

Lady Meacham merely stared up at me with a beaming smile as I steered Charlotte away from the old gossip.

We rushed through the dwindling guests and with a final nod to our host and hostess, I rushed Charlotte toward the drive leading up to the house. "Do you mind walking? It's not very far, or should I fetch the landau?" I asked, thinking of Charlotte's comfort.

"No, I would rather walk." Charlotte rubbed at her neck where I had previously gripped and let out a long sigh.

"I'm sorry today wasn't perfect. Farquhar and Raffles' war over their egos has swept me into a mess," I said, taking her free hand in mine as we walked through the lengthening shadows cast by the jungle on either side of the packed dirt.

Charlotte stopped, and it took me a second to realize. She gave me a lopsided smile. "It was perfect. As perfect as Sophia and I could make it. Farquhar is an evil man, and we cannot let him think he ruined anything for us."

Ignoring our location, I pulled Charlotte into my arms and slanted my mouth over hers before she could protest. I tried to infuse my kiss with all the love and pride I felt for her. Reluctantly releasing her lips, I watched as her eyes tried to focus on my face while both our breaths came in short, sharp gasps.

"I am a lucky man," I whispered.

She frowned at my words. "We only married a few hours ago," she teased back.

Her comment reminded me of the little time we had together, and I stepped out of her embrace and once again held onto her hand. "I must leave on a packet first thing in the morning. The sooner I leave, the sooner I hope to return."

"You wish to be here for the Bugis when they come trading." Charlotte surmised with her quick business sense.

"Indeed," I said as we left Government Hill behind and made our way through the darkened European Quarter. It was quiet this time of night. "I would also like to get back to my beautiful bride who will surely be pining away for me while I am away." I gave her a sly smile over my shoulder.

Charlotte laughed at my comment and shook her head at my pained expression. "When you come home, you'll see how I've fared with your own eyes."

My steps slowed as we walked down my street. We were almost home, my heart pounded in my chest at the thought of my large bed ready for us upstairs. After all, I thought while shaking my head, I was no green boy to fumble over my first girl. Searching for something to say, my mind came upon our conversation outside the church this morning.

"Did you want to tell me what was bothering you this morning?" I asked as I opened the front gate and watched her hips sway as she walked up the path to the front steps. Her shoulders stiffened slightly.

Quickly closing the gate, I cursed. Why did I have to bring up something that upset Charlotte now, even as I was mentally undressing her?

"I apologize; I should not have brought the subject up," I said quietly, taking her hand again and leading her up the stairs to the front door.

"No, it just seems so unimportant with the rest of the day's events." Charlotte stared into my eyes. I saw a need to let the matter drop as well as a slight sadness.

"Do not let Farquhar worry you," I started, but she held a hand to my lips.

"We already agreed to forget that man." She stood on her tiptoes and pressed a kiss to my mouth.

Using my free hand, I opened the door and bent my knees to pick Charlotte up in my arms. I grinned down into her face. "Welcome home, Mrs. Hawk."

Laughing, she pulled my head down for another kiss as I stepped over the threshold.

"Welcome, home Mr. Hawk, Mrs. Hawk." A disembodied voice intoned from the dark and Charlotte nearly jumped out of my arms in fright, a small squeak on her lips.

"Dutta!" I shouted as a match lit up a candle sitting on a table in the front foyer. "You nearly frightened us to death!"

"Apologies, Master." Dutta bowed, his forehead drawn together in concern. "I only wanted to welcome my new mistress to the house."

Charlotte removed the hand she was holding to her throat, and I let her feet touch the ground. "Thank you, Dutta. You are very kind to meet me."

Nodding in approval Dutta turned to face me. "I am taking the liberty of packing your things for the packet tomorrow. Is there anything else you require this evening?"

"Only some privacy," I growled, pulling Charlotte toward the stairs. I felt Dutta's eyes on me as we climbed.

Once we reached the upper landing, I picked Charlotte up again and carried her in my arms.

"How do you suppose he knew you were leaving tomorrow?" Charlotte asked as I shoved my bedroom door open with a shoulder.

"There's not much that happens in Singapore he doesn't know about." I sighed as I set Charlotte down on her feet. "I sometimes wonder if he has a gypsy crystal ball out back or a cauldron where he can see the future." Turning Charlotte around, I set to work on the tiny seed pearls holding her dress together. "I'm sorry, Charlotte. Do you want to stay here while I'm away? It might be lonely."

"I'm your wife. This is your home." She shrugged. "I belong here now. Besides, it will be a relief to get away from Father and Freddie for a bit.

Instead of asking her to elaborate on the comment I concentrated on placing kisses on every piece of skin I exposed down her back. My attentions made the tiny hairs on her skin stand on end. By the time I released the last button, I gave into the urge to lick my tongue from the base of her spine all the way up to the top of her neck. "You aren't wearing a chemise under your dress."

Charlotte's voice turned husky. "You'll have to peel the silk from my skin as it is."

"Very happy to oblige you, Mrs. Hawk." I chuckled as I turned her around and began pulling the silk and lace creation from her shoulders, revealing the creamy expanse of her chest, watching the rise and fall of her breasts as her breath quickened. Shoving the rest of the material over her hips, I took a moment to caress the soft skin at her waist. "Is this what you want?"

"Since the moment I laid eyes on you." Charlotte's voice was a whisper. Her need matched my own. With a groan, I thrust my tongue into her mouth again as I used my hands to bare the rest of her flesh.

&

Staring up at the ceiling I tried to ignore the gray light of dawn seeping through the curtains. Instead, I concentrated on the warm body snuggled next to mine. Sometime during the night, we had thrown the covers off the bed. I rubbed a soothing hand down Charlotte's back, memorizing the feel of her skin. She had been a virgin. I was surprised and pleased when I took her for the first time. Later, I felt like a cad, and now I was too tired to sort through all my swirling emotions.

She had loved my friend Bishop, but she had not given him her body. What did it mean that she had offered to share my bed once before we were married? Did she love me more? Or was she playing a game as Sarah Buck had said? Charlotte sighed and rubbed her nose into my chest. I would do well to ignore Sarah Buck and her accusations.

"Is it morning?" Charlotte asked as she tried to lift her head to look at the window.

Gently increasing the pressure of my wandering hand, I held her in place wanting to enjoy the moment. "It's still the dead of night," I said, smiling at the lie.

Charlotte murmured something and inhaled deeply. "I wish you didn't have to leave for Calcutta this morning."

"I have very little choice in the matter." I reached out and stroked Charlotte's hair. The thick brown waves hid auburn highlights that fascinated me. "They have threatened to freeze my father's pension as well as the investment payout he is due from his time at the East India Company."

"Is it a large sum?" Charlotte asked and lifted her head and rested her hands on my chest.

The sight and feel of Charlotte moving around naked momentarily stole my attention, and I had to focus on her last words. "I have no idea. I received the shares in Thistlewaite and Son as a separate settlement. However, even though it has been months since my father has been declared dead, the lawyers in Calcutta can't sort through his will. I have no idea how much money may be left."

My breath froze as she played with the hairs that covered my chest. "I suppose your mother will receive the pension."

"I guess it depends on what my father decided," I said vaguely, not wanting to ruin the moment by discussing my philandering mother. "None of it matters. I have my wages and the shares in Thistlewaite and Hawk, the money in my father's will is moot."

Charlotte placed a kiss on my chest, and I groaned in response. I planted a kiss on her giggling mouth and rolled her over.

A loud knock on the door interrupted us, and I did not hold back the growl in my throat. "Someone better be dead."

"Sir, Raffles is here to see you, and your trunks need to be taken down to the ship." The door muffled Dutta's voice.

"I'll be down in a minute," I ground out, peering into Charlotte's disappointed face. "Damn the East India Company to hell and back."

"They certainly know how to ruin a man's morning." Charlotte stifled a giggle as I threw myself from the bed and began searching for a pair of trousers.

"And a man's reputation besides," I said as I pulled one leg through a pair of linen pants and hopped a few times to get them over my thighs. "They will try and destroy my father. I know it."

"Your father was the best captain the East India Company ever employed. He protected company ships his entire life. They would never dishonor him." Charlotte sat up in bed and reached for a discarded sheet to wrap around her body.

What if my father had not always been a protector of the East India Company? He may have led the terror campaign of the ghost pirate ship against company interests. It was a small world; I was not the only one trying to find the identity of the ghost ship captain.

Looking down at Charlotte I said, "You're right, of course. They have no possible reason or evidence to conclude my father was anything but loyal." I hoped the words were true. My search of the origins of the ghost ship had turned up nothing. I could only hope any other search had proven fruitless. I began to fasten the buttons on a fresh shirt quickly. "I need to see Raffles, but will you come down to the wharf with me?"

"Of course," Charlotte agreed with a half-smile. "I miss you already."

I bent down and captured her lips in a searing kiss. Groaning, I stood back up and walked out the door cursing the world.

I scanned the small dining room on the lower level of the house. Dutta had laid out some breakfast dishes. Raffles stood at one end of the room admiring the neighbor's back garden, coffee in his hand. Dutta stepped forward to serve me, and I waved my hand. "Please make sure my trunks get stored aboard the packet."

"Yes, Mr. Hawk." Dutta paused by the door and turned. "Mrs. Hawk's personal maid arrived this morning with her belongings."

"Good, make sure you make her feel welcome." I wanted to add that I was sorry not to be here for all the changes that were happening in our lives.

Taking in my state of undress, Raffles cleared his throat at the sound of my voice. "I am sorry to bother you this morning, but I didn't want you to leave without speaking to you."

"I understand," I said cautiously, while pouring a cup of coffee. I blamed Raffles for this mess and my stupidity at baiting Farquhar. "Have you come to apologize for dragging me into your little war with Major General Farquhar?" I asked bitterly.

Raffles let out a long breath. For a single moment, I wished I could take back the words. The last years had not been kind to him. His posting in Bencoolen was a farce, and he had lost his sons to tropical fever. My father would have been appalled by the way I was treating his old friend.

"You have every right to be upset, Nathaniel." Raffles set his cup down and studied my profile. "There will be a time for recriminations after you get through with Lord Hastings and his inquiry."

"The inquiry is a farce," I said, slicing a hand through the air for emphasis. "As you rightly pointed out, I am a private citizen, and they can take father's pension with whatever money belongs to it and give it to the devil." The rage I had been trying to control since Farquhar had shown up at my wedding reception was suddenly spewing forth. I had no idea it was strong. "For years, my father played the politics game along with you and the rest of your company friends. I never wanted anything to do with it, and yet here I am only months after his passing being forced to explain his actions to men who probably knew him better than me."

Holding up his hands, Raffles shook his head. "You're right; none of this should have anything to do with you, but is it not true the sons must pay for the sins of their fathers?"

His statement caused air I hadn't known I was holding in my lungs to escape in a burst. Was he speaking of my father and his possible betrayal, or of the guilt he felt over his own sons' death?

"You know that's a ridiculous statement to make." I reined in my temper with little grace. "You are not to blame for anything that happened in Bencoolen."

Shaking his head solemnly, Raffles stared at me, his large brown eyes hard. "How I wish you were right." He held up a hand to stop my next words. "The fact is, my administration in Bencoolen will cost me more than the lives of my sons. It will cost me a pension and any revenues I might have gained from my works with the Royal Geographical Society. My future is a tangled mess. The East India Company will force me to pay restitution for fiscal decisions I made that cost the company money." He took a deep breath. "They will do the same to your father's estate."

"There is no way you can know what will happen in Calcutta," I said shaking my head. "Besides, my father was a ship captain; he hardly made decisions affecting fiscal programs."

Raffles gave me a half smile before his face turned grim. "He was the most successful pirate hunter the world had ever known, but he didn't always get his man." He let his statement sink in. "He lost a brand-new warship, and it cost the company thousands of pounds."

"It cannot be legally possible for the East India Company to charge my father for any of those things." I felt my aggravation rise. "They were beyond anyone's control."

"Some might argue he was in control," Raffles said in a solemn voice. "They will bury you, Nathaniel, and before you have realized what has happened, your life will be broken into so many pieces you can never put them back together again."

A movement out of the corner of my eye made me turn toward the entrance to the dining room. Charlotte stood on the threshold with her hand to her throat. Her cheeks were pale. Even if she heard only the last few words of Raffles warning, it was enough to scare her.

The overwhelming need to comfort her made me reach out to her. She willingly came into my arms and rested her head on my shoulder. Glaring at Raffles for a second, I soothed my hands down her back.

"There is nothing to worry about, my darling," I said in a voice I hoped sounded calm. "I will be back in a matter of weeks, and in years to come we will laugh at how worried we were over this nonsense."

She nodded and looked up at me. Her fathomless blue eyes bore into my own, and I saw the same fear she held yesterday at the church. With Raffles present and the morning rapidly disappearing, there was no way I could get to the bottom of what was bothering her.

"Mr. Hindly dropped by with some papers he thought you might need, and your trunks are at the wharf." Charlotte turned, and I watched the expression on her face turn vacant. "Sir Raffles, how wonderful to see you this morning. You will forgive my rudeness at not greeting you right away. I am a newlywed, after all." She walked over and held out her hands to the older man.

I listened with half an ear as I left the dining parlor and made my way to the study. Idly, I wondered whether Charlotte would transform the room into a drawing room. I would miss the leather and dark wood, but I wanted her to be comfortable in her new home. Hindly rubbed the stump of his right arm as I walked in.

"What do you have for me, boy?" I asked briskly.

"Mr. Thistlewaite sent this stack of papers for you to attend to before you leave this morning." Hindly pointed at a small stack of papers and said, "This is for when you get to Calcutta." He picked up a handwritten note with the words Hatton Solicitors on the top. "Mr. Thistlewaite said it was the name of Captain Hawk's solicitor in Calcutta, and that they handled all his legal needs."

Obviously, Cornelius thought the inquiry and Lord Hastings were much more severe than he let on yesterday.

"Thank you, Hindly. Let's get these papers signed so I can spend some time with my wife before I leave." Walking over to a small desk where quills and an inkstand sat, I put my mind to the contracts that needed attention.

Chapter 6
Charlotte

Touching my fingers to my lips, I pressed hard and watched as the packet carrying my new husband disappeared from view. We celebrated our wedding vows all night, but this morning there was a strange urgency to his kisses and small touches, something I never felt before. It was as if he wanted to possess a part of me before he had to leave.

"With God's aid, by the time Mr. Hawk returns, we can put Frederick's sorry mess behind us and move on," Bigham said. His presence by my side normally evoked a feeling of reassurance. This morning, however, it only reminded me of my meeting with Zheng Jing.

"Did you find out anything last night?" I forced my attention away from the harbor. My legs felt weak, and I was glad the long muslin skirts hid my weakness from the people roaming the wharf. Bigham held out his hand, and I placed it on his sleeve as he led me down the street.

"I tracked that little French bastard, Lavroche, down into a hell, the slums of the Chinese Campong." Bigham guided me through the throng of people. I bent my head toward him so he wouldn't have to shout. "He told me he didn't know the men your brother lost to at cards the other evening."

"Do you believe him?" I frowned as I recognized a familiar figure ahead.

"Absolutely not!" Bigham stated. "The man is involved in something. Whatever it is, he is in deep enough with men who scare him more than I. No amount of threatening would get me any information on the other men." As I let out a breath, I felt Bigham's eyes on me. "Lavroche told me the men come into Singapore every once in a while to enjoy a game of cards, and they quickly left after realizing their good fortune."

"Damn," I swore under my breath and ignored the startled looks from several people. "I was hoping we could accuse them of cheating and regain some of Frederick's losses."

"Even if we had found them, it would have been almost impossible to prove they cheated; it's too many days after the card game." Bigham waited a moment before continuing under his breath. "We would have had more luck robbing them."

Weighing his statement, I wondered if I would knowingly commit such an act. It didn't take me long to realize there was no question. There were very few things I would not contemplate to protect my father, brother, and, now, my husband.

"Mrs. Hawk." Cornelius Thistlewaite stepped away from another man he was speaking to greet me. "Let me extend my best wishes once again on your marriage. We had so little time to talk yesterday."

"Mr. Thistlewaite, a pleasure to see you this morning." I held out my hand to him and hoped my voice sounded enthusiastic. "Our lack of time socializing yesterday had nothing to do with either of us."

"Major General Farquhar is a damned bounder." Thistlewaite raised his voice, and several pairs of eyes darted our way. "We shall have to make do without Nathaniel for a few weeks. I insist you dine with me this week."

I studied the other man on a long exhale. His face was a social mask of welcome; only his eyes betrayed his true feelings. I knew his feelings toward me were less than amiable and, unfortunately, I knew he had every right to his feelings. "I would not want to put you out Mr. Thistlewaite. You will be busy with Mr. Hawk away." Not to mention dining alone at his house without another female would give grist to the gossips. There were enough assassins for my character already.

"I insist," Thistlewaite said with a false smile. "I will have my assistant put together a small party of agreeable guests and send out the invitations." He took my hand and raised it to his lips. "Nathaniel made me promise to keep an eye out for you."

"How gracious of you to accept." I acknowledged the other man's protection and the warning in his voice. My husband would hear of any misstep. "I look forward to receiving my supper invitation. Good day, Mr. Thistlewaite."

"Good day Mrs. Hawk," Thistlewaite responded and looked at Bigham. "Mr. Bigham," he said before turning back to his companion.

"Not very friendly," Bigham observed, as we walked down the foreshore. Without many men around during the low trading season, the area in front of the warehouses and offices of the traders and ship owners of Singapore was pleasant. "He bought the Monarch from you. I would have thought you should be the one standing on your dignity."

"What makes you think our little scene had anything to do with the sale of the Monarch?" I asked curiously.

"Other than business, there is nothing else the man can hold against you." Bigham shrugged and took out a gold pocket watch to check the time.

Bigham had no idea how I had manipulated Thistlewaite and his late wife into buying the half-finished Monarch. I prayed he never found out.

"We haven't much time before your meeting," Bigham said looking out at the small junks lined up on the foreshore. "I think it will be faster and safer for us to take a boat across the river. The fewer people who recognize you in the Chinese Campong, the better."

Nodding in agreement, I watched as Bigham negotiated a fare with a couple of coolies standing near their junks. I was more nervous about meeting with Zheng Jing this morning than yesterday when I walked down the aisle. Zheng Jing was a dangerous man if half the rumors surrounding him were true. Aside from any nefarious dealing he had with the Brotherhood, he was a sharp businessman who had built his Chinese consortium from nothing. I would have to use extreme caution when dealing with him.

Bigham waved me forward, and I lifted the shawl I wore around my shoulders until it covered my hair and the lower half of my face. The material was hot and offered only a little protection from the sun, but it shielded my identity from curious gazes.

I sat warily on a bench in the back of the boat. Bigham faced me, and the coolie waited a moment before pushing the small craft away from shore. He used a large pole to navigate the junk away from shore.

"Do you think it's a good idea for you to accompany me?" Knowing hard coins paid for loyalty, I glanced at the coolie, who appeared absorbed in navigating the current. "He told me to come alone."

"You meeting with him, let alone wandering around the Chinese Campong district alone, was never going to be an option," Bigham replied with finality. "He would have known someone was bound to come with you," Bigham continued after a moment of silence. "I wonder if he thought you would bring your husband."

We deliberately tried to keep our conversation vague hoping not to reveal too much of our business. "If Zheng Jing's plan was to meet my husband, he'll be disappointed."

"He will have heard of the circumstances of your spouse's departure from Singapore. I'm sure everyone is speaking of it this morning." Bigham shot me a warning glance to stay quiet as we neared the shore on the Chinese side of the Singapore River.

Bigham placed a hand under my elbow as he guided me from the junk when I stepped back onto solid ground. Lifting my skirts, I walked up to the foreshore and glanced around the brightly colored buildings where the Chinese traders and mediators plied their trade. They were so different from the staid and boring warehouses of the European side.

"Shall we?" Bigham asked after paying the coolie. I placed my hand on his arm once again as a street urchin sidled up next to us.

"You come with me, sister," the boy said. I looked down into his face. His large ebony eyes and appearance seem to be that of a ten- or eleven-year-old.

"I am afraid we don't have time for the gaming dens today," Bigham said with an amused chuckle, then pulled me around the urchin.

"No, brother," the boy said, stepping in front of us again. "You stay, and I will take the sister where she needs to go."

Bigham shook his head. "Anywhere she goes, I go." Bigham pointed to his chest.

The urchin contemplated Bigham's stance for a minute before nodding his head. "Your funeral, brother." The boy turned and began walking away.

Straightening his waistcoat with a hmph, Bigham followed the boy away from the foreshore pulling me along with him. I adjusted the wrap around my head and shoulders with my free hand as we wended our way through narrow dirt streets. My hand tightened on Bigham's arm as we stepped up to a red painted door behind the urchin. He knocked in a pattern and hopped from one foot to the other as he waited.

A panel cleverly worked into the wood opened, and two eyes peered out. They narrowed as they took in Bigham but nodded as they recognized me. When the door opened, the man on the other side gave the urchin a coin before waving us inside.

"Follow me, please." The large man's voice was gravelly and his Chinese accent thick. The inside of the small building was plain but clean, and I tried to get a picture of why Zheng Jing would want to meet me here. Bigham followed me up the steps to a second floor that opened to a large storage area. Large bundles of goods wrapped in protective coverings lined the walls. Zheng Jing sat on a wooden stool facing us; a teapot and three cups sat on the table in front of him. He stood up.

"Welcome, Mrs. Hawk, Mr. Bigham." His hand swept forward, indicating the two stools in front of him. "Please, take a seat."

I had attended enough afternoon teas and at-homes for the invitation to elicit an automatic response. Without thinking, I moved forward, trying to keep my gaze on the man in front of me rather than the men lurking in the shadows.

"Thank you, Mr. Zheng Jing," I replied as I swept my skirts into a modest arrangement and sat on the stool. I felt Bigham take his place beside me. I let the silence stretch for a few more minutes. He was the one who wanted to see me.

"Do you know what is in these bales, Mrs. Hawk?" Zheng Jing walked away from the small table and ran a hand lovingly down one of the bundles.

"No, Mr. Zheng Jing, I suppose I could guess," I said slowly. In fact, the packets could carry anything from silk to spices and gunpowder. They appeared nondescript.

Zheng Jing smiled back at me and used his right hand to remove a dagger from the inside of his impeccably cut suit. Bigham flinched beside me, and I willed him to stay calm. Zheng Jing chuckled when he saw the other man's reaction. "Had I wanted you dead, Mr. Bigham, I would not have brought you all the way down here."

Bigham did not relax, and my anxiety became almost unbearable while I watched Zheng Jing take his dagger and plunge it into the nearest barrel. The blade's edge must have been impossibly sharp as it sliced through the coverings. A substance that looked like dried leaves began pouring from the inside of the barrel. Zheng Jing held up his hand and caught some. He brought it over to the table and held it out to us, then dumped it into the teapot on the table.

"The most valuable commodity in the world," Zheng Jing commented as he took his stool once again. "Aside from opium."

"Tea," I said under my breath and wished the bales had been full of opium.

A boy carrying a large, steaming pot stepped up to the table and poured hot water over the tea leaves.

The smell of tea permeated the air, and Zheng Jing said, "As you know, the East India Company has a monopoly on tea traded with China." I could only nod as I felt a lump grow in my throat. "My little consortium does not think this is fair, but we do not want to risk our ships and trading business on murky deals with privateers and black market goods. That is where Carstairs and Son can help me." Zheng Jing poured the cups of tea. He lifted his own out in front of him. "To a profitable partnership."

Chapter 7
Nathaniel

Calcutta, the city of my birth. I had hoped never to step upon the shores of the Hooghly River again. Fate was a cruel mistress in the best of times, and the recent months were especially trying. The packet had made reasonably good time up the Malay Peninsula. We made several stops to exchange letters, packages, and general gossip around the far-flung corners of the East India Company's holdings. It was tedious. Charlotte's soft body invaded my dreams, while worries over what the East India Company might have found concerning my father's affairs crowded my days.

I arose with the rest of the new watch at the whistle an hour before. We followed the pilot boat up the river into the interior of India. Several smaller crafts were plying the waters as well as a few merchant ships. The big season was over, but there were always men looking for adventure and a bit of commerce.

Leaning over the railing, I took in the quiet breeze as we sailed past small farm dwellings. I could see the inhabitants of the farms working their way through the morning chores, gathering firewood and collecting water. A man wearing a turban and a loincloth herding half a dozen water buffalo watched as we passed. The man's gaze was wary, scanning the decks of the packet, looking for danger.

The constant animosity between the Indians and the European settlers was a large part of the reason I hated Calcutta. There were days, even weeks when it felt like the whole city was ripe for a rebellion. A single incident could act as tinder to inflame a widespread riot.

The packet reached the last bend in the river, and the deck swayed to the right as we maneuvered through the middle of the channel. As I squinted, I could see the outline of Fort William in the distance. The sun rising over the horizon made my eyes burn. The starburst shaped fort built by the East India Company stood as a sentinel at the beginning of the city. It looked as it had in my youth.

I tried to count the number of redcoats on duty, patrolling the high walls, watching for danger on land and water.

"Mr. Hawk, we will be sorry to see you depart this morning." I turned to see the second mate approaching with one eye on me and the other eye on the banks of the river.

"Mr. Woodley, the pleasure has been all mine," I said with real affection. Mr. Woodley was a sailor from the close crop of his bewigged head to the heels of his boots. He was a man my father would have been happy to spend a few hours with on deck in fraternal communion.

Grasping the railing in front of us, he spoke without looking at me. "I don't suppose I could convince you to stay onboard, eh?" he asked, as I watched a smile creep up into his eyes.

"The thought of avoiding Hastings and whatever the East India Company has planned for me is tempting," I said, suddenly realizing how true the words were. How much easier would it be to set sail again, lose myself as an anonymous deck hand, and never face my responsibilities! "However, my wife must be the priority, and she is damned clever. It would not take her long to track me down."

"If there's ever a chance you might change your mind..." Mr. Woodley gave me a sideways glance. "There are a few ship captains and crews who still think it's lucky to have a Hawk onboard."

"Thank you," I said, wondering if it were true. As far as the world was concerned, the ghost ship captain had bested my father. The other man walked away and began shouting orders at the sailors. The sailors scrambled to tie up the sails and prepare the packet for landing. It would stay in port for a few days before leaving on its return journey to Singapore.

I scanned the shoreline and was surprised to see the number of changes that occurred in my absence. Calcutta had been a large, bustling port when I left as a young man, but it had apparently continued to grow. It appeared nothing would halt the progress and wealth of the British Empire. I took a deep breath and went downstairs and grabbed a few personal items. The ship's sailors would deliver the rest of my belongings later in the day.

The air was as I remembered it as a boy. It was hot but not as humid as Singapore. There was the bite of spices. However, the overall smell was humanity at its most basic and primitive. Refuse, human waste, and the rubbing of sweating bodies all coming together in the trading capital of India to meld into one living being.

The customhouse wharf lay ahead, and I braced my body and mind for the challenges to come. There was little chance of keeping my arrival in the city a secret for long. I would not have much time to find out what Hastings knew of my father before facing the inquiry. Unfortunately, the outcome of this fiasco would affect not only me but Cornelius and Charlotte, as well. Depending on what Hastings and his cronies had dug up, my father's entire life's work might be for nothing, and anyone who associated with him would feel it keenly.

The sailors' yells on the wharf caught my attention, and the ship bumped abruptly against the wooden pilings. Curses in several different languages filled the air, and I was happy there were no ladies aboard the packet.

The gangplank lowered to the wooden deck of the wharf. I turned and saluted the captain who stood on the forecastle. The captain acknowledged my departure with a nod before turning his attention back to his boson. Without further thought, I left the relatively quiet companionship of the packet and stepped back into the frantic life of Calcutta.

The customs wharf remained crowded. I watched as officials inspected cargoes and ship captains argued over bills of lading. As I reached the foreshore, I turned left and joined the throngs of people rushing to their morning's destination. I kept one hand on my purse and a wary eye out for street urchins. It had been a while since I had to keep an eye out for footpads, but Calcutta's wharves were notorious for child street gangs.

It was only a few blocks to the Thistlewaite and Hawk warehouse located on the Clive Street pier just past the bonded warehouses. Cornelius's father had won the warehouse, in another lifetime, playing cards against some unlucky nabob. When I was a child and my father was in port, he would take me down to the Thistlewaite warehouse. The bales and crates stacked up in the warehouse provided hours of entertainment for me. My father would sit and talk for hours with Cornelius and his father, smoking pipe after pipe full of tobacco. There were many times when days turned into nights, and we would wander home to an empty house. My mother had all but given up on our return; those were the best of times.

Standing outside the warehouse, I inspected the front. The only change from my younger years was the sign. Painted in broad strokes across the top of the building, were the words, Thistlewaite and Hawk. I stepped up to the door and pushed it open, hoping there would be someone around this morning.

The interior of the warehouse was dim, without the light from an open door or one of the small windows near the ceiling, there would be no light.

"What's your business?" A bulky man emerged from the gloom and stood beside me. He watched me carefully with hooded eyes. His cockney accent sounded even thicker as it ricocheted off the thin brick walls of the building.

"The business of Thistlewaite and Hawk," I said into the other man's frowning face. "I am Mr. Hawk, come to Calcutta on business. Is Mr. Rickman about this morning?"

"Aye, gov'nor," the man said as he inspected me from head to foot. "You're not much to look at as a man, but I guess you were always a scrawny child."

"Do I know you?" I asked, trying to get a better look at the man's face.

"Prob'ly not." The corners of the man's whiskered mouth tugged into a smile. "But I remembered you as a scamp running around wild." He took a deep breath. "Offices are up the stairs. You'll find Mr. Rickman in the second office." Then, the man turned and disappeared back into the gloom. He didn't even bother to watch me climb the stairs.

Shaking my head, I took the stairs up to a specially built floor where several offices were laid out. The light came from one of the larger rooms, along with the sound of quiet conversations. The clerks have already been hard at work for the morning. It was good to know Mr. Rickman ran the Calcutta end of the business efficiently. I rapped on the door and walked in after receiving permission from an occupant inside.

A man with light auburn hair, brown eyes and a straight nose looked up from a paper he was inspecting. "Yes, sir. Is there something I can do for you?"

"I believe there is," I replied, moving farther into the room and standing before the other man's desk. "I'm Nathaniel Hawk."

The other man's brows came together in confusion for a second before he quickly stood up. Holding out a hand, he said, "Mr. Hawk, a pleasure to meet you at last."

"Likewise." I shook the man's hand before sitting in one of the worn leather chairs positioned in front of Mr. Rickman's desk.

Mr. Rickman shuffled a few papers on his desk before sitting back down again. "I have to admit I expected you." I raised an eyebrow, and he continued. "All of Calcutta can speak of nothing but the inquiry into the ghost and the secret allegations against Captain Sebastian Hawk. The whole damn waterfront is in an uproar. Never let anyone say sailors are not loyal folk."

"Any rumor of what the allegations might be?" I asked pointedly. The more information I had, the better when I confronted Lord Hastings.

"No one knows for sure, and those who do know aren't talking." Mr. Rickman rubbed his chin for a minute. "Damned unusual to have valuable information locked up so tight in their ivory tower." Shaking his head, Rickman continued. "It's always the same: embezzlement, debt, or treason."

"I need somewhere to stay while I'm here," I said, mulling over the other man's words.

"The Auckland Hotel just opened up. It's across from Government House," Mr. Rickman said slowly, thinking of other suitable possibilities.

Catching his eye, I said, "I would rather stay here at the warehouse if there a spare bunk the clerks aren't using. I do not want to be readily available to that lot down at the East India Company. They are probably tracking all my moves as it is."

"There's a spare single room here in the warehouse." Mr. Rickman spoke slowly. "The foreman used it, but he returned to England a few weeks back, and we haven't replaced him. It's basic."

"You forget I lived onboard a ship for years," I said reassuringly. "As long as it's relatively clean, I'm sure it's all right."

"Great, I'll have one of the lads show you where it is." Rickman rose from his seat and went to the door. He shouted down the corridor, and I waited while he gave instructions to a young man.

Standing up to join them, I said, "Thank you, Mr. Rickman. I look forward to speaking with you on the business in Calcutta. Perhaps we can implement some of your practices in Singapore."

The man preened under the praise, and I felt his eyes on me as I left his office.

An hour later, I stood in the marble entrance of Hatton and Sons, my father's solicitors. The reception room was elegant, yet soberly decorated with leather chairs clustered around low desks. On the right side a two-story mural depicting a pastoral scene of the Indian countryside, complete with jolly peasants working the fields, hung on the imposing wall.

"May I be of service, sir?" A gentleman in a dark suit with a painfully correct cravat asked from behind a small reception desk.

"Yes." I hesitated for a moment, an unaccountable attack of nerves settled in my gut, and I cleared my throat. "My name is Nathaniel Hawk, and I do not have an appointment." Holding out the card Cornelius had given me I said, "My father was a patron of this firm, and I need to speak with this gentleman as soon as possible."

The other man plucked the card from my grasp and studied it for a second. He looked up at me with narrowed eyes, and I felt like a bug under inspection at the Royal Geographic Society. "Please give me a moment." Without further direction, the man left and walked into the heart of the building. I watched as he swept past the desks where clerks sat hunched over their work. He disappeared up a set of stairs at the rear of the building, and I turned to study the reception area again.

On the wall opposite the pastoral mural, a large painting of a sea battle took up the entire two-story space. For a moment, I was lost in the roiling waves and the pitching decks of the ships as they tacked to the left and right trying to find the maximum position to set forth their most damaging volley. Looking closer, I noticed the flags straining against the turbulent wind. The British flag flew from the larger ship. The other ship was French, according to the name on the bow. It stirred a memory from somewhere, but I could not put my finger on it.

"Mr. Hawk, a pleasure to finally meet you." A voice from behind ended my reverie. I turned and found a man who was probably near my age. He studied me with his probing blue eyes as if finding some amusement. His light hair fell across an eye as he held out his hand. "I am Markus Hatton, one of the sons."

"Mr. Hatton, a pleasure to meet you." I took the other man's hand, and we shook briefly.

Nodding toward the picture, Hatton said, "Your father and mine served aboard the HRH Adelaide during the war against old Boney." He studied the picture with a critical eye before turning back to me. "I'm sure you're familiar with the story."

I shook my head. "If I ever heard the tale, I'm afraid I cannot bring it to mind." I tried to think of any of the stories my father told of his boyhood serving in His Majesty's Navy during the Napoleonic Wars. "He rarely spoke of his time in the Royal Navy I'm afraid."

"Something he had in common with my father," Hatton inserted smoothly. "Shall we retire to my office? I expected you might turn up for pressing business with the East India Company."

"Yes, thank you for seeing me on such short notice." I walked next to Hatton as we followed the same route through the central office the clerk who greeted me took. "I had hoped to arrive in Calcutta early enough to have a few days to orient myself before the East India Company was aware of my presence."

"No hope for anonymity in the heart of the cult, as I like to describe the Company," he grinned before climbing the stairs to the second floor. "They have spies everywhere. In fact, assume everyone you meet is feeding the East India Company information about you."

I entered a medium-sized office lined with shelves of ledgers and books. A large desk stood in the middle near a small window that let in some natural light.

"Even you?" I asked, curious as to his answer. He took up a chair behind the large desk covered with papers.

"Of course," Hatton replied, shifting a stack of ledgers to the side and placing his hands where the papers had been. "If I weren't giving out at least small snippets of gossip about you and your father, the company would find it suspicious. Unfortunately, in the world of dirty East India Company politics, it's what you know and where it came from that keeps you safe from the sharks."

"What gossip have you heard of my father?" I asked bluntly.

"None," Hatton replied succinctly. "The very lack of a substantial lead in whatever Lord Hastings has against your father is worrying. It means he either has nothing and is waiting for you to give something up, or the accusations are so insidious no one is willing to discuss them for fear of implication."

"You don't think this whole inquiry was set up because of Sir Raffles and Major General Farquhar's little spat over the direction of Singapore?" I asked, watching as the other man sat back in his chair.

He let out a long breath. "I think the inquiry has many different reasons for existence. Sir Raffles' ongoing problems with the top brass at the East India Company are one reason. Your father was a loyal Raffles man." Hatton thought for a moment before speaking. "Lord Hastings is on his way out, and he will not be getting a 21-gun salute or a medal from the King. Instead, he will be lucky to keep his dignity after the massive personal expenditures he has made with company money. None of this is a secret. He could be looking to divert attention away from himself."

"My father had more enemies than just the Dutch and the French." I thought of all the times he had tangled with the clerks at the East India Company. It was not always easy to get gold for wages and supplies for his crew when he suffered constant questioning over his expenditures.

"You're right, of course. Your father never took the easy way out, always fighting for his men whether they were crew or not." Hatton watched me. "You don't have any other choice but to present yourself at Government House and find out what angle Lord Hastings is going to take. Treason or fiscally irresponsible behavior, rest assured it will be one of those two avenues. I have already made inquiries. You are not to have legal representation because technically the investigation focuses on your father. That does not mean, however, that you can avoid implication in any of his dealings." Hatton gave me a meaningful look.

I thought of the man standing on the deck of the ghost ship whose identity I had yet to trace. There was no way I would tell anyone, let alone Hatton or Lord Hastings, who I believed captained the ghost pirate ship. The other man remained silent, and I knew he was fishing for information.

"Years have passed since I sailed with my father. I was only in Calcutta to make a truce with him," I explained. "In truth, aside from the odd letter, we were not on speaking terms since I turned down my captaincy."

"Good. This is what I want you to say in the inquiry." Hatton peered at me intently. "I assume you have not been to an investigation." I shook my head. "Fine, if half of your exploits of a few months back are true, you should be all right under pressure. I remind you not to give any information away, even if it seems innocuous. Answer with yes or no when you have a chance and claim you do not know, if you can't. There's no point in helping them with their speculations."

I nodded. "It sounds like a court martial."

"This inquiry is more than just about your father and his legacy. Everything he accomplished, all the battles he won, men he saved and acts he committed while under the protection of the East India Company flag, could come under scrutiny." Hatton's brows came together. "Should the inquiry gain any traction against your father, other great men who built their lives on his success will also be brought down. Have you any idea of how much influence your father had?"

"Enough to worry high-ranking officials of the East India Company," I replied, not having any idea what Hatton was trying to tell me.

"Damn right. The majority of the men he served with loved him and those who hated him still respected him. His power at his death rivaled that of Lord Hastings. You can be sure of that." Hatton pressed his point home. "It would be very dangerous for Hastings to believe you held even a fraction of your father's power."

Shaking my head, I said, "This whole inquiry is ridiculous. My father was a sea captain. He was the best naval captain of his time. Some of the ways he scraped victory out of the jaws of defeat, I will never know, but he was a simple man. He sailed, he fought, and he enjoyed a smoke and a yarn. Nothing more, nothing less."

"Your father was so much more than the sum of his victories. He represented something fundamental to the psyche of the British Empire. You need to recognize what it is, or the principles your father fought for will be lost." Hatton's gaze pierced me.

I felt annoyed and angry with the other man suddenly. "You appear to be an expert on my father. Why don't you tell me plainly what you aren't saying? You obviously knew him better than I."

Hatton let out a long sigh and waved a hand in the air. "I grew up with stories of your father's feats. My father never forgot the debt he owed Sebastian Hawk. Perhaps you don't see who the man truly was because you were too close."

"Or too far." I stood up. "Thank you for the advice concerning the inquiry. I will present my person as you suggested to Government House tomorrow."

The other man also stood and watched me warily, looking as if he might be debating something in his head before he spoke. "Your father was a man of secrets. Not all the secrets he held were his own. It is now your responsibility to keep those same secrets."

Resisting the urge to throw my hands up into the air, I stared at the other man. "Any secrets my father might have held went with him to his watery grave. He never confided in me. Not even when I sailed under him on the Constance. He kept his council."

Hatton remained silent for a moment. "Once the inquiry finishes, I will be in a better position to complete the requisitions of your father's will. It was quite detailed, but much of it depends on the outcome of the inquiry."

"I look forward to settling my father's business affairs," I replied and held out a hand. For a moment, I thought Hatton was going to ignore it, but he slowly reached out and took my hand in a firm grip.

"You will be fine, I think. Just remember to watch your back; loyalty has a price at the East India Company. Your father understood, but he couldn't always reconcile himself to it."

Chapter 8
Charlotte

I tugged my lace gloves into place and looked up at Cornelius Thistlewaite's residence. I hadn't been back to it since his wife Margaret died, and I planned to avoid the street altogether. Images of Margaret's pale face swam before my eyes as I thought of her last hours bleeding out. The doctor had been helpless to save her.

"Mrs. Hawk, are you going up?" A woman's voice sounded from behind me. "You appear to be wool-gathering."

"I apologize." Forcing a mild expression onto my features and forcing my gruesome thoughts away, I turned to Sarah Buck. "Shall we go up together?" I asked and opened the small iron gate and motioned for her to proceed.

Sarah Buck inclined her head and stepped in front of me. Her clinging perfume clashed with the light smell of jasmine from the hanging trellises in the front garden.

"How lovely to see you," Sarah Buck's breathing quickened as we climbed the stairs. "So unfortunate Farquhar ruined your wedding with his ugly scene. I'm surprised you can show your face in Singapore," she said.

Bridling at the insult, I felt my hands ball into fists at my sides. I had to take several steadying breaths to regain my composure. "Let me assure you. The Major General had no effect on my or my husband's countenance at all. We enjoyed the day immensely." It was true for the most part. His departure the next day had been much sadder, as well as the meeting with Zheng Jing, which I was still trying to forget.

I followed Sarah Buck up onto the porch. She hesitated before using the door knocker, giving me a sideways glance. "I have to say you're much calmer than I would be in your circumstances."

"What circumstance are those?" I asked with a sigh. This was going to be a long evening, and I had other more important matters to occupy my time. Such as finding out who swindled my brother and how to escape the trap Zheng Jing had set for Carstairs and Son.

Sarah Buck used the knocker and tilting her head gave me a pitying smile. I wanted to smack her face. "Why, dearest Charlotte. I thought Nathaniel would have told you before he left. Well, I never believed I would have to be the one to tell you."

I forced the words out of my mouth. "I have no idea of what you speak, Mrs. Buck, and please refrain from using my husband's Christian name." Rapid footsteps sounded on the other side of the door, and relief flooded me.

"I'm carrying Nathaniel's child, Charlotte." Sarah turned back to the door as it opened and Cornelius Thistlewaite's butler's image illuminated in the entrance.

Blood drained from my face, and black spots danced in front of my eyes, while my breath came in short, sharp gasps. On the periphery, I was aware of Sarah Buck greeting the butler warmly and stepping inside the house. My legs felt like lead, and my gaze dropped to the floor. I needed to control my breathing. Otherwise, I would end up in a heap in the entranceway.

Even knowing the other woman was enjoying my reaction, I still could not muster my natural poise and calm. A feeling I had never actually felt before ran through my veins and choked my throat. Betrayal was a part of my past. Bishop had left me, and Freddie time and again proved he was incapable of loyalty, but never had I felt such a sense of helplessness.

Staring at Sarah Buck's smirking face was not helping. I glanced at the butler who wore a slight frown on his face. His lips were moving, but no words reached my ears. I focused on him alone and the rushing sound in my ears dissipated slowly.

"I beg your pardon, Mrs. Hawk. Are you feeling well?" The concerned butler appeared to be considering fetching his master.

"Yes, thank you," I murmured and thought of a lie that was not completely unbelievable. "I have not been in the house since your mistress passed away. It was all a bit overwhelming for a moment."

The butler stood to the side and swept a hand forward. "We also miss her very much." He opened his mouth as if he might say more, but his jaw shut with a click.

There was no way I could avoid the look of satisfaction on Sarah Buck's face as we went through to the drawing room. Even knowing the other woman was laughing at me could not bring forth my anger as it normally would. Instead, I wanted to go home and hide under the covers of my bed and wallow in self-pity. The bed I shared with Nathaniel. I swallowed hard, trying not to think of how many times he had taken Sarah Buck in that same bed.

As I recovered, reason began to eat away at my thoughts of betrayal. I knew Sarah Buck had slept with Nathaniel once, months ago and he had promised never to go near her again. The gossips had her sleeping with any number of men since her husband's death. If she were indeed pregnant, any number of her lovers might be the father of her child. I entered the bright drawing room behind the other woman. It was the same as it was when Margaret Thistlewaite lived. The unnerving thought that she might bustle up to me and offer a pre-dinner drink had me pausing on the threshold.

Cornelius Thistlewaite finished greeting Sarah Buck and turned his cold blue eyes in my direction. "Mrs. Hawk, I am so happy you could make it to supper this evening. I know how very busy you are at Carstairs and Son."

"Nonsense." I held out a hand for him to take. "You and I are family now." Watching with a bit of satisfaction as Cornelius's lip curled slightly in dislike while taking my hand.

He kissed my fingers and tucked my hand into the crook of his elbow. "And family looks out for one another." He nodded at a server. "Would you care for a sherry?"

"Yes, thank you." I reached out and lightly took the proffered crystal glass from the silver tray. I scanned the room over the rim of the glass. Aside from Cornelius, Sarah Buck and me, Mr. and Mrs. Meacham were present. A pair of more incorrigible gossips would be hard to find.

"I would be remiss if I didn't warn you of the hazards of associating with undesirables, my dear." Cornelius made the endearment sound like a curse.

My gaze fixed on Mr. and Mrs. Meacham. "Sometimes I think we judge peoples' reputations unfairly."

"As Nathaniel is away from Singapore, I feel I must warn you against any association with Zheng Jing. He is a dangerous man and very little good can come from mixing in his circles." Cornelius saluted Mrs. Meacham when she looked over at us.

Sipping again, I locked gazes with Mrs. Meacham, who was busy trying to step away from Sarah Buck. "I have no idea what you mean," I said. My voice held an irritating quiver. The fewer people who knew of my new business partner, the better. I might stand a chance of escaping the gallows.

"Don't lie to me," Cornelius said in a hard voice. "You have a dirty secret, and I intend to find out about it. Do you understand me?"

I nodded at Mrs. Meacham who stepped up to us and began chattering incessantly. She spoke of my wedding day in detail. Thankfully, she only needed the odd murmur and sigh to continue, and I let my mind wander. Cornelius must have had Bigham and me followed. He knows we met with Zheng Jing, but I was sure he had no idea the topic of discussion. Cornelius would not hesitate to use my potential treason against me. But thankfully, he was still in the dark.

Cornelius had moved away and was now speaking with Sarah Buck. I watched the two of the out of the corner of my eye and felt time drag. The sooner we ate, the faster I could escape this fiasco. Between Sarah Buck and Cornelius, I felt completely drained.

"Good evening, Mrs. Meacham, Mrs. Hawk. Could I speak to you for a moment?" Bigham had finally arrived, and I hoped he was the last guest.

Mrs. Meacham frowned at Bigham but retreated with a promise to continue our discussion later.

"She is in fine form this evening," Bigham commented as a server handed him a glass of scotch.

"You have no idea," I said, resisting the urge to wipe a hand across my face.

"I have news regarding Frederick's friends," Bigham said with a flat expression on his face. I could tell whatever he had finally dug up would be of no use.

Cornelius's voice rang throughout the drawing room, "Now we're all here, shall we go through to the dining room?"

After what felt like an eternity, sipping tea in the drawing room after supper concluded and I stood. "Cornelius, thank you so much for a lovely evening. I do hope we can do this again soon. When Nathaniel returns from Calcutta, perhaps?" I questioned as I shook out my muslin skirts.

"I will certainly be expecting an invitation," Cornelius replied, and I felt his eyes on me as I made my farewells to the rest of the guests. I wished I could avoid Sarah Buck, but she made sure to say her goodbyes before I left.

Bigham met me at the door as I thanked the butler. "Let me escort you home," he said as he followed me out into the sultry night.

"I don't want to inconvenience you," I replied warily, finally able to give into some of the exhaustion I felt. My temple had ached dully as the servants served the first course. The ache had turned to a throbbing pain by the time we finished supper.

"At least let me walk you to the beginning of your street. It is on my way home." Bigham held the front gate, and we stepped out into the street. The European Quarter was quiet, a few men and women still walked through the thick, night air, but the evening was finally nearly over.

"You said you might have found a lead on the men Freddie played cards with the night he lost our money." I wearily thought of all the tangled lies that made up my life.

"It appears Frederick might not have been their only victim," Bigham said as we approached the end of the street. "There are a few others who describe losing large amounts of money to the same men."

"Does anyone know who they are?" I asked, knowing there was very little we could accomplish even with their identities.

"I'll keep trying." Bigham turned to me. "Are you sure I can't walk you home? You're not well."

"Thank you, Mr. Bigham." I wanted to smile, but I knew it was more of a grimace. "Solitude is what I need right now. I will see you tomorrow."

"Good evening," he said after a long last look then walked toward the wharves where I knew he had lodgings.

I wandered down my street. It was empty, and shadows fell from the trees and houses across the packed dirt road. All I wanted was some peace.

Muffled footsteps sounded behind me, and I twisted to admonish Bigham for his protective streak. Instead, another body slammed into me, and a dirty hand clamped over my mouth. Instinct had me flailing my arms and legs and trying to bite down on the hand over my mouth. A rough male voice swore, and one callused hand went down my bodice and grabbed my breast and squeezed tightly. I shrieked in protest.

"Listen well, lovey. I've been told to warn you." The man squeezed my breast painfully again as he dragged me into the shadows. "You are a beautiful piece of fluff, and I don't mind getting creative with my lesson, but I won't have to as long as you cooperate. Do you understand?"

I nodded my head, and the man sighed as he let go of my breast and held me close to his body.

"Call off your dog, Bigham. He won't find what you're looking for, and if he did, we'd have to kill you both," the man threatened. I smelled stale tobacco and ale. "This is way bigger than your brother or you, and my bosses don't mind taking care of obstacles permanently. Do you understand?"

I nodded again.

"Good girl." The man suddenly let go of me, and I was alone once again in the dark shadows. A sob escaped my lips as I sank to my knees and choked out panic.

Chapter 9
Nathaniel

As I sipped a beer at an inn not far from the warehouse, I watched as sailors and men of business enjoyed a pint or two at the end of a long working day. The barmaid caught the wave of my empty mug and nodded before I went back to brooding on my first day in Calcutta.

The meeting with Hatton had irritated and disappointed. As a man my father trusted with his personal affairs, I hoped for a little more support and less of a lecture on my father's complicated life. I walked back to Clive Wharf in the sultry heat and dust of the Calcutta morning. The city had come to life in the last couple of hours and become the port of my childhood. Men wearing sarongs led water buffalo pulling carts through the hard-packed streets where they rubbed shoulders with impeccably dressed nabobs and European businessmen.

I spent the rest of the morning and afternoon with Mr. Rickman going over accounts and different operations protocols. The man appeared willing to show me the Calcutta service. It was a lesson in how different the trade was between Singapore and Calcutta. I had no doubt Singapore would eventually grow into a port just as profitable and busy as Calcutta, but for now, Calcutta was still the larger jewel in the East India Company's crown.

Thinking of Singapore made me yearn to be back with Charlotte and the life we were building together. We had spent only one night together in wedded bliss, but it was the first night of a lifetime together. I only needed to curb my impatience. Hopefully, it would not take her long to become pregnant. The thought of her swollen with my child made me smile as the barmaid set the full pint on the table and collected the empty tankard. She winked at me in return.

From my position in the tap, I scanned the crowd. I came down to the inn, hoping to find more information on either the accusations against my father or a lead on the ghost ship. Mr. Rickman had assured me that rumors circulated over the attack on the ghost ship, but no one had any reliable information on her or her crew.

"Not seen you around here before." A man with a thick Cornish accent sidled up next to me.

"I haven't been in Calcutta since I was a young man," I answered truthfully. It was possible one or more of the men in this tap sailed with my father. "My name is Nathaniel Hawk."

"Hawk, eh?" The other man looked me up and down. "Thought I might have recognized you." He shook his head. "Damn shame what those clerks are doing to him." The man reached out and took up his half a pint, his sleeve stretched back enough for me to glimpse a tattoo I had seen before in Singapore. The dark blue ink depicted two hands clasped together. He saw me looking at the marking and quickly moved to cover it.

"I've only been in Calcutta since this morning," I said, hoping to prompt the other man into giving me more information.

"Aye, well, you've already got yourself a couple of company keepers." The other man rubbed his day-old white whiskers then jerked his head to indicate two relatively well-dressed men sitting at the front of the taproom near the windows. They quickly returned to their conversation as I glanced over at them.

Curious, I asked, "How can you tell they're company men?" The two men could have been clerks at any firm's warehouse as far as I could tell.

"They haven't got shit all over their shoes." The other man chortled with laughter at his joke. I grunted in response. "They came in right after you and have barely taken their eyes off you. Usually, we would have run them out of here. The Lonely Mistress is no place for the likes of them. But we were curious."

"I've always thought the direct approach was best," I said, picking up my pint and striding over to the two men with a confidence I did not feel. The old sailor might be setting me up. On the other hand, if the East India Company was following me, I wanted to know of it. The two men did not look up until I was standing at the edge of their table. "Do I know you?" I asked in a voice loud enough for the rest of the tap to hear.

The man on the right, dressed in a plain brown jacket with an unremarkable cravat looked up with a face devoid of expression. "No," he replied tersely.

"My friend over at the bar thinks you've been paying me an undue amount of attention." I used my pint to point at the old man standing at the bar, who was watching my exchange with great interest.

"Your friend should mind his own business, and so should you," said the man on the left. In the silence that followed, he made cursory glances at the other occupants in the tap, who apparently made him nervous.

I sat down next to him on the bench. "Why has the East India Company sent you to watch me?"

"What makes you think we are company men?" the man in the brown jacket opposite asked. "We've come in here to enjoy a pint like everyone else."

"This isn't a company tap; you don't belong here." I hoped the old man had not set me up.

"Is that what the old man told you?" The man opposite sneered, "I think the old sea dog was trying to get a rise out of you. Why don't you scurry along back to the bar and leave us in peace?"

"I think you work for the East India Company, and I want to know why you're following me." I looked the first man in the eye.

Out of the corner of my eye, I saw other patrons in the tap turning to hear the man's answer.

"Why don't you prove it?" The other man leaned across the table with a snarl on his face. "We know who you are, Mr. Hawk. I can assure you there are more people interested in you than the East India Company. Your father was a dangerous man to know, and here you are in Calcutta drinking ale with the rest of the so-called reformers."

"I have no idea what you're talking about," I said. "Who are these reformers?"

"No need to play coy with us, Mr. Hawk," the man sitting next to me said. His bobbing Adam's apple gave away his nerves. "We all know your father meant for you to take on his legacy."

"Everyone knows I turned down the opportunity for life at sea many years ago. I'm a trader now." I frowned at him.

The man sitting across from me laughed without humor. "Not that legacy, Mr. Hawk. The one involving your father's other more salacious and treasonous acts."

"My father was not a traitor." My voice went cold, and I stood from the bench. "I will kindly ask you to step outside for spreading malicious gossip."

"You're sitting in a known haunt of the Brotherhood, are you telling me your father was not a traitor and that you're not involved in his business?" The other man pushed his half-full tankard away. "I really cannot decide who's supposed to believe the lies you're spouting. You or me?"

Slowly lowering my tankard to the table, I used my other hand to reach out and grab the front of the man's shirt. I jerked him forward before he had a chance to adjust his posture. "Listen here you little maggot, my father was loyal to the Crown and the East India Company—to his detriment it appears. Men like you, who live beneath him, have no right to comment."

The man I sat next to decided the interview had taken a turn for the worse and reached out to try to unlock my fingers from the other man's jacket. "It's time to leave!" he said in a loud, quivering voice.

I twisted the material of his shirt tighter until I heard satisfying choking sounds coming from the man I held, before letting go and shoving him away. "Don't let me ever catch you disparaging my father again, you runt."

The newly released man's face turned crimson, and I barely had time to step back before he launched himself off the bench, his fists held up belligerently in front of his chest. "You're nothing, Mr. Hawk. A boy who rode on the coattails of his father's greatness to find his father was no hero after all!" Finishing his piece, he launched a wild right hook at my face.

Ducking, I brought my fist up, trying to connect with the other man's chin. "Someone should teach you a few manners, boy."

I had to lean back to avoid the punch, and barely had time to close my eyes as the other man brought his half-full tankard up, smashing it into my face. Stars erupted behind my eyes, and I let loose of some virulent curses as I staggered back a few steps into a solid wall of humanity. Unable to open my eyes or even lift my head, I tried to ward off my attackers with flailing hands as I regained my senses.

Aware of a solid form behind me, I heard someone say, "You little sods!" Assuming the worst, I braced myself for a beating. Instead, I felt hands on my elbows, forcibly moving me to the side. In the next instant, the entire tap erupted into crashes, curses, and the sound of meaty fists hitting soft flesh.

I opened my watering eyes to find several sailors surrounding the pair of men who, whether they worked for the East India Company or not, had apparently worn out their welcome. Two men took it upon themselves to grab each one by the collar and shove them roughly out the door. Through the front windows of the tap, I saw both of them land on their arses on the hard ground.

"Here you are, lad." The old man I had been standing next to at the bar shoved a glass in my hand. "It won't straighten your nose, but it will keep the pain away for a bit."

I winced at the sight of my bloodied hand holding the small glass. I shook my head to get some sense back into my brain and tipped back the contents and drank it in one gulp. Whatever the alcohol, it burned steadily down my throat until it hit my belly where it exploded and threatened to come back up. The old man noticed my distress and began to pound his fist on my back.

"What the hell is that stuff?" I croaked out between gasps.

"A unique brew," the old man said as he handed me a damp cloth and indicated I should take one of the vacated seats left by the East India Company men.

"You're either really brave or really stupid," the old man said as he took the bench opposite me. The barmaid came by and cleaned up the spilled tankards, and I ordered two more with the wave of my hand.

"Most people who know me say it's a little of both." I winced as I felt around my battered face. My nose felt broken. My eyes had already swollen to the point where keeping my vision clear was a challenge.

The door to the tap opened with a bang, but I was too engrossed in cleaning up my face to bother looking around at the newcomer.

"Mickey." A familiar voice intoned, and I looked up in surprise. "Thanks for keeping an eye on my friend until I could get here."

Recognizing Finlayson's voice, I called out, "You call this a job well done?" Waving a hand in front of my face, I continued, "I'm surprised you can recognize me!"

"I would recognize your ugly mug anywhere." Finlayson grinned and took the seat opposite me after the old man named Mickey stood up.

"What are you doing in Calcutta?" I asked in a small voice. "I thought you had a bit of revenge to dish up."

A wicked grin lit up Finlayson's face, and my eyes narrowed. "Not to worry, old friend; it's all in hand."

I grunted in response, wondering what he had been up to since he left Singapore a couple of months back. It was probably better not to ask and claim ignorance.

The barmaid set a tankard of ale in front of Finlayson and two of the small glasses of Mickey's mystery alcohol. Finlayson dropped a few coins into the girl's hand and winked. I raised the small glass, intending to down it in one gulp again when Finlayson's hand shot out.

"Neptune's balls! Don't drink that; it'll probably make you blind!" Finlayson plucked the drink from my grasp.

"As you can see, that would make little difference." I indicated my swollen face. "Besides, I've already had one." I spared a glance over to the bar where Mickey saluted me with his glass and drank it down in one. "What the hell is it?"

"The dregs of the rum barrel." Finlayson pulled a long face. "I wouldn't even feed it to my dog if I had one." He picked up his tankard and drank a couple of mouthfuls of ale. "I assume you're here to see Lord Hastings."

Wincing, I took a drink from the full tankard of ale in front of me. "Does everyone know my business?"

"This is Calcutta, the wind carries rumors and farts," Finlayson commented crudely. "I *am* surprised you got here so quickly."

I shrugged and watched the other man. "No choice, really, the good Major General saw fit to hand me my summons at my wedding reception."

"Bastard," Finlayson swore with gusto. "He's still pissed we managed to outmaneuver him with the Dutch."

"And he dares to call my father a traitor. He planned to hand me over to the Dutch, while we were negotiating a peace treaty with them." My hands balled into fists.

"What did Sir Raffles have to say?" Finlayson asked as he cupped his tankard between his work-worn hands.

"The usual, not much. Watch my back; don't trust anyone." I sighed and banged my tankard on the scarred wooden table a few times. "The problem is that with his weakened position in the East India Company, my list of allies is none. Even my father's lawyer told me to be prepared for the worst when I met with him earlier."

"Who's your father's attorney?" Finlayson asked interestedly.

"Mr. Hatton, he's part of a large firm, I would guess he's a younger son running an office out here." I thought of the young man with the serious expression. "I was hoping he could tell me what Hastings has in store for the inquiry."

Finlayson shook his head. "Even with my connections, I haven't heard much. It's unusual, but not unique. The company tends to dig a moat and pull up the drawbridge when they know they are in the shit. Hastings is wounded and going down fast. Once he leaves Calcutta, all his power will vanish."

"Damn, when I saw you, I was hoping you might have a few leads for me." I was genuinely disappointed. Finlayson was an old ally, and he normally had a great ear for leads.

"What did the two company men want?" Finlayson asked suddenly, and my thoughts jerked back to the minutes before the fight. With my nose throbbing and my head feeling like it might split in two, it was hard to concentrate.

"They accused me of being a traitor." I thought back to the accusations the man in the brown jacket had made. "He was rambling on about the Brotherhood, but I thought it operated only in Singapore under Zheng Jing."

Finlayson's expression suddenly became wary, and he looked at me intently. "You said it yourself. When the East India Company is against you, reliable allies can be hard to find."

"Zheng Jing may be a hero to some." I thought of the way the dockworkers and even the Chinese mediators gave the man more respect than I figured he deserved. "But make no mistake: He is into something dangerous, and I sure as hell don't want to know what it is. Even if he has some leverage against the company." I took another drink of my ale.

Sighing loudly, Finlayson looked at me earnestly and said, "It's a shame you came to know of the Brotherhood in Singapore, but I assure you it is an organization that has far surpassed the borders of that small port." He waited while those words sunk into my brain.

"Are you telling me Zheng Jing's claws extend farther throughout the East?" I lowered my voice and glanced around the tap. The men enjoying the ales had become eerily quiet. Suddenly, the young man sitting across from me was a stranger, and I wondered how big a mess I had stumbled into.

Finlayson shrugged his shoulders. His eyes became intense as they bore into my own. "Zheng Jing is one man. A powerful man to be sure, but he is neither the beginning nor the end of the Brotherhood." Taking a swallow of his ale, he fortified his next words. "The Brotherhood is in response to the tyranny of the East India Company. Take a good look around you, Nathaniel, and tell me what you see."

I sat back on my stool and took a good look around the tap. A few men watched my every move while others were content to ignore me. At first, the room looked like any other wharfside tap, servicing the men who plied their trade on the sea. I was struck by something I hadn't noticed when I first entered. These were men who knew each other well enough to trust having their backs to the front door. They spoke in hushed tones that did not carry far. The standard rowdy behavior found in taps along the waterfront was missing.

"It's quiet," I noted, with no real idea of the significance of that observation.

"This is known as a place where men who are members of the Brotherhood can come and exchange news and gossip without the fear of the East India Company finding out." Finlayson nodded to the barman. "Think of it as a sanctuary." Finlayson appeared to be mulling over something, and he finally set his left forearm on the table and rolled up the slightly damp and dirty linen of his sleeve. On his inner elbow, where the skin was most sensitive, was a tattoo of two hands shaking.

I swore as I saw the tattoo on his arm. "Don't tell me that's what I think it is." My mind flashed back to Mickey who wore a similar mark. "What have you done?" My breath felt caught in my throat.

Finlayson rolled his sleeve back down. "The world is not black and white, Hawk. Your father taught me that."

"Do *not* bring my father into this discussion." I heard the steel in my voice. "Besides, what you say isn't true. He believed men were either good or bad, and it was up to the good ones to keep the world safe. He devoted his entire life to defeating pirates and those who threatened the innocent."

"The Royal Navy and the East India Company are hardly the innocents." Finlayson scoffed.

"You're missing the point." I slammed a hand down on the table not caring what the other patrons thought of the action. "He fought his whole life for loyalty and honor. There was never any gray area for him."

"I don't think you knew your father very well." Finlayson's voice was low, and I heard a thread of pity in it. He was suddenly very interested in the scars worked into the wood of the table.

"He was my father," I said and pushed away from the table. "We sailed together for years. I know everything about my father." As the words came out of my mouth, I knew they were a terrible lie. No one, including me, could ever know Sebastian Hawk. And if he was secretly plying the waters as a pirate ghost ship captain, I realized I knew even less about him.

"Good." Finlayson looked up from the table. "You know he would tell you to take all the help you can get. The Brotherhood is not a friend of the East India Company. We want to help you."

"Listen." I lowered my voice even though I knew everyone in the tap strained to hear my every word. "If you're in trouble with these people, we can work something out."

With a note of barely controlled exasperation, Finlayson looked at me and said, "What you don't seem to realize, Hawk, is that you are already a member of the Brotherhood."

"Unless set upon while asleep and given the same horrendous tattoo as yours, I know I'm not a member of the Brotherhood. I would remember joining." I let out a long breath.

"Anyone who is against the East India Company is a friend and ally of the Brotherhood." Finlayson held up his hand to forestall my next words. "There is more at stake here than Sebastian Hawk's career. We have a chance to take some power back from those who have used and abandoned honorable men because they did not fit into their neat ledgers. We can finally see some justice."

"I am *not* included in your we?" I stood up and tossed a few coins on the table. "And you're wrong. No one can take on the East India Company and hope to come away the victor. They own the table, the cards, and the game. My father would have given you the same advice."

Shuffling from behind the table before Finlayson could waylay me, I nodded at Mickey, who still stood at the bar, a faint smile on his face as he watched me leave. Outside of the tap in the fading light of day, I winced from the pain in my face. Hoping to find a mirror back at the warehouse, so I could see how much damage the company men had done to my face, I turned and faced the grim prospect of having no allies as I faced my personal Goliath.

Chapter 10
Charlotte

There was nothing I could do about the tear stains left on my cheeks after my night of crying. My mind faded into nothingness after the man had warned me against pursuing the men who had tricked Freddie at cards. I had pulled myself together enough to get home. Dutta gave me a worried look, but he said nothing as I took a lit candle and went up to the master bedroom. Remembering the feeling of rage that overcame me as I stared at my marital bed, a shiver went up my spine. After tearing all the bedclothes from the mattress, I lay on the warm wooden floors and cried for hours, not caring what anyone thought.

This morning, after a fitful night's rest, I scrubbed my face and determined to face the world. I was a survivor. The last few years proved this, and I would get through this current catastrophe, too. Standing outside of the neatly kept building where I knew Bigham kept his rooms, I glanced left and right. My instincts warned me someone might be following me. But I knew they might also be nothing more than residual distress of the attack.

I knocked discreetly on the painted black door and waited a few minutes before knocking again. The need to warn Bigham of the danger he was courting by making further inquiries into the card cheats gnawed at my conscience. The sound of shuffling feet finally came from the other side, and I waited impatiently. An elderly woman threw the door open with enough force to have me stepping back in surprise.

"Forgot your damn key again?" The words were out of the woman's mouth before she even had a chance to get a good look at my face. After a second's pause, she continued. "Who are you?"

"I'm Mrs. Hawk," I responded without hesitation. It was better to be honest in this situation; all I needed was someone to get wind of my visit to a bachelor's quarters. "I need to see Mr. Bigham at once; he is my man of business, and the matter is urgent."

The old lady gave me an appraising stare and moved out of the way for me to step into the narrow corridor. I stared at her for a minute, and she let out a deep breath. "He's on the third floor, on the right. Tell him the morning meal will be laid out as usual."

"I will pass on the message." The words were out of my mouth before I climbed the first step. Working my way up the steep staircase, I could hear loud snoring and the sounds of banging coming from the other rooms. It was early, but I was hoping Bigham would be up already. I knew from experience he was usually at the warehouse early.

A little out of breath, I turned to the right on the third floor and found the door I hoped belonged to Bigham. I took a short breath and knocked loudly on the portal. It did not take long for the door to open and for Bigham's large frame to fill the doorway.

"What the devil are you doing here?" Bigham asked in a surprised voice before leaning out and looking up and down the hall. He grabbed me roughly by the arm and dragged me into his room. I didn't have time to look around before his face loomed above mine. "You're a smart girl, and I, therefore, do not need to tell you all the disasters that could happen if word of your visit here this morning got around Singapore."

I felt anger building up inside my chest. Bigham had no idea of the danger that entangled him. "You know I would never have come here unless it was important." I felt my control slipping away, and I bit my lip and stared out a small window that looked out onto another building.

"Of course." Bigham stepped back to give me some space. "You look like hell."

A small laugh escaped through my tight lips. "I cannot believe why you're not married," I said drily before looking back at Bigham. The next minute would be hard, but I needed to get through it without panicking. "Last night, after I left you at the end of the street." I paused and focused on the incident and tried to be logical. "A man grabbed me." I saw Bigham flinch and reach out to me. I waved his hand away. "He warned me about the dangers of sticking my nose into affairs that do not involve me. He also told me to make sure you ended your inquiries into the identity of the men who cheated Freddie."

"Did he hurt you?" Bigham's voice was cold.

"No, he said he was warning me." I swallowed hard as I reviewed the rest of his threats. It could have been so much worse. "We need to focus on our other problem and forget about the money Freddie lost. Even if we knew who these men are, they and the money have long left Singapore, so there's no recourse either through the courts or other means." I let my words drift.

"I disagree," Bigham said with force, and I watched him, surprised. "Whoever these bastards are, we've got them worried. They sent a man to harass you. It means we're close."

Panic filled my chest and bile rose in my throat. I knew I had to use reason. "There is no point in pursuing the matter. They're dangerous men, and I won't have you or anyone else hurt, or worse, over nothing, because that's what this is: nothing. We have to accept our losses and focus on Zheng Jing." Even saying the black-market trader's name made me nervous.

"He's probably behind this whole thing," Bigham said and slashed a hand through the air. "It's a little convenient to find he owns the debt slips and just happens to have a solution to our little problem. He is up to his damned bollocks in this mess. Who else do you think he has blackmailed?"

"It hardly matters." I sighed dismissively. "We are not going to pursue this."

Light flared in Bigham's eyes, and I tensed, waiting for some new revelation. "We have no idea how far this plot reaches. If I were to find more information that linked Zheng Jing with the card players, we could use it against him and get out of his carefully laid plans."

"You *are* right about one thing." I straightened my back and walked toward his door. "We have no idea how deep this treachery runs. Zheng Jing might be working with the card players, and God knows whomever else. Our righteous indignation will be little shield against whatever revenge they decide to take against us."

"We need to see this through, for the good of everyone in Singapore." Bigham's blue eyes went hard, and I knew he was going to play what he believed to be the winning card. "Mr. Hawk would agree with me."

"Unfortunately for you, Mr. Hawk is not in Singapore," I said with bitterness, thinking of Sarah Buck. "He's off dealing with his troubles and hardly has the time or resources to deal with mine." I placed a hand on the brass doorknob and turned to leave.

"Uncovering a black-market conspiracy in Singapore involving Zheng Jing and his associates could help Mr. Hawk with the East India Company. The only thing they hate more than pirates is smugglers." Bigham's words brought an image of a gallows sweeping into my head.

"You do not need to remind me." I thought of walking up those lonely, wooden steps to my doom along with Bigham, my father, and Freddie. "We do not know whom we can trust."

"Sir Raffles would be a good place to start," Bigham suggested, and I looked back at him.

"He's on his way out. Dr. Crawfurd has already taken over much of the running of Singapore from Raffles and the good Major General." I said the last with a sneer. "For now, we follow Zheng Jing's rules. I concede; if there is a chance to get out of this mess, we should take it. But it has to be safe for everyone. I cannot have another person's death on my conscience."

"Another person?" Bigham frowned.

I opened the door. "Please do as I ask and forget this scheme for now. We need to act like it's business as usual at Carstairs and Son."

Taking Bigham's grunt as agreement, I swiftly stepped back out into the hallway, eyes cast down. I flew down the stairs and out the door. Sighing in relief, I headed back to the European Quarter going over my conversation with Bigham. The terrible feeling that Bigham would continue to pursue the matter clouded my thinking until I had convinced myself to turn around and try another form of persuasion.

"My dear Mrs. Hawk; how lovely to see you so soon." Cornelius Thistlewaite was leaning against a building at the end of Bigham's street.

Eyes narrowing at the other man's smug expression, I didn't bother to hide my irritation. There were no social strictures we needed to maintain here. "Mr. Thistlewaite, out enjoying the morning air?" I had the distinct impression he had someone follow me.

"Mornings are my favorite time of day here in Singapore. It can be quite cool before the sun comes up." Cornelius pushed away from the building. "I believe this is the street Mr. Bigham, your man of business, lives on."

I walked by Cornelius and continued down the road hoping he would go away. Unfortunately, I felt his large presence beside me after a few steps. "You are remarkably well informed, sir. He is breaking his fast if you wish to speak with him." There was no point in denying I had an interview with Bigham this morning. Whoever Cornelius had set on me would already have given him the details.

"No need to bother a man at his meal; it only causes indigestion." Cornelius laughed at his joke. "You are about your business early this morning." He left the sentence open.

"And happily concluded," I said with a polite half-smile. There was no way I would volunteer any more information to Cornelius than needed. He was neither a friend nor an ally.

"Your husband would be interested in knowing your early morning ramblings." Cornelius prodded.

"I hope you're right," I said as we passed a few men on their way to work. "We will have something to discuss when he returns from Calcutta."

"You're up to something." Cornelius growled and gripped my elbow, bringing me to an abrupt halt.

"Yes, I am," I said, watching as Cornelius's eyes widened a fraction. "I am trying to salvage my father's business from the dung heap."

Cornelius shook his head. "I thought you already played your part as the heroine when you convinced me to buy the Monarch."

"Surely, you don't expect me to discuss my business affairs with a competitor." I stared into his eyes boldly. We stood in the middle of the street for longer than politeness dictated.

"It was a mistake for Nathaniel to marry you." Cornelius let go of my arm. "You are not to be trusted, and I will make sure he knows it."

A part of me wanted to argue with him, while the rest of me only wanted to get away. It had been a hellish twelve hours, and I needed to regroup. "Nathaniel loves me; he will never listen to your lies." I felt confident as I said the words. The fact that I was starting to doubt my feelings for him, especially after Sarah Buck's news last night, was inconsequential.

"I will be watching," Cornelius warned and walked away without a backwards glance.

I rubbed my forehead and wondered how I was supposed to stay one step ahead of Cornelius while dealing in black-market tea for Zheng Jing.

Chapter 11
Nathaniel

"The carriage you wanted is waiting out front, Mr. Hawk." The old man from the previous day called through the closed door to my little sanctuary.

"Thank you, I will be out in a moment," I called back and looked at my broken face in a small mirror. The old man had snapped the larger bones back into place when I returned from the inn on the previous evening. Unfortunately, my nose would never be straight again, and I wondered if I could ever breathe out of my nostrils.

Picking up my hat from the bed, I stuffed it on my head and left my sanctuary. There was nothing more I could do about my appearance, and if Lord Hastings took issue with me, I could only ask him not to have his lackeys pick fights.

"Good luck today, sir." The old man opened the door to the coach, and I stepped inside.

"Not much to be done now," I replied, sitting back into the worn cushions of the coach. The driver whistled, and the horses jolted into motion. The coach ride to Government House was a luxury I fully intended to enjoy while I was in Calcutta. Not being sweaty and dusty upon the arrival at one's destination was an extravagance compared to Singapore.

I wondered what Charlotte had been up to these past few weeks. She was certainly caring for her brother and her father, but I hoped she was taking time for herself. She had been worried about something before we even left the church for the reception, but I had put her off telling me, wanting the day to be perfect. I snorted as the carriage rounded a sharp corner. Now, here I was in Calcutta while she remained at home, alone. I hoped she wouldn't take too long to get over my newly flattened nose.

A sharp rap from above, along with the gradual slowing down of the horses, had me staring out the window. The palatial Government House stood out against the background of gardens. It looked as it had when I was a boy. As a child, I remembered my mother readying herself for balls and banquets held at the opulent building. Now I knew why she took such care of her appearance. She had probably been meeting any one of her numerous lovers. I had never been inside.

Pushing the thought aside, I alighted from the carriage and paid the driver. The traffic on the streets was picking up with the usual carts, buggies, and palanquins. I stepped off the curb onto the walking path leading up to the massive, forbidding structure. Someone once told me Wellesley built it as a symbol of the East India Company's power in the East. It certainly fit the part.

The further I progressed up the path through the formal gardens, the rest of Calcutta faded away in a haze of noise. The shouts of hawkers and drivers didn't penetrate the sanctuary of the English-style garden.

I tried to compose my thoughts as I walked up the great staircase to the building's main entrance. I found the complex intimidating when I was younger. Now that I had lived in London, it was just another ostentatious piece of architecture. Two guards stood at the top of stairs guarding the entrance. They wore red military uniforms and held rifles with bayonets pointed in the air.

The clearing of a throat caught my attention, and I looked toward one of the pillars surrounding the entrance. My two friends from the previous evening watched me with narrowed eyes. I was satisfied to see both looked as battered as I. The child in me wanted to make a rude gesture and continue the fisticuffs from the previous evening.

"Mr. Hawk, I don't believe I've had the pleasure." A cultured voice snapped my attention back to the two soldiers at the entrance. In between the two rigged-out guards stood a man who held out his hand. He was dressed in an impeccable blue suit of trousers and jacket his cravat tied in an austere knot.

I shook the other man's hand. "You have me at a disadvantage," I said, peering at the other man's features and trying to remember whether I had met him before.

"Officially, I am Viscount McCarr." McCarr released my hand. "However, while I am working in the capacity of Lord Hasting's private secretary, I'm known as Mr. Salcombe."

"A pleasure to meet you, I'm sure," I said.

"I wish it could have been under different circumstances." McCarr shook his head as his light blue eyes studied my expression. He turned and indicated the open door. "If you will follow me."

Passing the guards on the threshold of Government House, I felt as if I had stepped into another world. The heels of my polished boots rung out against the white marble of the floor, and I tried to keep my eyes from straying to the enormous oil paintings framed in gold lining the walls. This was a world away from the trashy, poverty-stricken streets I had come through to get here.

"It's a bit extravagant for my taste," McCarr commented, as we passed room after room. The servants were already about their morning tasks, silently slipping through the grand hallways. McCarr lowered his voice, "We bought our title a couple of generations back, but I don't think it's ever really fit."

Not having a response for the other man, I nodded. "Will I be seeing Lord Hastings this morning?"

McCarr straightened as he glanced over at me. "He was informed of your arrival in Calcutta yesterday morning." He hesitated for a moment as we stopped in front of a pair of white painted doors with more gold trim. "I would like to say the men were ordered to make sure you did not find trouble in the city while you were here. They were not authorized to engage in any way with you."

"A spy is still a spy." I looked at the other man. Despite his friendly demeanor, there was something slithering underneath his steady blue gaze. "I doubt you would be apologizing if I had never found them out."

I watched as a small tight smile crossed the other man's lips. "Forgiveness or permission, Mr. Hawk; we all play the game."

The doors opened, and I found myself staring into a large room. This room was an interesting contrast to the rest of Government House. Instead of white marble, the decorator had used dark wooden paneling. A row of windows that reached from the floor to the ceiling stood on the right side, overlooking one of the formal gardens letting in an abundance of natural light. In the center of the room, a long table stood with numerous chairs laid out on either side. At the far end, a portly gentleman sat at the end of the table along with a couple of other men. They all looked up and stopped their discussion as the door opened.

"Lord Hastings, may I present Mr. Hawk," McCarr intoned in a loud voice that echoed off the walls.

The man in question nodded his head but refrained from speaking. I followed McCarr into the room, intensely aware of the other men's stares. There was no question I was in enemy territory now, and Raffles' words came back to me. Any one of these men would be willing to stab me in the back to further their careers at the company. Hell, Lord Hastings would see me hanged instead of my father if it would save his position.

As I followed McCarr into the room, the only sounds were our footsteps and the shuffling of paper. McCarr indicated a chair not far from where the rest of the group sat, then took his seat.

Silence filled the room for several heartbeats, and I wondered if they were waiting for me to make the first move. As a seasoned card player, I knew it would be far better to sit back and work out their strategy. They apparently had discussed how this interview would proceed. I already knew McCarr was supposed to give me the impression he was on my side.

"Good of you to join us, Mr. Hawk. Though I hoped I would have seen you yesterday." Lord Hastings voice reminded me of an elderly grandfather rebuking a grandchild over tardiness. I said nothing in return, as the man had not greeted me. "Your father would never have been late."

I fought a smile. If Lord Hastings wanted to push me, he would have to find something much better to use than my father. Others had judged my life against Sebastian Hawk's, and I had always been found wanting. Pretending to pick a piece of lint from my black jacket, I said, "Since my father is dead, you would have waited a very long time."

Out of the corner of my eye, I saw McCarr cover his mouth on a small cough. The two other men at the table continued to watch me with disinterested expressions.

"You should know the allegations not only against your father but also against yourself are serious offenses. We are fully prepared to prosecute you both to the fullest extent of the law." Lord Hastings leaned forward, the grandfatherly expression he had worn previously wiped away. In its place, Lord Hastings had become every inch the Governor General of India.

I couldn't resist poking the overstuffed administrator again; I looked into his eyes. "As I said before, Captain Sebastian Hawk is dead. Unless you're willing to search Davy Jones's locker for his mortal remains, you stand very little chance of hauling him up by the neck until dead."

"Do not play the obstinate fool with me, boy." Lord Hastings voice boomed throughout the nearly empty room. His face had become a mottled red. "I know men like you, Mr. Hawk." Lord Hastings pointed a sausage-like finger in my direction. "You think because you're a son of the colonial empire, the East India Company owes you something. Let me tell you. We owe you nothing." He swiped his meaty paw through the air for emphasis.

McCarr used the moment of silence that followed to interject. "Lord Hastings, it might be better to get on with the formal questioning." He nodded at me. "Mr. Hawk has been infinitely cooperative in coming to Calcutta on such short notice."

Lord Hastings snorted and sat back in his chair never taking his eyes from me. It was, however, McCarr who asked the first question. "How well did you know your father?"

I settled back into my chair and schooled my features. This was a game I could play. "As well as any man, I suppose."

The man seated on Lord Hastings's right began scribbling down something onto a sheet paper. The man seated opposite with a large, red bulbous nose spoke next. "Would you mind clarifying that statement?"

"He was at sea for most of my childhood, but even onboard the Constance, he was the captain. I was only another kid to be trained as an officer," I explained. There was nothing in that statement they probably didn't already know.

"You spent your childhood with your mother here in Calcutta?" McCarr asked, looking up from his notes with interest.

"Yes," I replied, wondering where this line of questioning might lead.

"Her brother is a slaver, very poor society." Lord Hastings made the comment with a twist of his mouth. "Such a dirty trade."

"I couldn't agree more." I didn't bother to explain I meant both of his comments. Lord Hastings harumphed in response.

The man with the red, bulbous nose asked, "When you were aboard the Constance, did you have any reason to believe your father was working against the East India Company?"

"Isn't that a question you should ask the purser?" I stared at the other man, not breaking eye contact.

The man with the bulbous nose cleared his throat and looked down at his papers. "A midshipman by the name of Alex Mahoney?"

Mr. Mahoney was a scrupulous purser, counting every damn bean, cup of grog and wages owed and earned. "Yes, Mr. Mahoney was the purser while I was aboard the Constance."

"He was aboard the Diligence along with your father." McCarr filled the little silence. "In fact, many of the men who served on the Constance were with your father on the Diligence. Those who were not are either retired and not to be found or dead. A strange coincidence has made you and your friend Captain Masters the only living members of the Constance crew that we can track down."

I remained silent. McCarr had not asked a question, and I was not going to start blabbering like an idiot. With effort, I relaxed further into my chair. There was no rack in the corner or cat-o-nines sitting on the table. I was perfectly safe.

"It is very odd that we cannot find these men." Lord Hastings's chest puffed out and his eyes narrowed. "The whole thing smells of a conspiracy." Again, I kept my mouth closed.

"Were you ever privy to deals or concessions your father made with pirates?" The man with the bulbous nose asked.

"No." I gave the man a frown. "The idea is utterly ridiculous."

"Why is it nonsense for your father to be making money on the side with pirates or with enemies of the East India Company?" The man with the bulbous nose said. "He was an astute military man who wielded enormous power."

"Had my father been making deals with pirates and such, there would be evidence of his betrayal," I said stubbornly, refusing to believe anything these men had to say. "To be frank, I cannot believe you allowed Major General Farquhar to ruin my wedding and force me to come to Calcutta to answer these ridiculous questions." I attempted to stand up. "This is a waste of all our time."

"You will sit, Mr. Hawk, or we will decide your father's fate without your input." Lord Hastings's eyes were cold and calculating.

I sat back down again. "As I have reminded you, my father is dead. Nothing you decide here will change the fact."

"We control how much of your father's pension will be paid out to his estate." The man with the bulbous nose pointed out. "Even if you do not need the money, your father supported your mother for most of her life. Surely, you can stay and answer our questions for her sake."

Out of the corner of my eye, I saw McCarr's body shift, and I knew he was watching me carefully.

"My mother normally does very well for herself without my father's contributions. As for cooperating, I am sitting here and answering your questions to the best of my ability, but at this point, I wonder if you even know what questions to ask." I finished with a long sigh.

"Your father was a man of secrets," Lord Hastings spat out.

Wanting the interview to be over I answered back, "As I have been reminded several times since his death."

"There's evidence linking your father to dealings with pirates, men of fortune, and smuggling rings all around the world." The man with the bulbous nose shifted some papers in front of him. "He was likely a traitor to his country."

Before I could think to say anything against the outrageous slander, McCarr spoke. "Do you know of an organization called the Brotherhood?"

I tried to hide my alarm at the mention of the apparently not so secret organization. "There are always rumors."

"The Brotherhood is more than a rumor, Mr. Hawk. It is a group that has worked in secret to undermine the power of Great Britain." Lord Hastings's voice held a pompous thread. "They are a threat to the very existence of the fabric of the British Empire and all its dominions."

"You were seen drinking yesterday at an inn with known sympathies to this underground organization, Mr. Hawk." McCarr's stare never wavered.

"Thanks again for the broken nose. I don't suppose there will be any compensation for it," I asked dryly.

"Were you meeting with your co-conspirators yesterday hoping to get your stories aligned before you came in today?" The man with the bulbous nose inquired. "You were not very friendly when you discovered they were agents of the East India Company."

"In fact, they were not happy to be found out." I thought back to the two men who had been waiting out front of Government House to see me. "The fact I was drinking in a tap with rumored allegiance to a group of men who many believe do not exist is pure coincidence. I went there for a pint, like everyone else."

"I assure you the Brotherhood is very real, Mr. Hawk." McCarr sat back in his chair. "And they are dangerous."

Frustration welled up inside me. "I am not a member of this Brotherhood if that is your next question." The words tumbled into the room, and the three men who were interrogating me looked at each other. A silent communication passed between them before McCarr spoke.

"We think you might be telling the truth, Mr. Hawk. Nothing in your behavior leading up to your arrival in Singapore last year indicates you have any ties to the Brotherhood or your father." McCarr took a deep breath and plowed on. "But there is evidence to suggest your father was a member of the Brotherhood. In fact, we believe he was deeply involved in many of the organization's more clandestine activities."

"Impossible." The word was out of my mouth before I could think properly. Was it impossible? Who had been the captain of the ghost ship? There was something in my gut that told me I had seen my father. He had secrets even when I was aboard the Constance. He held his secrets close. I thought of Finlayson, showing me his tattoo. He knew my father; it's how we became friends and allies last year. There was a big problem with all of this. "There's a man in Singapore who is rumored to be the head of the Brotherhood. I know my father; he would never have dealt with this man."

"You are referring to a man named Zheng Jing?" The man with the bulbous nose read from his notes. "He is a Chinese mediator and, in recent years, has headed a consortium of Chinese traders. They recently bought a couple of ships of their own."

"Yes. I have heard the rumors like everyone else, but there's no proof." I went over my dealings with the man. "Among his Chinese compatriots, he's highly respected, but most of the European traders try to ignore him. I do not see how Zheng Jing can be the leader of an organization you say has such a far reach."

"We do not think he is the head of the Brotherhood, Mr. Hawk," Lord Hastings interjected. "But he is our best lead in finding out who is. We have tracked this organization's activities for years, since before your father's death. We thought he might finally lead us to the top of the organization."

"He was working with you against the Brotherhood." I was confused. "I thought you believed he was a member of the Brotherhood."

"Your father was never given a brief on the Brotherhood. Neither was his friend, Sir Raffles," McCarr explained. "The whole operation was given to Major General Farquhar when he took over the administration of Singapore. We had heard rumors here in Calcutta that Singapore would be the next port to become infested with these terrorists."

My eyebrows rose into my forehead. "I have been told the Brotherhood is about helping sailors and forming a community."

"Precisely what they want you to think, Mr. Hawk." Lord Hastings broke in again. "They want you to believe they set up innocent schemes to aid the families of drowned sailors or to find men work who need it. In fact, they're trying to subvert the realities of how this world works. The poor are here to do their masters' bidding, without question. The powerful have the responsibility to see to the welfare of the rest of the population. This exchange has worked for hundreds of years. Here in Calcutta, we can see the perfect relationship between the rich and the powerful and their responsible kindness to the rest of the population."

"I still do not see what any of this has to do with me," I said stubbornly. First, they accused my father of being a traitor, and now they appeared fixated on the Brotherhood. Neither subject was one I knew much about.

"Everything and nothing, Mr. Hawk." McCarr sat back in his chair. He looked like a man who had finally finished with the pleasantries and was now on to the purpose of this whole meeting. "We have little doubt your father was somehow involved in the Brotherhood. However, if the fact became known that he was actively working against the East India Company, all his years of hard work would have been for naught. Let us not previcate. He fought wars, and he won battles; if his reputation suffers, the East India Company and some very powerful officials in London must answer some seriously difficult questions."

"You want to bring down the real Brotherhood and save your reputations." My mind was working quickly. "In fact, you must to save face, especially with the Dutch since we have just made a treaty."

"Yes." Lord Hastings hissed. "The problem is that little bastards like Farquhar do not know their place. He was supposed to find evidence against Zheng Jing, not pursue his personal vendetta against bloody Raffles." I watched the other man's blood pressure rise dangerously as his face reddened.

"This is where you come in, Mr. Hawk." McCarr gave me a practiced smile I was sure he must have worked on hundreds of clerks hoping to get a pat on the head from their master. "We need someone to watch Zheng Jing; he will eventually contact his superiors. When we catch them, we will exonerate your father, and any contact he had with the Brotherhood will quietly disappear for our mutual benefit."

"What makes you think I can find anything on Zheng Jing?" I shook my head in disappointment. "The man doesn't even like me, and the feeling is very mutual. Besides spying is a dirty game played by men with no notions of loyalty or honor."

"Please, Mr. Hawk." McCarr gave me a condescending smile. "Spying is a man's work. Besides, we just need for you to send us the names of men whom he counts as acquaintances. Eventually, he will give up the game."

"What if I stand up right now and tell you to stuff this up your arses," I said aggressively. There was no way I was even going to find information on Zheng Jing. The very wharves of Singapore seethed with his informants who always surrounded him.

"You have no choice, Mr. Hawk." Lord Hastings pressed forward, his belly fitting snugly against the table. "I would have continued using the monetary threat of your father's pension and assets against you, but I think you believe you're too intelligent not to need the coin. So, I will make myself very clear. If you do not find the information we need to take down the Brotherhood, the East India Company will see to your ruination. Do not think this is personal, Mr. Hawk. My days of power are ending, but there's enough at stake here for this to be bigger than you or me."

I looked into Hastings's eyes, and I saw the truth in them. He was deadly serious, and I had to decide whether I wanted to lie in bed with the devil.

Chapter 12
Charlotte

"My dear, thank you for having us this afternoon." Mrs. Meacham peered around the masculine study at the front of the house with a critical eye. "You must be so disappointed that Mr. Hawk had to leave Singapore in such haste."

I set my teacup down into its matching porcelain saucer and smiled at the most incorrigible gossip in all of Singapore. "It was a great trial to have Mr. Hawk called away to Calcutta, but we have the rest of our lives together to enjoy each other's company."

Mrs. Meacham's daughter, Agatha, sniffed. I doubted she could help herself with such a pinched nose, the pained expression she regularly wore, giving the impression she was either ill or surrounded by a bad smell. "Still, the Major General should never have come to the reception. Terrible manners, indeed."

As always, the two of them were digging for information, anything they could pass onto the rest of the circle of gossipmongers. I was sure the fact I had not remodeled the study into a decent drawing room would be all over Singapore by nightfall.

Everyone already knew of my dislike of Farquhar, so I saw no reason to dissemble. "The Major General lacks manners, in general, dear Agatha; we cannot expect him to behave within the bounds of proper society. He is a soldier, after all."

Agatha sniffed in response, either in agreement or disagreement; there was no way to tell.

"Have you had any word of Mr. Hawk since he left Singapore?" Mrs. Meacham asked before popping a pastry into her oversized mouth.

"I'm expecting to receive something in the next packet. Mr. Hawk would have only arrived in Calcutta in the last week or so if the weather afforded it. Otherwise, as we all know it might have taken longer." I smiled and nodded at Dutta to enter the study and refresh the pot of tea. The sight of the fresh tea leaves made my stomach sink, and I had to force my gaze away.

"Calcutta is so much more civilized," Agatha said and looked out the front windows of the drawing room. "I keep begging Papa to consider moving back to India, but he has refused."

"Silly girl." Mrs. Meacham rapped her daughter's hands were her pink fan. "Your papa knows what is best for your future." Agatha set her pinched gaze on her mother but did not reply.

There had been a rumor the girl was in love with some clerk at the East India Company. Unfortunately, his family had not been good enough for the upright Mr. Meacham, and he moved his family to Singapore.

"I'm surprised Mrs. Buck is not here this afternoon. If I remember correctly, she is a particular friend of yours." Mrs. Meacham said, changing the subject when she realized she was not going to get any more information about Nathaniel and the East India Company.

My smile grew tight as I thought of my rival. Mrs. Buck had successfully informed the entire population of Singapore of her good news. Every time I stepped into a conversation, I was reminded of Nathaniel's infidelity, whether he was the father of her baby or not. I was glad Nathaniel had not sent a letter back from Calcutta yet. My heart still hurt from Sarah Buck's revelation. I needed time to figure out how I was going to process the fact she might be carrying my husband's child. The feeling of betrayal sat like a stone in my gut while Cornelius and Zheng Jing did their best to entrap me.

"We are familiar acquaintances, nothing more," I said, picking up the teapot and pouring out a measure into Mrs. Meacham's empty cup and my own.

"I daresay we will all be counting the days until the child arrives," Mrs. Meacham slyly remarked as she reached for the sugar.

Agatha snorted, and for once, the look on her face relaxed. She looked years younger without the frown. "You mean you want to prove if the rumors have merit?"

The sinking feeling in my stomach and light-headedness that was creeping into my brain were becoming familiar companions these past few days. I set the cream down, unable to hide the tremor in my hand. "What rumor?" I tried to make my voice casual, but knew I had failed when Agatha's gaze fixed on me, a pitying smile on her face flashing before she resumed her usual pinched nose expression.

"Which one, Mrs. Hawk?" Agatha asked and reached for her cold cup of tea. "There are several rumors circulating over the sire of her baby. One says it was a ship captain from the Junk season just passed. The man was willing to ease the pain of a merry widow before he made the dangerous run back to London. Another rumor would have the child's sire as any number of men who frequent her bed."

Mrs. Meacham inched forward on the settee. "My dear Agatha, you should not be discussing such things as you are not a married lady, yet," she admonished. Then, lowering her voice, she added, "I have it from a very reliable source that Mrs. Buck has gone through her widow's portion and has invited men into her bed to…well, you know." Mrs. Meacham nodded her head once and winked at me.

"Mother, you're ridiculous," Agatha exclaimed. "She's speaking of the world's oldest profession, Mrs. Hawk. I'm very sure your delicate sensibilities will not be offended by knowing everyone believes Mrs. Buck is a kept woman."

"Agatha, close your mouth this instant!" Mrs. Meacham's voice had gone up an octave. "This is not how I taught you to behave in polite society."

"Mother, if this is an example of how I'm supposed to act, then I do not believe it fits the word polite." Agatha rose from her place on the other side of the table. "Mrs. Hawk, you should know many people believe your husband is the man who is keeping Mrs. Buck. I for one do not believe a bar of it, but I would want someone to tell me rather than whisper behind their hands."

"Thank you, Agatha. It is not always easy to be the one telling the truth." I rose from my seat. There was no way I would comment on whether I thought my husband was keeping Sarah Buck as his mistress. "The afternoon does wear on." I let my words fade away.

"We should be going, Mother," Agatha said with some steel in her voice. The other woman still looked slightly stunned at her daughter's forward behavior. The small part of me that was not dying inside thinking of Nathaniel's betrayal admired the girl; perhaps I had read her wrong.

"I would be pleased if you came again." I turned toward the doors leading Agatha out of the study hoping Mrs. Meacham would follow on our heels.

The front door closed on Mrs. Meacham and Agatha, and I let out a long breath. Instead of going upstairs to the room where I knew damned well Sarah Buck had been naked, I went back into the study. I looked over all the flat surfaces. They might have started in here. A few kisses, Nathaniel would have pushed Sarah's bodice down. Stop it. My fists clenched as a sob rose from my throat. I stumbled toward the chair and let out the tears that had been threatening since Agatha made her revelation.

"Madam." Dutta had moved silently into the room. I continued to sit away from the door, and he made no move to enter the study. "May I clean up the tray?"

"Yes, thank you, Dutta." I reached for a silk kerchief I kept in the sleeve of my dress. It had been my mother's, and I kept it for luck. I rubbed my thumb over the intricately threaded design. It had not given me much luck lately.

Dutta finished clearing the tea tray, but he did not move from in front of me.

"Is there something I can help you with, Dutta?" I asked with a watery smile.

"This was dropped off for you while you entertained Mrs. Meacham and Miss Meacham." Dutta held out a tightly wrapped piece of paper. I stared at it for longer than necessary and felt an urge to refuse the missive. What if it was from Nathaniel?

I plucked the letter from Dutta's hand. "Thank you, Dutta, I was supposed to dine at my father's this evening, but I think I shall stay in. I will write a short note excusing myself if you deliver it."

"Of course, Madam." Dutta politely stepped back and took up the tray leaving me in solitude with the letter.

I flipped over the envelope looking for an address written in a familiar hand. The front of the carefully folded paper was blank except for a small round red stamp with several Chinese characters and two hands shaking. Frowning at the symbol, I used my thumbnail to dislodge the plain wax seal and unfold the piece of paper. A coin fell out of the folds and landed in my lap. I studied it for a moment. The design was like the stamp on the front of the paper with one crucial difference. Only the shaking hands remained, the Chinese lettering was absent. I read the three lines written across the page in red lettering.

> A boy will come for you at eight.
> Come alone with the coin.
> Burn this.

Without a doubt, I knew this was a message from Zheng Jing. It could have been from the men who had threatened me before, but my instincts told me otherwise. Turning the coin over in my hand, I realized there was no escape from my future. There was no point in speculating whether Zheng Jing had set up this whole scenario to gain access to Carstairs and Son's ship. I would dance to the tune of his damned jig to save the necks of my father and my worthless brother.

My life might be forfeit, and I wondered if Nathanial would even care? Sarah Buck's triumphant face rose in my memory from the dinner at Cornelius's house. Would they marry right away? Is it inevitable that I should fail?

I went to the large, darkly polished desk on the other side of the room. I found a flint in one of the drawers and used it to light a candle sitting on the top of the desk, usually used for melting sealing wax. Once the wick was alight, I put the paper to the flame and watched as the message turned to white ash, dropping the remaining corner into the candle's dish.

I held the coin tightly in my hand, staring at the remains of the letter. A moment of madness flickered through my brain. What if I just let go? My breath came in little pants, and I wondered what it would look like if I just allowed everything to burn down around me. Revel in the chaos of not caring and dance away from everything and everyone.

Yellow birds, fluttering against the window, settled on the sill. Their still forms brought me back from my thoughts of escape. I had responsibilities to my father, my brother, and even to Nathaniel, regardless of whether he deserved my loyalty.

Chapter 13
Nathaniel

"You will have to forgive Lord Hastings," McCarr spoke to me under his breath as we watched Lord Hastings and the other two men leave the room through a door on the opposite end. "His time in India, as well as with the East India Company altogether, is running thin."

"I've heard the rumors." I stared at the closed door at the other end of the room while thinking over Lord Hastings's last words. "It appears I don't have much of a choice."

"Mr. Hawk, everyone has choices." McCarr indicated the door we had previously used. "Please follow me."

With little recourse to do otherwise, I followed McCarr back out into the opulent hallways of Government House. Lord Hastings and McCarr were playing a dangerous game, and I was to be the cannon fodder in the first volley. "I will catch the next packet home, Mr. McCarr. This whole venture is a waste of time, you know. You haven't gotten any new information for me, and I don't give a damn if you think my father was a member of this so-called Brotherhood. I believe you're the ones with the most to lose."

McCarr glanced at me and gave me a weary look. He pointed at the walls and then to his ears. "Mr. Hawk, I think it would be best if you came to my office to sign the official documents saying you're not cooperating with the East India Company on this matter."

"I have to sign something?" My voice incredulous, I blurted, "I suppose some sod of a clerk will have to write it out in triplicate and send it off to parts unknown."

Clearing his throat to cover his laughter, McCarr observed, "My office is not far." He then began purposely walking down the road, lengthening his stride enough to make me ignore my surroundings in order to keep up.

We turned a corner, and I saw a young man in a red uniform straighten as we approached. McCarr nodded to him and opened the door the young man guarded. I stepped through into a well-appointed office crowded with stacks of paper, shelves of ledgers, official-looking seals and devices scattered over a wooden desk.

The door behind me shut with a click, and McCarr moved to the side of the room while I took a seat. "Rum?" he asked.

"Scotch, if you have it." The sun had barely reached the midday mark, but after my morning, I needed a drink.

"I heard your father was a rum man." McCarr set a crystal glass on the desk in front of me and moved to his chair, glass in hand.

"After our interview this morning, you must have realized I'm very different from my father." I reached for the scotch and took a sip. It was a superior blend, and I hummed my approval.

Apropos of my satisfied hum, McCarr raised his glass in a salute. "There are some perks to putting up with all the bollocks of the company. After pausing to take a sip, he looked at me frankly as he gathered his thoughts. "I apologize for before, but you never know who might be listening; the Brotherhood is everywhere. Even the damn servants have taken up the cause."

"Maybe their cause of equality for all men is a worthy one." I watched the other man as I set my glass down.

"Christ and all his apostles! Don't let Hastings hear you say that! I have to listen to a speech on the proper order of man at least twice a day." McCarr set down his glass. "I would have handled this completely differently. Hastings wanted to threaten you into submission. The fact is, if you do not cooperate, he can and will make your life impossible. You're newly married with a business to run in perilous times; you cannot afford to make the company your enemy."

"So what do you propose?" I was genuinely curious to know what this man thought. "I was surprised the interview was not a formal inquiry."

"As I indicated before, the Brotherhood is everywhere. They have infiltrated the very fabric of the empire, and there is no way to get rid of them unless we take the beast's head off." For the first time since meeting him this morning, McCarr seemed to become serious. "I propose a simple exchange of information. Right now, Zheng Jing is our best lead into the Brotherhood."

"I'm surprised you haven't gotten a lead here," I said slowly. "This is the jewel in the crown. I thought you company folk would guard it jealousy."

"We do." McCarr stared across the desk without looking at me. "There are Brotherhood members everywhere, businesses like the inn you drank in last night fairly shout their allegiance. But we cannot find men who are any better than street thugs. The city is well established, and the leaders well hidden. Singapore, on the other hand, is another matter. Even though it's growing exponentially, it's smaller and much harder to hide in."

There was something wrong with the whole connection between Zheng Jing, my father, and the Brotherhood, but I couldn't place my finger on it. "Are you sure there's anything sinister about the Brotherhood, something more menacing than a bunch of men wanting to stick together for mutual support?"

"These men are involved in all manner of black-market trading, piracy, even treason against the Empire," McCarr said with finality. "We cannot take their threat seriously enough. The fact we cannot find anyone who worked with your father is worrying on many different levels. It may only be a coincidence, but what if someone is covering their tracks? You never know what might turn up on your doorstep."

"You don't need to frighten me. I have already paid for my father's legacy. Captain Collaart tried to kill me last year, with a little help from your friend, Major General Farquhar."

McCarr appeared embarrassed. "He's no friend of mine, I assure you, and we called out his actions as soon as word reached headquarters. It's part of the reason we're sending the Major General home. He likes power too much."

"I'm happy to hear it," I said, thinking hard. "Why not keep Raffles in Singapore? He has been good for the port." He might have gotten me mixed up in a mess or two, but I was loyal.

"Believe me when I tell you, Sir Raffles has his problems. When the company decides his time is up, we'll take care of him." McCarr stared at his empty glass.

For a moment, each of us kept his thoughts to himself. To break the silence and move the conversation on, I said, "The idea of being used as a spy sets my teeth grinding, and I don't like feeling backed into a corner. But my father was loyal to his country and the East India Company. I suppose if there's a way to honor his memory and his legacy, as well as stay in the company's good graces; I shall have to do it."

McCarr's face lit up. "I'll try and keep you out of politics as much as I can."

"I'm not sure I can help you at all." I pursed my lips as I thought, inadvertently twisting my broken nose and making it throb with pain. "I have met Zheng Jing, and we are *not* friends."

"The business with Mrs. Sarah Buck's widow's portion?" McCarr asked. I looked at him quizzically. "Don't be surprised. The company has its spies. Gossips mostly, but they're quite useful."

"Among other reasons, yes. I cannot think of a good reason for getting close to the man." I tried to think of different reasons and discarded them all.

"We have set something up, and I know you're not going to like it at first but hear me out." McCarr crossed his legs. It was evident he had a vested interest in the plan. "Zheng Jing has been trying to expand his little consortium for a few years now; it's part of the reason he moved to Singapore in the first place. There are certain members of the East India Company who do not trust him because of the Brotherhood and other less reputable reasons."

"He *is* Chinese," I said flatly.

"Yes, well, we are men of our times," McCarr replied vaguely. "The point is: However efficiently we may have curtailed his progress, he's one damned resourceful man. This coming Junk season, he has contracted the services of a Dutch trading and shipping company to bolster his capacity."

"Zheng Jing is going to work with the Dutch?" I was shocked. "He's living and trading in a company port. Isn't that treason? My father would never be a part of anything that advanced the interests of Britain's enemies."

"The Dutch are no longer our enemy; we signed a treaty, and now we get to play happy families." McCarr's voice dripped with sarcasm. "As for the second point, I don't think you realize how far the Brotherhood extends. We believe it's an infection of global proportions. Moreover, one-half of the organization may have no idea of the goings-on in the other half."

"What do you need me to do?" My voice was barely a whisper. I was sure I would hate the answer.

"Zheng Jing has no idea we have a deal in place with his Dutch contacts. It's simple enough: Captain Groot of the Dutch shipping company Groot Verzenden will come into Singapore and trade with Zheng Jing. He will have more than enough goods to trade with other houses, but the East India Company will issue a friendly warning to anyone attempting to trade with the Dutch."

"So much for the treaty," I sighed.

"Just because we now have to let them into port doesn't mean we should buy their wooden clogs," McCarr grumbled and lowered his voice. "Because of this inquiry, you will be publicly on the outs with the company."

"Giving me a reason to trade with the Dutch and therefore get closer to Zheng Jing." I thought it over. This plan was obviously in motion for quite a while, but its principal actor, me, was only just now being installed. My eyes narrowed as I looked at McCarr. Raffles' words of warning coming back to me: Trust no one. "How do I know you aren't going burn me for trading with the Dutch? You could be setting me up for something you think my father might have done. I got the impression Lord Hastings would like to drag my father's reputation through the gutter."

"He would," McCarr said with conviction. "At this point, he would sell his mother to the brothel owners in Turkey if he thought it would help him keep his position here in India."

"Why are you helping me?" There was something about McCarr's motivations I couldn't understand. He could have continued to allow Lord Hastings to threaten me, but he decided that wouldn't work and tried another avenue.

"Mostly because I think you and I have much more in common than you think." McCarr sat back in his chair and was silent for so long I thought he might not continue. "Our fathers made sure there was no escaping their esteemed, if somewhat precarious, legacies, and our mothers are whores."

The fact the other man had just called my mother a whore had no effect on me. She was a whore, and I had spent my childhood trying to defend her even when she ignored me and treated me like an unwanted pet.

"How will I communicate with you? If you believe there are leaks here in Government House, I assure you it will be next to impossible to get messages to you without the Brotherhood or even Zheng Jing knowing of them." I needed the details on how this operation was going to work, because after I left this office, there was no coming back.

&

Midday had come and gone by the time I stepped out the sweeping front doors of Government House. The guard had changed during my meeting, and the building had become busier with clerks and administrators rushing to complete their work for the day. I stuffed my hands into the pockets of my trousers and went down the stairs to the path that would lead me to the street. Out of the corner of my eye, I watched as two shadows detached from one of the tall pillars and followed me away from the building. My nose twitched as I walked through the Calcutta haze.

The two men from the previous evening followed me through the gardens at a discreet pace. There was no reason to confront them now. If they wanted a fight, I would give it to them, but I was more concerned with booking the next passage to Singapore.

I left the confines of the manicured gardens of Government House and jostled my way through Calcutta's crowded streets. The morning's events played over in my mind. My game between the East India Company and Zheng Jing and the Brotherhood was far more dangerous than Captain Collaart's infatuation with me. As the newest member of a conspiracy with the East India Company, I wondered what my father would think. After my conversation with Finlayson the previous evening, his insinuations about my father and the Brotherhood made me uneasy.

As if summoned by my thoughts, Finlayson waved to me from across the street. I groaned inwardly and thought furiously. I could tell no one of my alliance with the shady Viscount McCarr, or Mr. Salcombe, whichever persona he was wearing on a particular day. Not ten minutes from striking my deal with McCarr and I was already on the path of lying and covering my tracks. There was a reason the profession of spying was not honorable.

Looking both ways down the street, I quickly crossed, narrowly avoiding a carriage and a couple of tightly strung donkeys pulling a cart. I reached the other side of the street and stopped in front of Finlayson. He looked up at me for a minute before glancing away. No matter our argument from last night and his membership in the Brotherhood, I felt the pull of responsibility when I stared into his face.

"Have you had lunch yet?" I asked, trying to keep our conversation light and comfortable.

Finlayson looked back at me and studied my face for a minute. He sighed loudly and shook his head. "I've been waiting for you to come out of Government House." I opened my mouth to ask him several questions, but he held up his hand. "Our conversation did not go well last evening, and I was worried you might be carted off to a prison ship without my apologizing."

"You're going to apologize for joining the Brotherhood?" I asked, confused.

Shaking his head, Finlayson let out a bark of laughter. "Of course not. I would apologize for not seeing things from your perspective. You're only trying to look out for me."

Not wanting to discuss the Brotherhood out on the street, I asked, "Where can I get a good pie?"

"That's easy." Finlayson nodded his head toward the river. "Not far from Thistlewaite and Hawk there's an inn that does a fantastic curry chicken pie. Just like mum made."

"I thought your family hailed from Yorkshire," I said as I followed him down the crowded street.

"Well, she would have made, if I had known her." Finlayson shook his head. "And if she had known of curry powder."

As I looked at Finlayson, I was thinking about how I could get him to talk about his connections with the Brotherhood without raising his suspicions. Hastings might be on his way out of office, representing only a fleeting threat, but McCarr was a different story. He would follow and eliminate every lead in connection with the Brotherhood. Glancing at Finlayson out of the corner of my eye, I knew there was no way I could stop him from his current path here in Calcutta.

Finlayson halted in front of a poorly painted building a block from the wharves on the river. I raised an eyebrow, wondering if Finlayson's definition of a good pie was the same as mine.

He laughed as he saw my expression and shoved the door open. "Come on. When have I ever led you astray?"

I walked through the door behind Finlayson and watched as my two shadows merged with the shadows of the warehouse across the street. We sat at a table in the busy tap and ordered two pies and ales. Companionable silence descended as we waited for our ales. I was wondering how I could broach the topic of his connections with the Brotherhood, and I was also sure he was trying to think of a way to question me about the inquiry.

The barmaid returned with our ales, and Finlayson cleared his throat. "How long do you have in Calcutta?"

Clever. He was going to try the indirect route.

"I'm not sure." I picked up my ale. No lie there. "It depends on the next ship, packet, whatever floats and will get me back to Singapore the fastest."

Finlayson's eyes widened as he stared at me. "The inquiry is over?"

"My part in the questioning is finished." I let my real bitterness at Hastings and McCarr reverberate through my voice. "Though I wondered why I bothered coming at all."

For a moment, I thought Finlayson looked relieved before he sat back on his stool playing with his tankard. "It did not go well?"

"They had their minds made up ages ago. Nothing I said would have changed how they thought of my father—or me, for that matter." I had to tread a careful line here. "No announcement of the decision yet, but I know a conspiracy when I see one."

But *did* I know how to spot a conspiracy? The thought ran through my head. My father would have smelled this whole inquiry months ago and would have had plans to thwart it. I, on the other hand, was left holding the losing hand. For once in my life, I needed my father's guidance, and he was either dead or, more likely, pirating his way around the globe captaining the ghost ship.

Finlayson took a long drink from his tankard before placing it back down on the scarred table with more care than necessary. "It's what the Brotherhood thought would happen. Are they going to repudiate you?"

I shrugged my shoulders as a girl set the pies in front of us. "Should we be talking so openly of the Brotherhood here?" I asked, watching the barmaid walk into the back.

"This is a friendly place," Finlayson said as he waved a hand around in the air encompassing the tap. "We have no need to watch our speech here." He pointed out the window. "I see your old friends are still about this afternoon."

"Hmmm." I picked up my pie. Taking a bite, I set to chewing the water crust pastry, enjoying the flavor of the curry on my tongue, a taste of my childhood, when I could get it. My mother hated anything she deemed oriental or exotic, including food.

"They won't follow me to Singapore," I said between bites.

"You know the East India Company better than that." Finlayson gave me a stern look. His face transformed from the young man I knew into an older version who had seen too much.

"Farquhar is getting the boot." I thought of the man's double cross last year, which almost ended in both our deaths.

"I think I should come back to Singapore with you," Finlayson said as he pushed his empty plate away.

He was offering to go with me. I didn't have to try and convince him. In Singapore, I could watch out for him and protect him, unless this was a Brotherhood plot. Perhaps he needed an excuse to travel to Singapore and make contact with Zheng Jing.

"You don't need to come back on my account." I let out a long breath. "As you well know, I'm more than capable of looking out for my interests."

Finlayson's eyes narrowed, and he swiped a hand through his hair. Frustration poured off him in waves. "You think this is some Brotherhood conspiracy. Believe me, when I tell you the Brotherhood only wants what is best for the men who ply their trade on the sea. Many of the members sailed with your father." He stalled for a second. "They only want to make sure you're protected now he's gone. After what happened with Collaart, you can hardly believe the East India Company is going to watch your back."

"I never expected them to come to my aid," I replied, thinking of Raffles. But I knew I was lying. Being completely honest, the boy in me had worshipped Stamford Raffles and my father. I thought Raffles would protect me, but his power was gone.

Even though I had already made the decision, I took a deep breath as if coming to a great decision. "There is always work to be had at Thistlewaite and Hawk, even in the off-season. I must admit, I could use your help. So yes, come back to Singapore with me." I watched as Finlayson's face brightened. Holding up a hand, I stopped his next words. "Don't thank me too quickly. I'm not going to join your Brotherhood, and if you believe coming back to Singapore will convince me otherwise, you're wrong. I have had enough of the Company and any other person or organization trying to control me."

"Deal." Finlayson's smile spread across his face. "Just know the Brotherhood will be watching out for you."

Knowing every ear in the tap was concentrated on our conversation made me pause for a minute. However, the need to draw a line or state my purpose further compelled me to speak again. "I have heard from several people the Brotherhood is corrupt and dangerous. It rules with men who have only one goal in mind, and it is not the betterment of man."

"Don't believe a word of what Lord Hastings said of the Brotherhood." Finlayson snorted. "Or his toady Salcombe."

"What do you know of Salcombe?" I asked too quickly. Finlayson could not miss my immediate interest.

"He's dangerous for all his talk of wanting to be called Mr. Salcombe, and his mixing with the clerks. Lord McCarr is a part of the establishment, never forget it." Finlayson stood up readying to leave. Under his breath, he said, "Someone powerful backs him. Salcombe's boss is much higher up than our poor Lord Hastings."

I followed Finlayson out the door of the tap and watched as he flashed my two shadows a rude hand gesture. "Shall we find ourselves berth on the next ship to Singapore?"

I nodded in response and thought of Finlayson's words. I never thought McCarr could be working for someone higher than Hastings, but as I went over my private interview with the man, some of the things he said began to come together to make a larger picture. There were pieces missing, but the ones I had led me to believe I was in much more danger than I previously thought. It might be prudent to keep Finlayson and his Brotherhood friends close. Even with Zheng Jing in Singapore, the enemy of my enemy might gut me in a dark alley, but Finlayson had already proven his loyalty. I could count on him at least.

Chapter 14
Charlotte

"I am pleased you were free to meet with me again." Zheng Jing sat behind a large polished table.

Grimacing, I took the seat offered to me by one of Zheng Jing's henchmen and took my time organizing my skirts before looking up. "I might have declined the invitation had I realized there was a choice involved." My voice was steady, but my nerves thrummed to my quickened pulse. The coin Zheng Jing had sent me this morning burned into the palm of my gloved hand. Reaching out slowly, I placed the coin on the table between us with an intentional snap.

"Sometimes we do not realize we're reaping the choices we made long ago," Zheng Jing replied casually without glancing at the offering. "I hope you haven't decided to go against our little arrangement."

"Did you send that man to attack me?" I asked, hopefully sounding bolder than I felt. "It seems very strange to me that my brother would happen to lose at cards, and now we find ourselves in your clutches."

"Is that how you feel, Mrs. Hawk? I hold you in my clutches?" Zheng Jing lifted his hands and clenched them in front of his face for a second, studying them intently, before settling them back on the desk.

"You have drawn me into your nefarious scheme," I challenged.

"A small business proposal you have seen fit to honor." Zheng Jing sighed. "Besides, you cannot blame me for your current state. Your father and your brother have a penchant for gambling."

I knew Zheng Jing was behind this entire scheme, but there was no way I could ever prove it. The man was too powerful and damned smart. He would never give anything away.

"Why have you brought me here?" I gave up trying to escape. The look on Zheng Jing's face made me think of a bird eyeing a particularly juicy worm.

"You have not brought Mr. Bigham with you." Zheng Jing shook his head. "I would like to discuss the role you're going to play, however, without your man."

Zheng Jing never finished his sentence. I sniffed and slashed the air in front of me. "I run Carstairs and Son. There is no need to involve Mr. Bigham or my father and brother. If I am going to commit treason, they need to be able to deny all knowledge of the details. It's true, Mr. Bigham knows about our arrangement, but he will not be privy to any harmful details."

"Will your husband be a problem?" Zheng Jing asked, cocking his head. I was suddenly aware of the other man's interest in my answer.

"My husband has his problems." I looked Zheng Jing in the eye defiantly.

"Indeed." Zheng Jing sat back in his chair, and I had the impression he was lost in thought on another matter entirely. After a minute his gaze sharpened, and he looked back at me. "The Bugis season is fast approaching. You will need to trade very well to salvage your finances for the big Junk season. I have several Bugis traders who work exclusively with me. They will approach you, and you will trade for their goods as normal. Money and property will exchange hands, except instead of the silk or nutmeg you've negotiated for, I will load your ships with tea."

"Won't the crews of my ships expect something is off?" I asked clenching my hands in my skirts to hide my anxiety. "What of the customs officials?"

"You need not concern yourself with officials, either here or in Portsmouth. Those ends of the transaction are my responsibility. Once your ships have landed in Portsmouth, the men in my employ will buy the goods marked as tea from your captain, for a fair market value." Zheng Jing pursed his lips. "Do you have any questions?"

"What if Mr. Bigham doesn't buy from the proper Bugis sellers?" I asked seeing several flaws in Zheng Jing's plan. There's also a chance my captain will sell the goods to the wrong buyers in Portsmouth. I'll have to bring more people into the conspiracy." I shook my head trying to calm my anger.

"I can assure you we have contingency plans in place, should our first sellers or buyers be rejected." Zheng Jing's lips curved into a smile that did not reach his eyes. "I have been doing this for a great many years, Mrs. Hawk. There is some risk to all of us should my plan fail. However, if you continue to play the game, we will all be winners."

Stamping down a snort and the urge to roll my eyes I said, "Is that a quote from one of your philosophers?"

"Perhaps." Zheng Jing's gaze did not waver. "I have outlined my expectations. You won't expect to hear from me until after the season has finished. It is far too dangerous. We both have reputations to uphold."

"What if there's a problem? How can I contact you?"

"Should anything unforeseen arise, I assure you, I'll know about it before you." Zheng Jing reached into a pocket of his jacket and pulled out a solid gold watch. "That's all for today, Mrs. Hawk. You will excuse me. I have several other appointments to keep." He stood up but made no effort to reach across the table to shake my hand or to indicate in any other way that the meeting had ended.

I stood on slightly shaking legs and nodded toward Zheng Jing before walking toward the stairs. The silence was better than any response I might have given him. Thinking through our meeting and the contact we had shared previously, I wondered if there was a social protocol for addressing the man who was blackmailing you into committing treason. Mrs. Meacham probably knew the rules of decorum in such a situation. I would have to ask her one day.

Pulling the hood of my cloak up to hide my face and hair I walked away as twilight descended on Singapore. The more distinguished members of society were either at home or attending a social evening. The less respectable citizens of this far-flung port were headed in the direction of the Chinese Campong looking for their evening's entertainment precisely in the neighborhood I was now standing in. The thought of someone recognizing me down here had my feet flying down the dirt track.

The same urchin who had led me to Zheng Jing's warehouse followed closely on my heels. To avoid any awkward questions, I kept my gaze riveted on the ground. Unfortunately, this course of action made me stumble into several different people, and I had to apologize over my shoulder as I made my escape. I spotted the drawbridge over the Singapore River ahead and sighed with relief. There were any number of reasons I might be roaming around the European Quarter at this hour. I might even come up with a plausible explanation for having no escort.

Sweat trickled down the side of my face, but I resisted the urge to push back the hood of my cloak and itch the trail it made running down to my chin. Not much further and I would be safe. Out of the corner of my eye, a familiar face swam through the crowd. I stopped, not caring of the disruption my still form made. Instead of continuing across the bridge, I turned and followed the familiar face back into the Chinese Campong. A slow burn started low in my belly, and my breathing became rapid.

Freddie wandered through the crowd, eyes ahead as a tall man dressed in a light suit spoke in his ear. He was apparently heading out for the evening with one of his cronies despite his lack of either money or credit. Only this afternoon, his tailor had made an appearance at the house asking for at least the interest on Freddie's bill. Fortunately, I had money left by Nathaniel for household expenses, or I would have faced another embarrassing situation because of my brother.

Instead of continuing to the safety of the European Quarter and home to think upon Zheng Jing's demands, I stepped into the swarm of people going back over the bridge to the Chinese Campong. I told myself I only wanted to see where he was going. I needed to know what the allure of gaming and intoxication meant. It had ruined my brother's life, and now it threatened my father and me.

I caught sight of Freddie's fashionable evening coat swerving to the right, and I followed him down a poorly lit street. The refuse was tidily swept into piles, waiting for disposal. Unfortunately, it did nothing for the smell. I had jumped in a panic before I realized the noise behind me was only my little urchin follower. Thrusting him from my mind, I continued to follow Freddie. He could think anything he pleased.

Ahead, Freddie and his companion stopped in front of a green door with a large dragon painted in detail. The thought of Freddie wasting his evening in a gaming hell when I knew he had no coin set fire to my burgeoning temper. Stepping forward, I walked right up behind the two men.

"What are you doing here?" I demanded. I was annoyed to find myself bordering on hysteria.

Freddie's back straightened for a second before he slowly turned to face me. Out of the corner of my eye, I saw his companion speak in rapid French to the man who answered the door. Grabbing my arm roughly, Freddie pulled me into the shadows at the side of the building.

"What the hell are you doing here? Christ! This is no place for a gently bred woman!" Freddie's face turned from haunted to angry in a couple of seconds. "Did you follow me?"

"No Freddie, I decided it was a lovely evening to stroll the streets of the slums and spend the night gambling with money in a gaming den." I shook a finger at him. "I ask again, what are you doing here? You are supposed to be staying out of sight."

"Lacuste said he might have information on the gamblers." Freddie's voice trailed off.

"I told you to pursue that no longer," I said between clenched teeth, thinking of the disaster Freddie could inadvertently create by persisting with his interference. I added, "Go home and try not to lose any more money on the way!" I winced as my words hit home.

Freddie frowned and shook his head stubbornly. "I can fix this. You'll see. I can prove to you and Father I'm worthy."

"There is nothing to pursue. The men you gambled with are beyond our reach." Trying to reason with him, I pointed out, "Besides, you have no evidence they cheated you. Only speculation. Go home."

"It is a matter of my honor," Freddie complained.

"Was your tailor visiting me this afternoon asking for payment on your bills also a matter of your honor?" The last fumes of my patience were fast evaporating. "I'm dealing with the consequences of your damned foolishness, your 'honor,' and all the rest of your damned nonsense! You have no idea what you have led our family into!"

"I see you have finally had to get your hands dirty." Freddie examined my expression. "Not hiding behind Bigham anymore. Well, if you want to give up the power of Carstairs and Son, I'm right here."

"Will you ever grow up?" I said, barely resisting the urge to slap him. Instead, I turned on my heel and stalked away, ignoring his friend Lacuste.

"Wait! You cannot wander around here alone. Let me take you home," Freddie said behind me in a fit of gallantry.

"Don't bother," I threw over my shoulder. "I can't save you, and you sure as hell can't save me."

Chapter 15
Nathaniel

The wind ripping through the sails of the packet did nothing to distract me from the view of Singapore as we crested wave after wave coming into the harbor. It had taken five long days to get passage back to Singapore on the mail ship, long enough for the watchful eyes of East India Company spies to wear holes through my back.

My stay in Singapore was long enough that I could get the verdict of the inquiry first hand. The lawyer Hatton received a copy and passed it on to me. There were no surprises in the findings. The investigation found Captain Sebastian Hawk's guilt undetermined in the case of embezzlement and treason against the nation. I knew that if my mission with Zheng Jing should fail, new evidence, whether real or fabricated, would mysteriously find its way into the hands of Lord Hastings or the mysterious Viscount McCarr.

Added to my worries was the welfare of the man standing next to me. Every morning I woke up knowing I had to speak to him about his dangerous ties to the Brotherhood. Unfortunately, every night, I went to bed promising my conscience I would talk to him in the morning. Even with our impending arrival in Singapore, I could not bring myself to broach the subject. As if he could sense the direction of my thoughts, Finlayson shifted his feet on the rolling deck.

"Despite your feelings toward them, the Brotherhood supports you, as it would your father." Finlayson dived into the topic I least wanted to discuss.

Without turning to look at him, I replied, "How do you know that's what my father would have wanted?" Men scurried around us preparing the ship for docking. I didn't bother trying to hide the topic of our discussion. Early on in the voyage most of the crew had subtly disclosed their affiliation with the Brotherhood to me. At first, I worried that they suspected my secret deal with McCarr, but as time passed, I realized their interest in me had other motives.

Finlayson ran a hand through his thick dark hair and turned to stare at me. I kept my gaze ahead, knowing I was a coward in the face of his frustration. "Your father was a part of this," Finlayson began. "He was going to tell you once you reached Singapore, but he never got the chance. Why do you think someone targeted him? Only a coordinated effort against Captain Sebastian Hawk would have brought him down."

Unable to maintain my distance, I let my gaze fall on Finlayson's face. It was as open as it ever had been, but I sensed he was holding something back. I wondered if we shared the same secret. Had he seen the captain of the ghost ship, too? "It's no secret my father had enemies. If even a fraction of them decided to work together against him, I doubt it would have taken much imagination." I paused, wanting to emphasize my next thought. "If you're implying Farquhar had anything to do with the sinking of the Diligence, you might be right. But I find it hard to believe they would destroy a vessel worth thousands of pounds just to kill one man."

"But what if that man was the single greatest threat to the East India's dominance in trade all over the world?" Finlayson's eyes opened wider. "Your father was asking some hard questions, and he had allies." Finlayson raised a hand to cut off my next comment. "Not just sailors, but men of trade, who could make their fortunes because of the protection your father provided. He was working to change many things, and some men in the East India Company did not like where his changes were leading."

"I suppose they won because my father is dead." My voice was flat. "I told you once before. I have no intention either to join the Brotherhood or align myself with the East India Company." I thought of my mission to get close to Zheng Jing. Hopefully, I would not have to ask Finlayson to expose him to the company.

"He might be dead, but his legacy lives on." Again Finlayson's eyes were bright as he stared at me. The effect was unnerving.

Trying to break the tension, I shook my head. "My father made it very plain I was a disappointment. His legacy is his own and has nothing to do with me. Look how well I have defended it against the company bureaucrats."

"You're wrong," Finlayson replied as he surveyed the activity in the port.

Following his gaze, I let the anticipation of my arrival seep into my bones. Tonight, I would share a bed with my wife again! She probably was as eager and as willing to please as she was on our wedding night. I wanted nothing more than to spend the next week in bed, not giving a damn whether people realized what we were up to or not.

I braced my legs and held the side railing as the ship swept up to the edge of the wharf. Scanning the crowd on the pier, I watched as a young boy spotted me and trotted away, as another, slightly older boy sped away toward the East India Company warehouses.

"No point in trying to keep your presence in Singapore a secret," Finlayson muttered, watching the same lookouts I was as they scurried off to report to their masters.

"There are too many spies to keep anything a secret in Singapore." I made the statement as a warning to both Finlayson and myself. My involvement with McCarr and the East India Company would become public knowledge one way or another. In equally absolute terms, whatever plans Finlayson had with the Brotherhood would not stay secret for long.

As the wooden hull of the boat bumped against the side of the wharf, Finlayson looked at me and smiled slightly. "It's a good thing you plan to keep to your own business," he said, a hint of challenge in his voice.

"I'm glad you brought up business. Let's get you settled before you decide to commit anything illegal." I nodded to the purser. "Let's get off this floating tub; I have a mind never to take to sea again."

"Speak for yourself," Finlayson said, feigning a look of utter horror. "You are getting soft in your old age." I was secretly happy to see some of his old humor resurfacing.

"Watch who you're calling old." I shot back, walking across the gangplank as soon as the wood hit the deck of the wharf. "You might offend me. Besides, it's as though you're itching to go back to sea," I added as he joined me on the wharf. I dodged a few pointed stares and ignored the gawkers. The story of my leaving Singapore had apparently made the rounds.

Finlayson took in the mood of the small crowd waiting for the packet and observed sardonically, "You're as popular as ever."

"Some things rarely change. I find myself a marked man once again." I did my best to hold in a frustrated sigh.

"And you say you don't need the Brotherhood." Finlayson lowered his voice. Out of the corner of my eye, I watched him nod curtly at two men leaning against a stack of crates.

I pretended not to notice the glances cast my way as we walked down the foreshore to the Thistlewaite and Hawk warehouse. Finlayson let out a long whistle.

"Looks like you did well for yourself after all. It must be true that old sea dogs can learn new tricks." Finlayson followed me into the cavernous space.

The guards on the door both nodded at me, surprise on their faces. A shout from the second-floor offices caught my attention, and I looked up to see Hindly waving his hand madly. He raced down the stairs.

"Mr. Hawk, it's nice to see you back!" Hindly jumped the last couple of steps, and I was happy to see his strength had returned.

"Thank you, Mr. Hindly." I refrained from slapping the younger man on the back. "You might remember Mr. Finlayson here from his previous time in Singapore? He has graciously agreed to come work with us."

"Of course, Mr. Finlayson, how are you?" Hindly held out his left hand awkwardly.

Finlayson did not even blink as he reached out and took the proffered hand. "Mr. Hindly, you're looking well, I see you have fully recovered."

Hindly ducked his head, and I took advantage of the lull in conversation to ask about Cornelius. The sooner I met with him, the sooner I could track down my wife.

"Mr. Hindly, please see that Mr. Finlayson finds the clerk's quarters." I looked at Finlayson as I said the rest. "Tomorrow will be soon enough to put him to work."

"Thank you," said Finlayson as he smiled and adjusted the duffel bag on his shoulder. Giving his full attention to Hindly, he asked, "Come, you must tell me of all the goings on in Singapore. Where is the best place to drink? Play cards? Meet women?"

Hindly's face turned an interesting shade of crimson at the mention of women, and I resigned myself to speaking to him about the Shibari ladies. He apparently had not heeded my warning over spending his pay packet down at the whorehouses. I watched them walk to the rear of the warehouse. If I had to guess, I would say Finlayson was only a few years older than Hindly, but he carried himself in such a way that he looked far older.

Putting the problems of both Hindly and Finlayson from my mind, I went up the stairs to the offices with quick steps. I was only one meeting away from seeing Charlotte. I would track her down, sweep her off her feet, and spend the rest of the day and night in bed with her. I was counting on spending the rest of the week in a similar position.

After taking a brief glimpse into my office, which appeared unnaturally abandoned, I walked down to Cornelius's door. I hesitated a moment before knocking, wondering what I might find on the other side. Cornelius barked something that I hoped was "enter," as I turned the handle.

I was wrong. "Don't you have ears, or is it sense you lack? I told you I'm not to be disturbed!" Cornelius frowned, looking up from his ledgers. He stared at me for a moment as if he saw a ghost before he broke into a smile. "Nathaniel, my boy! It's damn great to see you!"

"You look relieved," I said as I took one of the faded leather seats in front of his desk. "Were you worried I might find more intriguing delights in Calcutta and never leave?" I laughed.

"We heard the inquiry's decision yesterday." Cornelius's face grew serious. "Came in on the East India Company mail ship. Bloody bastards."

"As people reminded me often, it could have been worse." I did not want to discuss the inquiry with Cornelius right now. "How have you been? How is Charlotte? I trust you kept an eye on her while I was away."

Cornelius's large white eyebrows came together for a moment, and I thought he would press me for information on the inquiry. Instead, he let the matter rest for now. "I had Charlotte around for a little dinner party I hosted," he said, leaning back in his chair.

"Did she look well?" I asked, staring at him closely while I waited for him to say whatever was on his mind.

"There are rumors, Nathaniel." Cornelius began quietly.

"Charlotte is a beautiful woman who has married an eligible bachelor. There will always be rumors surrounding her. Society dines out on women like her every evening." I waved my hand. I had no time for such nonsense, and I hoped Cornelius would understand my mood.

"They say she is involved with her family man of business." Cornelius persisted in the matter.

"Bigham?" I shook my head. "The two are close. They brought Carstairs and Son back from the brink of bankruptcy last trading season. I know there's nothing untoward between them." Cornelius's face held little reaction to my statement, and I pressed on. "I asked her about Bigham, and she assured me there's nothing between them. He's a smart trader, and she has done well to learn from him.

"I found her early one morning on the street of his boarding house," Cornelius said the last as if it were enough to convict Charlotte of all manner of licentious behavior.

"How do you know where Bigham lives?" I said, thinking quickly. "I'm sure it was only a coincidence."

"She was acting very suspiciously," Cornelius added.

"Maybe she had to deal with some business complication." I shrugged, even though a feeling of doubt was growing in my gut. "We have those from time to time."

"Rumor places your wife down in the Chinese Campong doing God knows what." He held up a hand. "Even shouting at her brother in front of a well-known gaming hell."

"There you have it." I almost shouted in relief. "Charlotte was merely bringing her brother to heel. I know Bigham has been trying to mentor young Frederick."

"I kept an eye on her for you while you were in Calcutta," Cornelius said, repeating himself. His face twisted into a frown, and he added, "I wash my hands of the business."

"Thank you for being a good friend," I said, quietly wishing he would tell me about his apparent underlying problem with Charlotte so we could work it through. Shifting in the seat uncomfortably, I wondered how much longer we would have this one argument between us.

"Speaking of my new wife." I tried to put emphasis on the last two words, "I should find her and assure my conscience that she has fared well." As I stood up and turned toward the door, I heard rapid steps on the wooden walkway beyond the door. I looked quizzically at Cornelius, but he merely shrugged before reaching under his desk where I knew he kept an absurdly out-of-date blunderbuss and a dull cutlass someone had given him as booty from a long lost Spanish galleon.

A brief knock sounded on his door before it swung open. I took a defensive position to the side of the door as Sir Stamford Raffles looked around the small office.

"God's bones!" said Cornelius as he exhaled and pulled the old blunderbuss out from under his desk. He let it clatter on the polished wood and open ledgers.

Raffle's eyes went wide for a moment before he eyed the weapon with a touch of derision. "Were you going to throw that at me? I doubt it could fire a damn thing."

"I assure you it functions very well." Cornelius frowned back at Raffles.

"Can you even get shot from that antique?" I asked, reaching for it.

Cornelius snatched the weapon back up and pointed it at me. His eyes narrowed. "Go ahead and find out."

Holding up my hands, I tried not to laugh. "You haven't even got a wick, Cornelius."

Raffles cleared his throat and interrupted my next words, and I turned my attention back to him. He appeared even more aged than when I last saw him, only a few weeks ago. He was grayer at the temples, and the lines around his eyes were more pronounced. As much as I wanted to rail against him for involving me in his argument with Farquhar, I knew deep down the company would have come after Sebastian Hawk's son in time.

"It must be important for you to face down a blunderbuss. Please have a seat," I said, gesturing toward a chair opposite mine.

"I read the inquiry verdict yesterday," Raffles began. "In the meantime, I have done my best to exonerate your father further, but I don't think we can salvage much of his pension with the company." He reached into his coat pocket and handed me a letter embossed with a large wax seal with the East India Company crest, as well as Lord Hastings's own personal seal. "I intercepted this on its way to Farquhar."

With a steady hand, I accepted the inquiry's judgment. I knew Raffles must have spies in Farquhar's office for him to get this from his nemesis. "Thank you for delivering this personally. It means a lot to me." I paused for a second, remembering the words of McCarr and Lord Hastings. "It would have meant something to my father."

"I don't know what lies Hastings has put into your head, but don't believe it." Raffles eyes grew intense, and I felt pinned by his gaze and reminded that he was not just a friend but also someone who people feared at the East India Company. "Your father changed much in the last years of his life, yet he always remained a good man."

"Are you saying my father was committing treason?" I asked, even though what I wanted to know was whether Raffles believed my father was a member of the Brotherhood like Finlayson implied. Unfortunately, if I mentioned my father and the secret organization, Raffles might try and put the two together even though they didn't fit.

The room was silent for several minutes. The air grew uncomfortable, and I saw Cornelius shift in his seat. He started to say something several times before he shut his mouth and watched Raffles.

Raffles appeared to gather his thoughts and chose his words carefully, his voice even. "I believe your father would have committed many crimes others would see as disturbing if he believed it was for the greater good." Raffles let out a long breath in relief. His explanation made no sense to me.

"Everyone bends the rules here and there to make what the bureaucrats say in London and Calcutta work in the real world." I dismissed Raffles assertion. "There is no way anything my father did was any worse than other sea captains."

"When will you stop looking at your father from the perspective of a boy?" Raffles said in a curt voice. It was the first time I had ever seen him lose his temper. "He was a man just like any other man, and I assure you he had enough follies to make up for the fact everyone thought he was a hero."

"As the son with whom he was always disappointed, I assure you, I am harboring no illusions about my father." I shuffled toward the door not wanting to have this conversation, especially because it might end my friendship with someone I valued.

"You have no idea who your father was." Raffles shook his head sadly and gained control over his anger.

"That is where you're wrong. I have made a very intense study of Sebastian over the years, and I can assure you, I know him as well as any man. Better because as his son, I am of his blood." I nodded to Cornelius and reached for the door. "If you will both excuse me, I need to find my wife."

"There are rumors," Raffles began as I opened the door to the office.

"Cornelius told me." I frowned over my shoulder at both men before settling my gaze on Raffles. "I'm surprised you would believe such tales."

Raffles shrugged. "I merely meant to warn you. It is hard to believe what your wife might believe after being alone these many weeks."

"My wife is not one for female histrionics," I reassured Raffles. "Now I am going to find her, tell her how much I've missed her and take her to bed. Cornelius do *not* send anyone to bother me."

Sweeping out of the room, I closed the door behind me. There was no sign of Hindly or Finlayson in the warehouse as I swept down the stairs. I would have to trust Finlayson could keep out of trouble for the day. Stepping out of the warehouse into the humid Singapore air, I glanced around at the sailors and dockworkers. I wondered how many of them were loyal to the Brotherhood and Zheng Jing. How much influence did the clever Chinese trader possess.

I turned to the left and with quick steps made my way through the growing crowd of people. Singapore was becoming busy with the promise of the Bugis coming soon to trade their wares. Cornelius and I could weather the small trading season relatively well even without the good graces of the East India Company. The Junk season was another matter entirely, but I had a few months to rehearse my lies before then.

"Good morning, Mr. Hawk." The guard out front of Carstairs and Son nodded his cap in my direction.

"Good morning," I replied, not knowing the man's name, an oversight on my part. These men potentially saw Charlotte every day. They would know her as well as I. It seemed to be a gross error on my part not to cultivate a loose friendship with them.

"Is your mistress around this morning?" I let the word "morning" hang in the air.

"Ainslie sir." The man spoke with a soft Irish lilt. Mrs. Hawk is inside, sir."

"My thanks, Ainslie." I pushed into the dim interior of the warehouse and stopped to let my eyes adjust to the dimmer light. Unlike Thistlewaite and Hawk, this warehouse did not have windows built high into the outer walls to let light filter through during the day.

Focusing on the two people standing in front of a worn wooden desk, I watched as Charlotte expressed her point by waving her hands. Bigham shook his head, and when Charlotte became agitated, he grabbed onto her forearms to stop her movements. The air froze in my lungs as I watched the couple and Cornelius's words came back to me. For a moment, the two people in front of me stared at each other before Charlotte yanked her arms away from Bigham's grasp.

It looked as if Bigham was pleading with her and, by her reactions, Charlotte had heard the arguments before. A part of me wanted to leave the warehouse and go home. Unfortunately, there was just enough false bravado within me to carry forward.

"Charlotte," I shouted across the space between us. Bigham and Charlotte dropped their conversation and stared at me. Bigham wore a look of relief on his face as he recognized me. On the other hand, as I stepped up to them, Charlotte's brows came together, and she regarded me with a closed expression.

"Mr. Hawk! It's nice to see you back from Calcutta!" There was no way to mistake the relief in his voice.

"Mr. Bigham, I'm happy to be home. Calcutta was a necessary evil, but I'm glad to be home with my new wife." I smiled at Charlotte, but the look she gave me remained cold.

"I forgive you, my love, for not meeting my ship since I did not send word of my return." I hoped a light joke might ease her expression. Watching the lines around her mouth grow tighter. I realized something terrible must have happened in my absence for her to react this way. Perhaps her father or Frederick had taken ill.

"Even if I had known which ship you were returning upon, I hardly think I would have come down to meet it." Charlotte sniffed loudly. Bigham shifted his feet uncomfortably, and I racked my brain to think of what I was missing.

"Surely, wives rejoice in their husband's homecoming," I said the words slowly.

"As much as their mistresses, I've heard tell." Charlotte's nose rose in the air.

Chapter 16
Charlotte

I watched with satisfaction as Nathaniel's eyes widened at my remark. It took him longer than I thought it might to catch my meaning.

"Charlotte," he murmured. "This is not the venue I would choose for this discussion. Let me take you home."

Shaking my head at him, I didn't care if I looked like a child. I knew if we were alone all my resolve to keep him at arm's length would dissolve. When I heard his voice and saw his lean figure standing only a few feet away from me, my heart began to slam into my ribcage, and my gut clenched. The urge to run to him and let him hold me was overwhelming. I wanted to tell him of my problems with Zheng Jing. Together, we could conquer anything, but we were separate. Sarah and her child stood between us as sure as a reef before the shore.

"As you can plainly see," I waved a hand around the warehouse before continuing, "I'm working, Nathaniel." My dismissal had the effect of waving a red flag in front of a bull. He stepped forward, ignoring Bigham and grabbed my arm.

"Is this how you treat your husband after he has been away?" Nathaniel's jaw clenched. "I told you I would explain."

"No explanations are required." I tried not to choke on the next words. "We seem to have a typical marriage after all." My words made his hand clamp around my upper arm and tighten, and I gasped in response. Bigham moved forward, and I glanced between the two men.

"I would not become involved in my personal affairs, Mr. Bigham." Nathaniel put extra emphasis on the word personal. "As it is, several people have informed me of the rumors circulating Singapore of your relationship with my wife."

Gasping, I wrenched my arm out of his grasp as Bigham's face grew stony.

"The only rumor going around Singapore is that of you and your mistress." I poked a finger into Nathaniel's chest. He turned his attention back to me. "Yes, sir. All of Singapore is agog with the impending birth of your bastard." Shaking my head, I felt one tear slip down my cheek, and I angrily wiped it away. "How could you, Nathaniel? And with Sarah Buck? You know how we feel about each other."

"I would prefer not to do this with an audience." Nathaniel suddenly looked tired, like all the fight had suddenly melted from his bones. "It has been a difficult few weeks, and all I want is to spend time with my wife."

"You are not the only one with problems, Nathaniel," I spat back like an angry fishwife when all I wanted to do was comfort him. I was a foolish girl. Even when he deserved my anger and derision, I wanted to comfort him.

"You know the extent of my involvement with Sarah Buck." He glanced at Bigham, and I watched his jaw work for another second. "There has been nothing after it. I swear it."

I closed my eyes, wanting to believe him, but men lied. Opening my eyes again, I studied Nathaniel's face. "I cannot forget the past." Another tear slipped down my face, and I cursed inwardly. "You have a responsibility to that child." I wanted to be the only mother of his children.

"That baby could belong to any number of men." Nathaniel reached his hands out to grab mine. His fingers were warm and calloused. He would comfort me if I allowed it.

"She has singled you out." I tilted my head to stare at the ceiling hoping to prevent any more tears from falling.

He tugged on my hands. "Come home with me. We can put this to rights."

Not wanting to fight with him anymore but also unable to give in, I shook my head. "I need time." Pulling my hands away from his grasp, I said, "The Bugis traders will have a significant role in the rehabilitation of Carstairs and Son's fortunes. Mr. Bigham and I will be putting in some long hours before we finish."

Nathaniel's hands clenched at his sides, and for a minute I thought he might commit some form of violence. He was a man on the edge, and I had done nothing but push him toward it. As much as I knew, he had to be hurting over the East India Company findings and his father. My pride was too much to bend to this man or any man's will.

"Fine." Nathaniel released a breath. "I will be home tonight, and I expect you to join me." He nodded at Bigham. "I trust you will have a good day." With that, he turned on his heel and departed. I watched as he retreated. The urge to chase after him and make everything right pulsed through me.

"Are you sure you know what you're about?" Bigham asked quietly.

"Do you have a comment to make, Mr. Bigham?" I was astonished he would say anything at all. He didn't turn to me, only stared at the door where Nathaniel had been moments before.

"Playing games with men is dangerous at the best of times." He turned his head and stared directly at me. "Playing games with a man such as Mr. Hawk is playing with fire, a dangerous, unpredictable fire that will consume you."

Sniffing at Bigham's tone, I said, "I have legitimate reasons to be angry with my husband. You will refrain from commenting further on my personal life."

"Of course, Mrs. Hawk." Bigham adopted the tone of a servant. It grated on my nerves. I was going to continue our argument when a boy came through the door and raced up to me.

Without speaking, he held out his hand, palm up. A coin with two hands shaking lay in the middle.

&

My heart thumped and dozens of questions swept through my brain as I followed the urchin across the bridge to the Chinese Campong. Zheng Jing had made it clear he would not contact me. I prayed there was a problem too dangerous for the man to continue his smuggling activities using my shipping company.

We did not turn down the familiar alley leading to the secret storage rooms Zheng Jing used to house his illegal tea. Instead, the urchin and I wended our way through increasingly close and refuse-strewn alleys. As I was about to tap the boy on the shoulder and inform him I wouldn't proceed any farther, he stopped in front of an opening.

The boy looked up and down the alley a couple of times before scraping a door away from a makeshift frame in a two-story shanty house. I looked the building over a few times with a growing sense of unease. Zheng Jing may be a treasonous smuggler, but he had never asked me to meet him somewhere this run down. Backing away from the opening with growing trepidation, I shook my head at the boy who had turned around to beckon me further. Perhaps Zheng Jing had decided I was more a hindrance than a help. God knows my brother would fall more readily into his plan than I had.

Oddly, I thought of Nathaniel's reaction if I died in some back alley shanty. Would he repent his actions with Sarah Buck? Or would he continue with his mistress? Either way, I did not intend to find out. Turning on my heel, I meant to try and find my way out of the maze. A few drunken laughs and lewd comments from down the alley had me turning back to the haphazard door. The curses of the drunken men had my ears burning. They were much more ribald than the salty curses of the warehouse workers and sailors I encountered on the wharves.

There was no hope for it; I would have to face the uncertainty of the shack or the inevitable confrontation with the drunken men. I found the urchin waiting with a single lit candle. He motioned for me to follow him up the stairs. The attraction of carrying a weapon had never appealed to me, but I vowed in this moment, in the future, I would bring something for my protection.

The shack had only two rooms, one below and one above. I stepped into the dancing shadows of the poorly lit second floor and searched the dark corners for my tormentor.

"I'm here." I let out an impatient breath. "What is it you want?" The strain in my voice made the question sound harsh.

"To see you admit to your crimes," Cornelius stepped out of the far corner, and I had to strain through the gloom to make out his bulky shape.

"Where did you get this coin?" I asked, too stunned at finding him here to hold the question back.

"Did you think only your lover had access to the Brotherhood's calling card?" Cornelius stepped up to the urchin and took the candle. The boy turned and went back down the stairs.

My conversation with Nathaniel this afternoon crashed through my brain. "You think Mr. Bigham is a member of the Brotherhood? You are utterly ridiculous. As nonsensical as telling my husband there's a rumor through Singapore we are lovers."

"But, my dear, there is a buzz in Singapore that you have a very particular relationship with your man of business Mr. Bigham." Cornelius's smile did not reach his eyes. Here was the man of business who had made his fortune by being ruthless.

"What do you want?" I asked, knowing the answer.

"Revenge for my dead wife, but you know this already." Cornelius studied me intently. "I know you were blackmailing her over the parentage of our child." My whole body tightened in response to the allegation, and I wanted to deny it. Unfortunately, he would know it for the lie it was after it left my lips. "Good girl for at least acknowledging with your silence the role you played in my wife's death."

"What would you have me do?" I wanted to know what his plans for me included. Surely, there was nothing he could do to humiliate me that Sarah Buck had not accomplished publicly.

"Why are you working for Zheng Jing and his band of merry marauders?" Cornelius laughed at my surprised expression. "It's a wonder you make any money trading at all, my dear Charlotte. You don't mind if I call you by your Christian name? We are practically brother and sister by marriage."

"Not even close," I muttered. Cornelius's brows rose, and I hoped he had not heard me. "Does your family blackmail one another?" I tried to push him off topic.

"My mother would have stabbed me in the back and boiled my bones if she could make a quick guinea from it." Cornelius's face looked set in stone. "Do not underestimate me, little girl. What is your involvement with Zheng Jing?"

A plan fitted into place, and I took a deep breath. "Carstairs and Son are looking to save money by hiring an outside mediator for the Chinese trading season. We need better connections and access to the best goods." I shrugged trying to feign an air of calm I did not feel.

"Why don't you tell me the truth?" Cornelius shook his head, and in the candlelight, he looked dangerous. The sheen of the gentleman trader stripped away.

"There is nothing more to tell." I felt my chin rise. There was nothing I could do if he chose not to believe me.

"When you feel like telling me the truth, send the coin back to me." Cornelius moved toward the stairs. He passed within a few feet of me. "Until you confess, there will be no absolution. When I find out what the two of you are up to, you might wish for a little absolution.

Chapter 17
Nathaniel

Pressing an ear to the door of the usually empty room at the beginning of the landing, I waited to hear any sign Charlotte might be awake. Nothing, the thick wooden portal did not even reveal whether she might be breathing on the other side. Dejected, I let my forehead rest on the painted wood for a minute and took deep breaths before leaving.

Without venturing farther into the house, I eased out the front door and into the relative coolness of pre-dawn Singapore. Hardly anyone was around this early in the morning. A few industrious servants carrying out their duties scuttled through the dark, but for the most part, the streets of the European Quarter were empty.

After the scene with Charlotte yesterday at Carstairs and Son, I came home alone, too angry to return to work and have Cornelius dissect my marriage. I spent hours trying to concentrate on the contracts and ledgers that had piled up in my absence. All I could think of was Charlotte's face as she revealed her knowledge of Sarah Buck's pregnancy. She was utterly devastated. I could understand on some level why the news of another woman carrying my child would be upsetting, but I cannot comprehend why she would believe Sarah Buck was my mistress.

I told her there was nothing between us after she had caught Sarah and me after our unfortunate encounter, and that I would never return to her bed. Obviously, my word means nothing to her. By the time she walked through the door, I was in a towering rage fueled by Cornelius's words over the rumors surrounding Charlotte and Bigham. Had she in a fit of revenge decided to bed her man of business? I was a man tormented.

A rustling to my right had me pausing and reaching for the pistol shoved in the waistband of my trousers. With the bad news from the East India Company concerning my father, I could not take any chances. It was a firm declaration that I was not under their protection any longer. My life was free for my father's enemies to take.

A gray face with small black eyes and a white beard appeared from behind a small hedge. The monkey studied me for a minute as if reacquainting himself with an old friend. I waited to see what he might do before the creature shook his head and turned away. I hope it was not an omen. Stupid to think such things. Only in the East would meeting a monkey in the morning mean anything other than what it was.

Sighing, I continued to walk down toward the wharves, thinking of Charlotte's angry words from last night. She wanted a divorce, a separation, anything that saw her far away from me.

But she only pricked my temper raw until we were screaming at one another. I finally retreated to the study she had started to use as a drawing room. Shutting the door, I drank my way through the contents of several bottles of Scotch before passing out. For all my promises that my marriage would not be the same as my parents, it was turning out to be eerily similar. Accusations of cheating followed by someone getting roaring drunk and passing out in the house.

This was something I did not know how to fix, and there was no one I could turn to for advice. My father was gone, and Cornelius had been against my marriage from the first. I would have to try and woo Charlotte back to my side on my own. In the early hours of the morning, I had almost resolved to march down to Sarah's house and demand an explanation for her actions. Only the thought of the scene I might cause prevented me.

A few sailors slept off the night's excesses in the shelter of the warehouses surrounded by the scuttle rats and other small animals. I picked my way down to the Thistlewaite and Hawk warehouse and used my key to open the lock. Inside, the guard stood to attention and gave me a bleary smile. I nodded to him and headed to my office to get some work done before the events of the day intruded.

A few short hours later, a rap on the door had me easing away from my desk as I bid the person enter. Finlayson stood in the doorway, and I suppressed a frown. I was hoping to speak to Cornelius this morning over a number of odd entries in the ledgers, but I had not heard him in his office.

"Good morning, I trust your first night back in Singapore was a memorable one." I smirked at the dark circles under Finlayson's eyes.

"I spent some time getting to know the locals again." Finlayson grinned and plunked down in the only other chair in the room. He relaxed and frowned at me. "I'm surprised to see you here, knowing you had big plans for the rest of the week."

"Your fishing exhibition is not going to turn up any new information than what the gossips are sniping over, so don't bother." I grimaced at my surly tone.

"It's true, then?" Finlayson asked. "You and Sarah Buck?"

"A gentleman and all that." I waved a hand in the air.

"Well, someone should have said something about ladies and all that," Finlayson said with a shrug.

"Don't you have work to do?" I asked, wanting to forget this topic.

"I'm supposed to be doing some work for Mr. Thistlewaite this morning, but he has yet to come in." Finlayson glanced behind him at the door. "I thought I would come in and bother you until he finally showed."

I frowned at my pocket watch. Cornelius should have been in long ago. I stood up without looking at Finlayson and walked to the door, stopping on the landing. Hindly stood on the bottom step speaking to a small boy.

"Hindly," I shouted down. "Can I talk to you, please?"

"Yes, Mr. Hawk, one moment." Hindly said something further to the boy and came up the stairs with the kind of energy only someone young could muster.

Without waiting for Hindly to greet me, I plowed into my concern. "Have you seen Mr. Thistlewaite this morning? Did he mention working from home yesterday before he left?"

"No, Mr. Hawk." Finlayson shook his head and used his stump to point down the stairs at the boy. "That is Mr. Thistlewaite's houseboy come to see if his master stayed here last evening." Finlayson stopped speaking and looked away for a moment, and a light blush crept up his cheeks.

"It's fine, Mr. Hindly, you may speak plainly." I knew Hindly would find it difficult to talk of his superiors negatively, even if it was the truth.

"Mr. Thistlewaite often spent the night here after having too much rum. Said he could not bear the thought of going home to an empty house." Hindly's voice filled with sadness. The news was not new to me. I had found him slouched under his desk numerous times. "But he left work yesterday, and I saw him. Mr. Thistlewaite told me to be good, and I would see him in the morning." Frowning Hindly continued, "He left early yesterday, said he had some unpleasant business to attend to."

Sharp as a warning whistle onboard a ship to warn the crew of danger, my instincts made my heart beat faster. "Did Mr. Thistlewaite give any clue as to what his business might have been?"

"No, he only made the comment about unpleasant business and left." Hindly looked over my shoulder.

"What do you think, boss?" Finlayson asked.

"He probably went to sort out some business and went for a drink afterwards." I tried to sound confident, but my gut was screaming at me that something was terribly wrong. "Mr. Thistlewaite obviously had a few too many and has spent the morning sleeping it off somewhere." Unfortunately, it just did not sound like Cornelius to not come into the warehouse even if he was at death's door. By the look on Hindly's face, he agreed with me. "Find the office manager and ask him if he knows what this business is that Mr. Thistlewaite was attending to last night."

"Yes, sir." Hindly walked toward the large office at the end of the corridor where the clerks bent over their ledgers and journals.

"I can make some discreet inquiries." Finlayson stepped in front of me. "There's a whole network of men waiting for you to call on them."

More like have me owe them a favor, I thought. I tried to think beyond Cornelius to my secret mission for McCarr. "We will wait another hour or so," I spoke before Finlayson could form an argument. "He might have snuggled between some woman's thighs, and if that is the case, I would rather let him be. Mr. Thistlewaite could use the softening influence."

He houseboy stood at the bottom of the steps looking unsure on how to proceed. I descended the steps quickly and tried to dredge his name up from the bottom of my memory. Drawing a blank on the boy's identity, I fixed what I hoped was a friendly smile on my face.

"You have come looking for Mr. Thistlewaite?" I prompted.

"Yes, the housekeeper says Mr. Thistlewaite would never miss dinner and breakfast. He must be in a bad way." The boy nodded with conviction.

I agreed with him. "Did Mr. Thistlewaite mention where he went last night?"

Shaking his head, the boy stamped his foot impatiently. "Maybe he went to play cards at his favorite place. I am to go there after here." He used his chin to nod at Hindly coming down the stairs. "But he told me to wait here."

Hindly came down the stairs to meet me, the boy and Finlayson who had followed me down. "The office manager says Mr. Thistlewaite should have been here this morning."

Nodding at Hindly, I looked back at the boy. "Could you take me to this card place?" I had a rough idea of where Cornelius liked to turn a hand, but I wanted to make sure Cornelius was not hiding anything from me. The boy would have a better idea of his habits than me.

"Yes, sir." The boy agreed and immediately scampered to the door. "Hindly, if Mr. Thistlewaite arrives here while I'm gone, be sure to tell him I wish to speak with him." I threw this order over my shoulder and did not wait to hear his response as I rushed to catch up to the small figure hurrying ahead of me in the now hot Singaporean sun.

Finlayson's presence beside me was more irritating than helpful. I wanted to tell him to go back to the warehouse, but to do what? Strictly speaking, I didn't have anything for him to do at this time.

"What was the job Mr. Thistlewaite wanted you for this morning?" I did my best to keep up with the houseboy who darted in and out of the small crowds of people headed for the Singapore River.

"Nothing important." Finlayson shrugged and did not glance my way. His tone was far too dismissive.

"If there is something you can tell me that will allay my fears for Mr. Thistlewaite, now is the time to say it." I let aggression tinge my voice.

Staring ahead at the drawbridge over the Singapore River, I felt Finlayson weighing his next words. He had only been back in Singapore for a day, and already he was hiding information from me. Critical information regarding the well-being of someone I considered family. This did not bode well for our relationship in regards to the Brotherhood.

"He wanted me to spy on your wife." Finlayson's voice sounded reluctant.

"What the hell?" I swore loudly, and several people stopped to stare at me as we walked to the bridge. "I hope you told him where he could go!" Cornelius's ridiculous obsession with Charlotte would have to end immediately. Once I found the old man, I was going to have a meaningful discussion with him on acceptable behavior and my wife.

"Not exactly." Finlayson pursed his lips. "I agreed to watch her man of business, Mr. Bigham, after asking a few questions. There are enough misunderstandings between us as it is."

Feeling as if I had to make explanations for Cornelius's behavior, I took a deep breath as we took our first steps on the wooden bridge. A crowd gathered on the north side, and looking over the railing, they caught my attention. Staring at the crowd, I persisted with my comment. "Cornelius's dead wife, my cousin Margaret Thistlewaite, did not like Mrs. Hawk, and I think her feelings have translated over to Mr. Thistlewaite. There is absolutely no reason to suspect my wife of any clandestine behavior," I announced with confidence I did not entirely feel.

Finlayson nodded in response to my explanation, his attention to the crowd gathered on the edge of the bridge. As if by silent agreement, we changed direction and walked toward the railing. I shouted for the houseboy to wait a moment as we shouldered our way through the crowd looking down on the Chinese Campong side of the river. Small junk boats littered the bank of the river, crammed one on top of the other until they formed a floating extension of the land.

Amongst the wooden crafts, soldiers resplendent in their red coats milled around, sweat dripping from their iconic black hats. Some rested their rifles over their shoulders, bayonets glinting in the sunlight. Several men, including an officer standing alongside the recognizable figure of Major General Farquhar, his absurdly large hat jerking around as he made some point to the men at large, they stood over a shrouded figure, discussing some detail or other.

"Fisherman, whore, or gambler?" Finlayson asked under his breath.

"Any or even all three of the above," I replied grimly. "It's becoming a much more common occurrence these days. Farquhar barely has time to investigate one murder when the next one occurs. Singapore is becoming as bad as Calcutta. The company should do something more about the lawlessness." I thought for a minute. "In fact, isn't that in the interests of your lot?" I cleared my throat and purposely did not mention the Brotherhood in public.

"Only so much can be done." Finlayson frowned and put a hand over his eyes to shield them from the bright sun. "Besides, there will always be an element of disorder here and in other ports far away from civilization. It's why men like us come here. We fit in."

"Am I included in that assumption?" I said, shaking my head and pushing away from the railing. "Give me a proper queue in London any day, for anything. The line may be long, but I know eventually, I will have my turn."

"You would be far better just to take your turn and walk away while the rest of the sheep wait." Finlayson followed behind me as we left the crowd to their grisly vigil.

"You did not learn such an attitude from my father," I commented as we began to follow the houseboy down the bridge.

Finlayson shook his head in disbelief. "You would be surprised at what I learned from your father. You do not know him as well as you think."

I grunted, not wanting to resume this tired old argument. The sooner we found Cornelius, the sooner Finlayson could get back to work. Doing what, I wondered? Indeed, not spying on my wife.

A red coat soldier stood in front of me, and my train of thought halted abruptly. Shaking my head at the rudeness, I made to step around him.

"Mr. Hawk. A moment of your time, please." Farquhar motioned I join him several feet away.

The soldier was young and looked eager to please. I comply with Farquhar now rather than having a public scene with only Finlayson as back up. I slowly made my way over to where Farquhar watched carefully, his expression dangerously neutral.

"What do you want, Major General?" I asked the question just before reaching him.

"Welcome back to Singapore, Mr. Hawk." Farquhar looked me over with a piercing glance. "Calcutta has made you forget your manners to your betters."

"That shall be a mystery to you until you see me meet one." My insolent reply earned me another glacial stare.

"What are you about this morning, Mr. Hawk?" His voice was crisp, and I felt the stares of the rest of the soldiers train on me.

"I believe my business runs under the category of none of yours." There was something satisfying in being deliberately disrespectful to Farquhar. It dredged up all the same feelings of my ten-year-old self, indulging in a prank I knew my father would not approve.

"In this case, it may have to do with the security of the citizens in this port," Farquhar smirked. "I can have you arrested and thrown in the pit." The soldiers held their breath waiting for the order to haul me away.

"My business partner did not come into work this morning and his houseboy," I waved at the boy who had once again stopped in his search for Cornelius to wait for me, "said he had not been home last night."

"Where do you hope to find him?" Farquhar's eyes narrowed.

"Under the sheets and with a woman wrapped in his arms, I have little doubt." I forced a smile. "However, I do not think Mr. Thistlewaite's personal life is any of your concern."

"Where were you last evening?" Farquhar barked.

Dread bubbled up and oozed through my gut and settled in my chest. This did not feel like the game I usually played with Farquhar. A quick glance around at the tense stance of the soldiers had the alarm whistling in my head again. The shrouded figure hauled onto one of the junks behind Farquhar caught my attention again.

"Who is it?" My voice no longer sounded like my own. I moved forward, trying to brush past Farquhar. He grabbed onto my arm and said something. I shook my head, unable to hear the words over the rushing sound in my ears. Countless faces of friends lost to me in battle and sickness flashed in front of my eyes, and I knew the addition of another face was inevitable.

It was easy to break Farquhar's grip on my arm, and I surged forward. A couple of soldiers rushed toward me with their bayonets pointed at my chest, but I didn't pay them any heed. Focused exclusively on the shrouded form, I used my hand to push the sharp blades away, my fingers and palms stinging where the metal had sliced them.

Falling to my knees, I reached out a shaking hand to the white sheet. I noticed now it was wet. Blood from my hand dripped onto the fabric and mixed with the other stains. People were shouting behind me, but my mind was oddly calm as I peeled the sheet away carefully, as if revealing a precious treasure. Underneath the sheet, a pair of familiar sightless eyes were glassy in death.

Cornelius's face was slack, and his fat jowls pulled at the corners of his mouth, giving his face an eerie look. The bog man did not look at peace after death, like some, I had known who died. Instead, his corpse screamed of an unfinished life, taken too early.

"Mr. Hawk this is highly inappropriate. You are interfering in a murder investigation." Farquhar's voice sounded annoyed and angry. "I will have you arrested if you do not step away."

"Where did you find him?" I asked without leaving Cornelius's side. I pulled the sheet lower looking for his cause of death.

Silence greeted my question, but I didn't move. With my hands bleeding now in earnest, I searched over his body and made to roll him over.

"Stop, Mr. Hawk." Farquhar sighed, and I felt him squat down beside me. "He was found in the tidal waters this morning by a couple of Chinese fishermen," Farquhar whispered and gestured to a small rip in the shirt Cornelius wore. "As far as we can tell, someone stuck him in the heart. A clean entry and exit, whoever it was knew what they were doing."

"An assassin?" My voice was bleak as I tried to register the implications. "The company sent an assassin to kill him to punish me."

"Not everything is about you and your father, Mr. Hawk." Farquhar's exasperation snapped me out of my stupor. "They certainly wouldn't bother to assassinate Mr. Thistlewaite to bring you to heel."

Standing up, I took the kerchief Finlayson handed me and tried to do something about the cuts. "You don't know that for sure."

"It is far more likely you had Mr. Thistlewaite killed to take over his share of the business." Farquhar's eyes were hard as he made the accusation.

"Of course, you believe I would kill a man who was like a father to me." My voice dripped with derision. "Better to steer the investigation away from the East India Company, the real culprits." Stepping forward, I filled up the space between us, "I will find out who did this, and if you or the company have even a hint of involvement. I will bring you down." Farquhar bristled. "I know. You can have me arrested for that. Come, Finlayson. We need to make arrangements for Mr. Thistlewaite."

"You'd better not leave Singapore, Mr. Hawk. No matter your accusations, you are the main suspect in Mr. Thistlewaite's death. I will be watching." Farquhar's voice rose as I once again approached the drawbridge over the Singapore River.

The houseboy stood forgotten in my grief. Tears streaked down his face, and I bent down to speak with him. "Go home and inform your mistress of Mr. Thistlewaite's death. Tell her I will be around in an hour." He nodded and took off at a run, his skinny legs pumping hard in the harsh sun. I watched him until he disappeared. Looking out over the harbor, I let my grief wash over me for a moment.

Cornelius had been a steady influence in my life for as long as I could remember. He had been the one to provide support after my father's death. I went to him for advice on everything, and now he was gone. Taking a deep breath, I thought, I need to know who did this.

Finlayson nodded beside me. "I can ask around; you know the Brotherhood would be more than willing to provide aid. Mr. Thistlewaite was a respected member of the community."

"We need to find out what his business was last night. My feeling is whoever met with Mr. Thistlewaite last evening is directly responsible for his death." I tried not to choke on the last word.

"It shouldn't be too hard to find out," Finlayson assured. "Singapore is small enough, and Mr. Thistlewaite was well known." He was silent for a minute. "We will unravel this."

"I want a name," I said with quiet conviction. "And when I have that name, I will kill the person to whom it belongs. There will be no mercy for the man who committed this crime. I cannot replace what they have taken from me." Cold certainty wrapped around my heart, and I knew revenge would keep my grief from overwhelming me. I would be strong. The petty argument with Charlotte was nothing compared to this. She was alive, and all she needed to do was forgive me. I would not allow her jealousy to ruin our marriage as it destroyed my parents. With a new conviction, I walked back toward the wharves.

October 1823
Chapter 18
Charlotte

"How do the ledgers look?" I asked without much enthusiasm. Through the large doors at the front of the warehouse, I could see the sun setting and twilight rapidly descending on the harbor. I thought of going home to the cold, empty house and shuddered.

"Charlotte." The concern in Bigham's voice was gentle but irritating. "You work too hard."

"Do I?" I studied his face for a second before sitting in one of the chairs in front of his desk.

"You spend more time here than I do." Bigham admonished and held up a ledger of the loans we owed to several people, including Zheng Jing's syndicate. "You have done well here. We are not out of trouble, but your instinct on the price of ginger in Europe this year was on the mark."

"There is a fashion for giving one's sweetheart a ginger confection in Germany. The trend is making its way through all the fashionable circles." I waved a hand. "You should read the ladies' digests."

Bigham shuddered in mock horror. "What would the lads say down the tap if I settled in on Sunday morning with my pie and a lady's quarterly?"

A burst of laughter escaped my lips at the picture Bigham's words conjured. The sound was rusty, and it was over as soon as it started.

"I was hoping to hear that laugh again." He gave me a lopsided smile and reached a hand out as if to touch my shoulder, but after a moment let it drop to his side.

Shrugging off his comment, I observed, "There hasn't been much to laugh at over these past few months." It was the truth. The death of Cornelius Thistlewaite had not only brought a new level of intensity to my husband, but it had a curious effect on the rest of Singapore. Cornelius's murder had sparked a ripple of outrage and a feeling of lost innocence among the European residents. People who had been the victims of unknown assailants had always been apart from the community. It struck a terrible fear in people, not least of all in me.

"You are not responsible for his death." Bigham sighed the words.

"Quiet," I warned, raising my hand and scanning the darkened corners of the warehouse. Only Bigham knew I had gone to meet Zheng Jing that night and found Cornelius instead. "We both know what happened."

"Did Zheng Jing ever say he killed Cornelius?" Bigham finally asked the question that I knew had been in the forefront of his mind for months.

"Of course not." I shook my head. "One does not admit to such things." I rubbed a hand over my eyes.

"It could have been footpads. No one has found any evidence otherwise." Bigham sounded assured.

Raising my stinging eyes to Bigham's face, I said, "My husband is still searching for the man who Cornelius reported meeting with that night." My voice was tight. "He believes this person is the one who killed Mr. Thistlewaite."

"We both know it isn't true," Bigham assured me.

I gave him a weak smile. "I don't know what's true anymore." Nathaniel had given me an ultimatum the morning of Cornelius's death. I was to forgive him for his brief liaison with Sarah Buck so we could get on with our lives, or we could separate. He could stay with a woman who hated him for the rest of his days as his father had hated his mother. At the time, I chose to forgive and try to forget. It wasn't easy with Sarah Buck appearing at all the same events as me, speaking of her joy of carrying a child. She coyly demurred to her late husband as the father of her child, while casting sly glances my way. Unfortunately, everyone suspected the truth because she had spread it by her lips.

Nathaniel had been all but silent on the matter. He did not acknowledge Sarah Buck as a mistress or even a former lover. I suppose it was true. One afternoon did not a commitment make. My marriage was an example of this. No matter how hard I tried to be a good wife, I still feared what would happen if Nathaniel learned about my interaction with Cornelius on the night he met his killer. This concern, coupled with the dangerous game I was playing with Zheng Jing, kept my nerves raw and my head throbbing. I lived every minute of every day in fear my whole world would come tumbling down.

Bigham reached out a hand and lightly touched me on the shoulder. "You're going to come through all this a much stronger person."

I clutched my hands to my stomach. "I cannot be any stronger than I already am." A wave of nausea struck me just then, and I took deep, steadying breaths that turned into sobs. Bigham squatted down on his haunches and tried awkwardly to provide some comfort.

Almost every night since Cornelius died, Nathaniel would come home in the wee hours of the morning and make mad, passionate love to me. Before the sun rose, he would be out of bed and off back to work. I hardly ever saw him, except in the dark, where the harsh planes of his increasingly sharp profile labored over mine to bring me exquisite pleasure.

The fruits of all those nights had now coalesced in my belly. Staring into Bigham's concerned face, I could not tell him about my suspected condition before informing Nathaniel. I had wanted to tell him right away, but we hardly had any time to interact. Everything was such a mess.

Pulling myself together, I gave Bigham a watery smile. "You're right. Things are already looking up. How much longer before we're free of Zheng Jing?" This was something I could control. I could manipulate and trade my way out of debt with Zheng Jing even if he held all the power now.

"A much longer time than even you suspect, Mrs. Hawk." The familiar cultured voice of Zheng Jing sounded from the dark entrance of the warehouse.

"What the hell are you doing here?" Bigham's voice thundered out across the warehouse floor.

"I see discretion is not one of your strongest qualities." Zheng Jing grimaced as he looked around. "We are not alone."

"We damned well are not." Bigham's temper was rising to the surface, and I needed to diffuse this situation before it blazed out of control. Look what Zheng Jing had done to Cornelius.

"You have come here," I said with icy clarity, staring directly at Zheng. "I believe you informed me that would never happen."

"Plans change; you should know that by now." Zheng Jing strode forward. Movement by the door leading outside showed a couple of large men watching over Zheng Jing. I wish I had the strength to overpower the man and kill him. A glance at Bigham showed he was angry enough to carry out the deed even with Zheng Jing's guards on the doors.

"Is that a threat?" Bigham asked, coming around the chair and putting his big body in front of me. "Don't think for a second we don't know you're responsible for Thistlewaite's death."

Zheng Jing strode right up to Bigham. A tic in his cheek was twitching furiously. He said, "If I were responsible, the blame would lie squarely on Mrs. Hawk's shoulders." He looked at me as I stood. "She should have kept her house in order."

Bigham growled only inches away from Zheng Jing's face. The Chinese man may have only been a few inches shorter than Bigham, but Bigham outweighed him by at least a couple of stone. The guards by the door cautiously stepped inside, eyes riveted on the scene unfolding.

I put a hand on Bigham's arm and shook my head when he finally looked at me.

"It's your party, as they say," Bigham snorted. "Just know someone is watching."

"The last man who was watching is no longer with us." Zheng Jing snapped.

"Enough!" I shouted at the two men. "What do you want? I ask again. It's dangerous for you to be here."

"Why? I'm your mediator." Zheng Jing looked around the warehouse partially filled with goods. The expression on his face made it clear he was not impressed. "We have business to discuss."

"You should have sent a coin." I tried to take some power back in our exchange.

"The coins might have outlived their usefulness," Zheng Jing asked. "You might want to take the risk, but I have no desire to make explanations to anyone, especially your husband. From now on, we meet here, and Mr. Bigham remains in attendance."

"No." I shook my head. "The less he knows, the better. This is dangerous."

"It's better this way, Charlotte." Bigham used my first name as a way to remind me of our friendship. "Better to have me here; this man will do anything to take advantage of you."

Zheng Jing's eyes narrowed, and a look of rage passed over his features so quickly that if I hadn't been watching him, I would have missed it. "Believe what you will, Mr. Bigham. No doubt you make such assumptions based on my race. I will have you know we were performing medical feats far beyond your capabilities while you were still grubbing around in the dirt."

"I base it on your actions alone, sir." Bigham drew in a breath. "You are a brigand who orchestrated this whole mess. The money Mr. Frederick Carstairs lost at the card table probably paid for the clothes you're wearing."

"You make many assumptions." Zheng Jing's lips curved into a sneer. A heartbeat later, he turned his attention back to me. "I suggest we leave the insults until a later date. Make no mistake, Mr. Bigham, I always remember when someone insults me."

Bigham inhaled angrily, and I looked at him quickly. I hoped he saw the caution in my eyes as he deflated and took another few steps back.

"The hour grows late," I persisted.

"A Dutch trader will be coming into Singapore this December to trade. I have been in contact with the company, and I will be the mediator for the sea captains." Zheng Jing cleared his throat. "

"You are going to trade with the Dutch now?" Bigham exploded. "Is there no limit to your depravity?"

"Very little, and you would do well to remember it." Zheng Jing snapped before continuing. "You will trade all your Bugis goods to him in exchange for a fair price, of course."

Resisting the urge to let my foot start tapping on the bare floor, I replied, "You will mediate for the rest of the goods with the Junk captains." I pursed my lips. "I suppose he will, in reality, be getting a ship full of contraband tea, rather than nutmeg and porcelain."

Zheng Jing's eyes turned stony, and the black depths pinned me to the ground. "You do not speculate upon my business, Mrs. Hawk. I think I have been very generous. Your Bugis goods will be sold out with little effort on your part."

"What of the goods I receive in return? Are they even worth trading?" I knew my tone was insolent, but my temper was frayed. There were limits to my endurance.

"Yes. I'm a businessman after all. The goods you receive in trade will be the same the Chinese will accept. I have a reputation to maintain not only in Singapore but in China, too." Zheng Jing looked around the warehouse again. "Do not think to cross me. I'm always watching. You wouldn't want your husband to lose another family member, would you?"

Terror once again poured through me at the thought of the power this man wielded. I felt as if I were drowning as I curtly nodded and turned away to see Bigham unleashing a look of loathing on Zheng Jing.

Bigham let loose a barrage of curses, and I knew we were once again alone. "I would like to string him up by the balls."

Not in the least bit shocked by Bigham's outburst I could not hold in my sigh of resignation. "You might like to, but I think he would enjoy it too much to bother."

Chapter 19
Nathaniel

Reaching for the sand, I sprinkled a liberal amount over the wet ink on the paper stretched out across my desk. I memorized the neat scrawl of Cornelius's previous entries and my cramped script underneath. Picking up the letter, I bent to the side and blew off the sand, inspecting the words to make sure none of them had run.

Months had passed, and I was beyond frustrated at the little progress I had made in solving Cornelius's murder. Despite my best efforts, there was no sign of the man who had stabbed him. I had no idea what led Cornelius out that night, or what business resulted in his death. Farquhar had been less than helpful. I had an alibi for the evening, but the Major General didn't appear to consider me the sole suspect. He spent his time trying to prove my guilt or harassing Raffles and the new First Resident of Singapore, Dr. John Crawfurd.

My hopes now rested solely on Finlayson and his Brotherhood brethren. Every now and again a snippet of information would turn into a lead that went into a dead end. It appeared whoever was responsible for the death of my friend and mentor was as elusive as smoke.

It seemed I would have to work very hard to live down my father's new, tarnished reputation, as well as my own. Farquhar's constant insinuations over Cornelius's death had led to speculation. I was responsible for his death. Men who had been friendly before now avoided me.

The Bugis trading season had been a lesson in how much Thistlewaite and Hawk relied on the good graces of not only the East India Company but also Cornelius's stellar reputation as a man of business. The Bugis were willing to deal with me, but I couldn't hire additional ships for cargo back to Europe at decent rates. Our ships were loaded to the gunnels with extra cargo to compensate, but I would have to find extra hold space if I wanted to keep our profits high.

"Mr. Hawk?" Hindly hailed me from the door, and I looked up startled. "Sorry sir, I knocked several times with no answer. I thought maybe you had gone home for the evening." He held a stack of papers balanced under his stump.

"Why would I go home?" I asked the boy with a layer of sarcasm.

"Your wife is there?" Hindly answered the rhetorical question with a question.

I sighed loudly; it wasn't the boy's fault my life had turned into a penny dreadful. "You have some papers for me?"

"Contracts for you to look over, sir." He fished the stack out from under his arm and handed them over the desk. He continued to stand in front of my desk as I looked at the top contract.

"Is there anything else you need, Mr. Hindly?" I asked without looking at him.

"It's just a couple of us lads." He paused for a second, and I looked up at him curiously. "Well, we're going down to the red door for a couple of drinks. I was wondering if you might want to join us. Seeing as you're not ready to head home for the evening." His face turned a painful shade of red at the last words.

"Thank you for the invitation, Mr. Hindly." I knew there was not only gossip about my involvement in Cornelius's death, but whispers had started over my relationship with Charlotte. Damn Sarah Buck and her indiscreet mouth. I had no idea what she planned to gain out of claiming her unborn child was mine, but she would get nothing from me. "However, I plan to finish up my work for the evening and spend a quiet evening at home."

"Yes, sir." Hindly turned, looking defeated before he stopped at the door. "It just seems that you spend a lot of time in the office." He waved his stump around to indicate Cornelius's old office. The one belonging to me now; I moved in shortly after his death to feel closer to him.

Smiling ruefully at Hindly, I said, "The running of Thistlewaite and Hawk takes up most of my time. In fact, I am now in awe over Mr. Thistlewaite's abilities. I have no idea how he managed on his own for so many years."

"He relied on the men he hired to carry some of the burden," Hindly spoke with conviction. "A ship is only as good as her crew."

Finlayson appeared in the door, his face flushed with exertion. "Never truer words were spoken, Mr. Hindly," he said, though he looked directly at me. After a pause for effect, Finlayson announced, "It has happened."

I sat up in my chair forgetting Hindly altogether. "You're sure?" My breath caught, and I felt the blood pumping through my veins. "If this is another false lead, I am losing the remainder of my patience."

"These things take time, Hawk. Thankfully, your patience has brought results, but we must go now." Finlayson jerked his head back down the stairs.

Reaching into the drawer of the desk, I took out my pistols and examined the shot and gunpowder. The old cutlass Cornelius kept under his desk caught my eye. The day Raffles burst into the office upon my return from Calcutta swam in my memory. Raffles had stood where Finlayson stood now. The three of us only worried over my father and the East India Company. Cornelius warned me of the rumors surrounding Charlotte and Mr. Bigham. He was persistent in his claims she was unfaithful, and I was insistent it was a misunderstanding.

Either way, she had chosen to stay and work on our marriage. I had decided the best way to curb her activities at Carstairs and Son was to get her with a child as quickly as possible and not to stop until she had too many underfoot to think of leaving the house.

"I'm ready." I stood and brushed past Finlayson and Hindly as I walked out the door. Perhaps tonight would be the night I finally got some justice.

"Where are we headed?" Hindly asked.

"Better for you to follow and keep your trap shut, Hindly," Finlayson said behind me.

"Maybe you should stay behind, Mr. Hindly." I glanced at the boy as I jumped down the last two steps. "This will not be a night for remembrance, and there is every possibility Farquhar will be after us."

"Mr. Thistlewaite was a good man." Hindly's chin rose in the air. "He gave me a job and treated me no different than the other lads. I'm going to ensure the implementation of justice." He nodded his chin for emphasis.

Finlayson looked in my direction for approval. I had little doubt he would put a stop to Hindly's involvement here and now if I wished it. But Hindly was correct. Cornelius had been a mentor and father figure to the clerks who had traveled far away from their families to seek their fortune. It only fitted at least one of them witness the vengeance I planned to release upon his killer.

"Let's go before this lead turns cold, too." My tone made it clear I was addressing Hindly as well as Finlayson. We all strode out of the warehouse into the night.

I had questions, but I knew they had to wait until we were private. The Brotherhood had finally made good on their vow to help me track down Cornelius's killer. My heart was in my throat as we hurried down to the river bank.

Finlayson nodded to a couple of sailors with bulging biceps standing beside an old junk. One of them stepped into the boat and settled with both long oar handles in his hands. "This will be the fastest way."

Hindly looked at the small craft with distaste. I knew he hadn't been back on the water since losing his arm. He would have to confront his fear of the water.

"Come on, Mr. Hindly." I stepped into the small craft making it wobble on the surface of the water. "Let's be prompt, if you please." I used my best captaincy voice and pretended not to notice his hesitation.

He stood staring a second longer before climbing onto the bench beside me. I reached out a steadying hand as his butt connected with the wood. "Thank you, Mr. Hawk." His response was so hushed I was the only one who heard.

The oarsman, still standing on shore, barely paused as Finlayson stepped aboard to push the craft away from the banks. The man working the oars threaded our way expertly through the other junks tied up for the evening, and we turned, heading out to sea.

None of us spoke. Hindly's remaining hand clenched the side of the boat so hard his knuckles turned white. Finlayson stared into the distance, immersed in his thoughts, and I did my best not to fidget. The oarsmen pulled against the tide, as the sea surged into the harbor.

We hugged the coast to the east of the main port. I knew from gossip a small encampment had started on the outskirts of the central port area away from the Chinese Campong. It was made up of gypsies and sailors looking to hide or escape the establishment of Singapore. It made sense Cornelius's murderer was hiding out here. The Brotherhood would have found him sooner if he had been wandering around Singapore.

The night noises of the jungle that had first disturbed me on my arrival filtered through the canopy of greenery on the coast. The water amplified the sounds. Faint lights in the distance spoke of some form of settlement. I watched them dance with the motion of the boat and was happy to have the heavy weight of my pistols weighing me down.

Clearing his throat, Finlayson spoke with caution from the bow of the boat. "Singapore is a freeport and runs without the interference of the East India Company for the most part," he began, "but this is no longer Singapore. This is no man's land. It's the rule of the strongest and the meanest. I would suggest you do your best to keep to yourselves as much as you can."

Somewhat confident, although the rowers were members of the Brotherhood, I asked, "The Brotherhood's reach extends all the way out here?"

"In some ways." Finlayson took a deep breath and looked away. "If there were contacts out here, the Brotherhood would not boast of them. For their safety as well as the reputation of the Brotherhood."

Hindly nodded his head curtly, and his hand went to the smooth piece of wood he wore on a leather string tied around his neck. It was the wood he bit down on as I let the doctor take his ruined arm.

I said nothing. Would it matter if I came out of this confrontation alive? I concentrated on the lights growing brighter as we neared the water's edge. People moved in the darkness, out of sight. I could feel their steady gazes on the boat. How good an idea was it to put my safety in the hands of the Brotherhood, let alone Hindly?

It was too late to back out now. The oarsman, who had pushed us away from the river before, stood up as we touched bottom. Finlayson jumped over the side and sloshed his way toward the beach. A dark shape came out of the shadows and waited for the boat to slide closer. The hull scraped against the bottom.

"This is as far as she goes, boys." Hindly wore an expression of relief as he followed Finlayson to shore. I held the edge of the boat and launched over the side, my gaze never wavering from the shrouded figure on the beach.

Finlayson spoke to him briefly before they both turned to me. "We need to hurry," Finlayson urged as Hindly staggered up beside me.

"Is there a problem?" I asked, trying to identify the man who had met us.

Sighing loudly and turning to follow the silent man, Finlayson waved ahead. "It appears that our man has more on his conscience than murder. He has racked up significant debts in Singapore at the card tables. The men he owes money to are currently taking it out of his hide."

"Will they sell him into slavery?" I wanted to know if there were a chance this man would escape the justice I had planned for him. An eye for an eye the Bible said. Even though I was not a religious man, this seemed fair to me.

"I don't know." Finlayson shook his head as we marched deeper into the forest. I felt eyes record my every move as we penetrated deeper into the jungle. Without warning, we stumbled into the middle of a small village. Huts were built from the predominant foliage and arranged haphazardly around a makeshift clearing.

Boys relit torches shoved into the soft earth. The man who had met us on shore led us to a hut near the end of the row. Finlayson spoke with a couple of men standing outside the hut before turning to me. "The man you seek is inside this hut." He waved at a Chinese man in the group. "Even though his crimes against you are grievous; it is up to this gentleman to determine the murderer's fate." I opened my mouth to argue, but Finlayson stopped me. "We are guests here because this man owes the Brotherhood a favor. He found Cornelius's murderer and has given you the courtesy of seeing the man who took your friend's life before finishing with his punishment."

"Thank you." I looked at Finlayson and nodded curtly. Stepping up to the threshold of the simple hut, I took a deep breath and prepared to push the mat aside.

But before I could move, Finlayson laid a hand on my arm. "I have been warned that if you kill him, your life will be forfeit to the debtors." He continued to stare into my eyes. "Give me your pistols as a sign of good faith."

Damn and damn. Tearing my gaze away from the door, I looked at the man who I owed for finding Cornelius's killer. "I don't need my pistols to kill him." Staring into Finlayson's eyes, I said, "I will do it with my bare hands."

Several men, the group, shifted their weight nervously, and the air hung thick with silence.

Finlayson held up his hands in surrender. "I leave the choice up to you."

My nostrils flared at my helplessness. I struggled to control my temper. Hindly's taut face did much to help me remember my responsibilities. I had to think of Charlotte's well-being; God knows her family never did. Not to mention all the people I employed at Thistlewaite and Hawk. It would be a poor way to honor Cornelius by letting down the people who admired and depended on him.

Glaring at the unknown man, I reached down and took hold of my pistols. A mad second passed while I contemplated trying to take down as many of these men as I could to accomplish my vow. Instead, I gave my guns to Finlayson. Barrels pointed toward me.

"Any other restrictions?" I didn't bother to keep the bitterness from my voice.

"No." Finlayson's fingers closed around the handle of the weapons. "Beat him all you like, just make sure he can face whatever these men have planned.

I looked at Hindly before I turned and pushed the crude door out of the way. The hut was dark. Only one candle lit the inside. A man lay on his side in the semi-darkness, curled into a ball. Another two men stood over him, watching his every move. One additional guard looked up and acknowledged my presence.

Circling the man who had killed Cornelius, I tamped down a sense of disappointment. I might have passed this man every day for a year, but bruises and damage marred him too significantly. His chest rose and fell in a shallow, erratic rhythm. Leaning down next to him, I held up my hands as the guard started forward.

"I am only going to ask him a few questions," I said to the beefy man who held a pistol primed at my head. "There are things I need to know," I choked out. He nodded and stepped back. Not wanting the guard to listen to this private conversation, I shuffled closer. "Do you know who I am?"

The slightest of nods answered my questions.

"Who am I?" I asked to be certain.

The man's throat and mouth worked as he tried to chew out the words. "Mr. Hawk. You are Hawk."

"Yes, I'm Nathaniel Hawk," I confirmed my identity. "Who are you?"

He shook his head and sobbed. The motion made him choke and cough. The guard came forward to watch intently while the racking sobs continued. He face grew slack again, the blood and saliva quivering on his lips indicated he was still of this world.

"Who are you?" I asked again.

"Don't you want to know why?" He asked and tried to open his eyelid. Through the narrow slit, I spied a chocolate brown iris.

"I imagine you did it for one of two things." I grew annoyed this man wanted to ask me the questions. "Power or money." Since you would gain little power from Mr. Thistlewaite's death, I can only assume money tempted you."

A long pause followed, and the man licked his lips. "Aye, money."

Wishing there were another way, I moved so my lips were right over the other man's ear. "Who are you?"

"Not important now, Mr. Hawk." The man said as he tried to crack a smile. "I'm a dead man. Either by your quick hand or the hands of those mercenaries out there." He took a deep, steadying breath. "I did you an unfortunate turn. Mr. Thistlewaite was a good man." His words were a confession, and I grabbed onto the front of his shirt and lifted him partially from the ground. The guard edged closer.

"Who are you, dammit?" I shook the man. The guard grabbed my wrist and shook his head. Letting go of the beaten man, I watched as he crumpled back down to the floor. I wanted to make sure I could revenge myself on his family if I couldn't kill him. Squatting back down, I waited until he opened his one eye to stare at me. "I will find out who you are. Then I will track every single person you care about and have my revenge."

The man whimpered and gulped in air. "You will kill them?

"Worse, I will make sure their lives are so excruciatingly painful. They will wish for death to come." I surged forward so I was only an inch away from the man's face. I let all the rage and anger I felt bubble to the surface. The intensity surprised me. "Don't think I will hesitate for a moment to obliterate every last morsel of you from the face of the earth.

The eye revealed his anguish at my words. I could see the terror for his family building inside him. I stood up to leave; disgusted with him and myself. If I were half a man, I would take the small dagger I have hidden in my boot and end this all here. But my damn responsibilities kept intruding on my will to forge my path.

"Wait." The man let out a strangled cry.

I stood over him for a full minute before squatting down again. "You are not going to tell me who you are. Now you know of my plans."

He tried to twist around and settled for lowering his voice. "I have information."

"I cannot save you from your fate, even if I had the desire." I shook my head

"No, but my family." He closed his eyes and swallowed hard. "I have a wife, daughters. You will know all soon. They're innocent."

"You are not," I replied. "Our time is up." I ran a hand through my hair. This had not turned out as I planned. My hands itched to beat the man until he no longer breathed.

He licked his lips. "You have enemies, Mr. Hawk. Terrible enemies, ones you will never suspect."

"It wouldn't be wise to play games with me," I said making a move to stand again.

"You will certainly end with a knife in your back if you do not listen to my next words." His voice was frantic. "I will give you the name in exchange for clemency. Please let my family alone."

"Tell me the name of this person who will kill me, and I will decide whether or not to save your family," I demanded.

"I have heard you're an honorable man. A man of his word, Mr. Hawk," he said as he contemplated my deal.

"There are those who would say otherwise, but I try to keep my promises," I replied vaguely, waiting to see if he would take the deal.

"Come closer, and I shall whisper the name," the man said.

"How do I know you will only tell me the name and not bite my ear off?" I said, frowning. "You've been playing a game with me all this time."

"Wait. I swear on the lives of my wife and daughters," he said anxiously.

Inclining my head toward his face, I waited for the man's teeth to sink into my skin. Instead, his breath was warm and smelled coppery from the blood he had been coughing up. With feather light softness, the man uttered the one name I would never have believed, even with yards of proof laid out ahead of me.

"The devil you say," I exhaled a long breath, too stunned to keep my voice down.

The man's eye flickered with fear as he looked at the guard who had advanced close enough to hear the rest of our conversation even in whispers. "The threat is real, and your mutual destruction too late to stop. There can be no deviating from the course now. Either you might be able to save yourself. Otherwise, you will both perish."

"Where is this threat coming from? The East India Company? How do you know about it?"

A humorless laugh escaped his lips. "Mr. Hawk, you have more enemies than the East India Company. You have no idea what awaits you in the dark."

"Enough." The guard looked down at his prisoner. The man had obviously revealed enough. I watched as the guard kicked the prone man once in the back with a sturdy boot.

Scrutinizing the man one last time, I turned to the door. Outside I breathed in the humid, salty air, but it did little to clear my head. My glance immediately fell on Finlayson, who watched me with a neutral expression. I held out my hands for the return of my pistols.

"I'm done here. Thank you for your help, such as it was," I said to the man who owned Cornelius's killer.

Finlayson handed the pistols to me. "I'm sorry if you didn't get the revenge you wanted."

We started walking back through the small cluster of huts toward the shore. Hindly trailed behind us. "To the contrary, my plan has only changed."

"In what way?" Hindly asked quietly.

"Cornelius's killer had some fascinating information, and I plan to exploit it. My enemies had better be on their guard because I'm coming for them. "I said the words aloud to infuse them with as much conviction as I could muster.

Chapter 20
Charlotte

I waited in the study with my hands curled into fists in my lap for Nathaniel to come home. Bigham was right. I needed to talk to someone, to feel the connection. Perhaps this baby would bring us closer together. After everything we had been through, we deserved some happiness. This child would be the start of our new lives.

As usual, he was late coming home. I knew he wasn't working, at the warehouse at least. Hoping to catch him at his office, I had gone there, wanting to walk home with him. Enjoy a simple pleasure. Unfortunately, I had been informed by an apologetic office manager that Mr. Hawk had left with a couple of others only minutes before.

I rushed home. Only Dutta was there, studiously preparing an evening meal. Taking a small supper in the study, I continued to wait, alternating between sitting restlessly and pacing the wooden floors. Why was this so hard? We had already agreed to make our marriage work and now there was no question of a separation. No court would grant it with the child on the way.

Sighing, I picked up a stack of papers and tried to focus on the words, but my simmering anger made it difficult. It was not only this evening but also every other one before it swam in my memory. "Had Nathaniel ever really wanted to try and make our marriage a success? He said he did. Unfortunately, his actions spoke louder than words. I was at home, and he was where? At the gaming tables? Drinking with his friends? In another woman's bed? The last thought made my blood thicken and my temper never far from the surface made my hands clench more painfully.

The front door opened, and the wall clock showed it was almost midnight. Nathaniel was at home unusually early. Was this a good sign? Or a bad one?

"What are you still doing up?" Nathaniel asked from the doorway. He was in the middle of unbuttoning the front of his shirt.

"I was waiting for you to get home," I replied and watched as he stepped slowly across the room to the sideboard.

"Scotch?" he questioned as he poured a couple of fingers.

"No, thank you." I wrinkled my nose.

"How could I forget?" Nathaniel picked up another decanter. "You prefer sherry." He held it up in silent question.

"Nathaniel, I was hoping we could talk." His lack of emotion annoyed me.

"It's been a long day." Nathaniel demurred as he turned around and pressed the glass to his lips.

"The months since your return from Calcutta have been long." I straightened my back. "And lonely. I thought we were both supposed to be working on this marriage."

"What more would you have me do?" Nathaniel's eyes narrowed.

"How about being present!" I said in a rush, my anger taking over. I pointed the finger at him. "This is the first time you have been home before midnight. Come home and eat with me, be seen with me at a dinner or dance. Acknowledge I'm alive."

Nathaniel drained another glass before setting it on the table. "Every night I come home and prove how much I am willing to make this marriage work." My face turned red at his crude words. He stalked around the table and faced me. I smelled the Scotch on his breath and something else. It was different and unusual. "What else do you want from me?"

"Were you with your mistress?" I choked out. "Is that why you're home early? You have a fight with your paramour."

"Christ's balls, woman," Nathaniel swore under his breath. "You have an overactive imagination."

"Is that what is growing in Sarah Buck's belly? My imagination?" I taunted and immediately regretted saying the words. This was not how I wanted the evening to go.

Nathaniel's eyes widened. "You married me knowing I had slept with her. I thought we were going to start over." He shook his head. "All for nothing, I suppose." His shoulders sagged, and he stepped away. He made a visible effort to regain control of his emotions.

Taking a deep breath, I thought frantically for a way to salvage the situation. I took his hands in mine. "Nathaniel, please sit." He nodded and sat on the silk-covered sofa next to me avoiding my skirts. "In so many ways, I wish this could have been different, but I see now how stubborn we both are." I tried to smile into his closed face. "I am with child." He continued to stare and remained silent. "You are going to be a father. Again." I finished lamely.

A long silence passed and he finally responded, "Is it mine?"

Shock made my head light and my stomach drop. Involuntarily, tears sprang into my eyes, and I felt my lip quiver. "What is wrong with you?" I stood up.

He stood up at the same time. "I think it's a reasonable question. Is it mine or is it Bigham's?"

I slapped him hard across the cheek. My hand burned, but it felt good compared to my humiliation. "How bloody dare you?" I screeched and stepped away from him. "I should never have agreed to this sham marriage."

"Is that what you were thinking on the morning of our wedding? In the carriage on our way up to Government House, something was bothering you. Tell me now what it was." Nathaniel looked earnest.

"What are you talking about?" I yelled at him. "I married you in good faith. As you said, even though I knew of your affair with Sarah Buck." I held my hands over my still flat stomach. "What did you think was going to happen if you came home and made love to me every night?" My exasperation made me stamp my foot. Laughter bubbled up at his idiocy.

Nathaniel stared down at me for several heartbeats before swearing under his breath and turning on his heel.

"Where are you going?" I shouted in frustration. "Why does our marriage always have to be this way?" He stopped at my words.

"To what are you referring?" Nathaniel asked without turning around.

Biting my lip to try and keep my temper. "We were in love once." The words were out of my mouth before I had time to think. Impossible to take them back now.

"You no longer love me?" Nathaniel asked as he slowly turned back around. "I ask you again, why did you marry me?"

My shoulders sagged, and I felt the full weight of the problems in our marriage. "I was a fool in love, I suppose."

"And now you're no longer a fool." Nathaniel's hands turned into fists.

"We were going to make this work," I said desperately. "We have no choice now. Our child deserves to live in a loving household."

Nathanial came toward me slowly. With deliberate intent, he held out his arms and enveloped me in his embrace. He was stiff at first. I let out a long breath and melted into him.

"I wish I did not love you as I do." Nathaniel's voice sounded strangled. "It would make my life so much more bearable."

The smell of sweat clung to his linen as I buried my face in his chest. Tightening my arms and eyes, I asked, "Why would it be easier? I thought love was supposed to be easy."

"Tell me your secret." Nathaniel kissed the top of my head. He felt me stiffen in his arms. "I will protect you."

I held my tears while continuing to bury my face in his chest. The thought of unburdening myself to Nathaniel and seek comfort in his strength was unbearable. I knew it was impossible. Zheng Jing had murdered Cornelius for stumbling on the truth, and I could never live with Nathaniel's death on my conscience. Despite the past few months, I loved him. It was probably why Sarah Buck hurt me so much.

"There's nothing to tell," I lied. The worst part was I didn't even sound convincing to myself.

"Very well." Nathaniel let go of me and stepped back. The look on his face conveyed hurt and betrayal. I wondered if he already knew my secret. Before I could say anything, he walked to the door and did not pause as he left the house. The door closed with finality, and I sank onto the sofa.

The tears I had no idea I was shedding ran down my cheeks and splashed onto my fingers.

Chapter 21
Nathaniel

Standing in front of the familiar red door, I wasn't sure how I had gotten here. The ugly scene with Charlotte continued to play over in my mind. I needed to escape, if only for a few hours. Using the underside of my fist I pounded on the door again. The shutter opened violently, and a scowling man's face appeared.

"It be you, Mr. Hawk," the man said in surprise.

"It be me." I let sarcasm infuse each word. "Can't a man get a drink in this town?"

The doorman studied my face for a minute. "Are you sure you want to come in?"

"No, I have decided to waste both of our time with this pointless conversation." My anger was winning out over patience.

I heard a loud sigh before the shutter slammed closed and the door opened. "Welcome back, Mr. Hawk."

"Thank you," I replied without much enthusiasm. I had not been back here since the night before my wedding. It was the same, except at the table where Hindly sat with a couple of the clerks. Finlayson had taken the place of Cornelius. I inwardly winced. This night was for forgetting everything. Hoping no one at the table noticed my entrance, I tried to blend into a crowd watching a game of faro near the bar.

"Mr. Hawk." I heard my name shouted across the room. So much for finding oblivion. Turning around, I saw Hindly sway a few times as he stood. He motioned for me to come over with his stump. His face was red, and I should have realized he would have been in a state after the evening's proceedings. My turmoil had enveloped me, and I ignored him and Finlayson.

Waving a hand in greeting, I changed directions and headed for their table. I spoke to a passing waitress and ensured the table would not be dry all night. Finlayson used his foot to push the remaining chair out from the table, and I sat down staring at the rest of them.

I reached for the glass a clerk handed me and took a drink. "Thank you." He nodded back in embarrassment, and I held in a groan. This was going to be a long night.

Finlayson asked, "What happened in the hut?"

Aware of several eyes, let alone sets of ears trying to listen in on the conversation, I took another drink before answering. "I don't know what you mean."

"I'm not surprised to see you down here this evening, Mr. Hawk." Mr. Meacham's voice boomed over the chatter of the rest of the room. He was one of the old guard and, as much as Cornelius put up with his nonsense, I thought he was nothing better than a gossiping old woman.

"Mr. Meacham, and why is that?" I asked, looking up at the portly gentleman. The rumors said his wife paid for his mistress so he would not climb up on top of her in the evenings.

"The good news, my dear boy." Mr. Meacham's comments had drawn a small crowd in the card room.

Rolling my shoulders, I readied for a confrontation. "Mr. Meacham, I'm afraid you will have to be much more specific." Was he referring to the fact he knew I had confronted Cornelius's murderer or that my wife was pregnant? Perhaps he was commenting on my problems with the East India Company.

"The birth of your son." Mr. Meacham tipped his glass in my direction. "Congratulations."

I stared at him for a full minute before I realized he must be speaking of Sarah Buck. Shock froze my body. I knew my face had gone blank, but my mind whirled over the day's events. The Brotherhood claimed to have found Cornelius's murder. The man whom they proclaimed had committed the foul deed gave me the name of the person who was betraying me. When I confronted her and begged her to tell me her secret, she had told me of her pregnancy. Did she know of Sarah Buck? Was she reacting to the birth of the other woman's child?

"Mr. Meacham, it's well known Mr. Hawk does not claim paternity of Sarah Buck's child," Finlayson spoke into my continued silence.

"No one claims them, my dear boy." He bestowed a clumsy wink on us.

Reaching out for my glass of Scotch, I was surprised to see my hand was steady. I raised it. "To Sarah Buck and the legacy of my great friend Captain Buck. May his son only be an asset to his memory." I swallowed the contents down in one gulp and shivered. Hindly and Finlayson finished off the rest of their drinks.

"As you are an asset to your family." Finlayson murmured for my ears alone. I snorted in response. The alcohol made the blood rush in my veins, and I felt alive for the first time since leaving the gypsy camp.

"Yes, indeed." Mr. Meacham murmured. He walked away after another minute when the table remained silent. I felt the relief of all those seated.

"I wouldn't have punched his face in," I said to the group, in general, hoping to break through the quiet.

Hindly shook his head and reached out to one of the bottles on the table. "I was tempted even if you were not, Mr. Hawk." He poured out rations around the table. "The girls all say his willy is tiny." Putting the bottle back down, he wiggled his thumb. "Like this."

A few of the lads laughed at his joke, and a couple of conversations broke out among them. Finlayson shook his head and studied his drink.

"Why do you know what the girls say, Mr. Hindly?" I asked across the table.

He held up his hand, the picture of innocence. "I promise, Mr. Hawk. I'm only talking and looking. Not touching and paying."

"Keep it that way," I growled back at him.

"Would Mr. Hawk like to touch?" The same woman from the night before my wedding sidled up to the table. She had the same length of silk rope hanging in loose folds down her front. I saw Finlayson frown at her out of the corner of my eye.

"I have a wife for that," I said quickly giving her an easy smile.

"Shibari is not always about intercourse, Mr. Hawk," the woman said informatively. My smile turned genuine at her staid word for sex. "It is about surrendering your power to another or taking it back. Lots of trust must be present between two people for it to work."

"I can count on one hand the people I trust in this world." I reached for the glass Hindly had poured for me. "And none of them, I can assure you, will let me truss them up like a Sunday goose."

"Mr., Hawk is not interested in your wares, woman." Finlayson snapped. I was surprised by his tone. The look on his face told me he was impatient to begin our previous conversation.

"Perhaps I can be persuaded to learn?" I reached out and fingered the silk rope. "What is your name?"

"Are you sure this is a good idea? You have a wife at home." Finlayson did not lower his voice. His insistence that I give up the game only made me more determined to try.

"Jade, you may call me Jade." Jade unwound another length of the rope and let it fall into my outstretched hands.

"Jade is a little obvious." I frowned at her. What was I thinking? I had enough problems without all of Singapore talking about how I had slept with a prostitute on the night Sarah Buck gave birth to my supposed son. Let alone the fallout when Charlotte's condition began making the gossip rounds.

"Yet easy to remember." Jade leaned forward, and I caught a glimpse of small rounded breasts underneath her red silk tunic, she wore a soft elusive scent I could not name. "I can give you complete control back, Mr. Hawk. I only need a few hours. Let me provide your escape."

The word escape persuaded me. I had walked in here this evening hoping to drown my worries over Cornelius and Charlotte. Only to be handed more problems in the form of Sarah Buck. The look on Finlayson's face meant I wouldn't get a moment's peace until I spilled my guts over what happened in the hut. I wasn't ready to confess I suspected my wife of trying to kill me or ruin me. Was it one in the same?

With a groan, I pushed back from the table and looked around. "It's been a trying evening, gentleman. I will see you all in the morning." Hindly's eyes were wide as he looked up at me. I could read the thoughts spinning out of control in his head. "Not to worry, Mr. Hindly. I will be on the wharves waving Raffles off like everyone else tomorrow morning." I watched as Jade called a younger girl over to the table. "I don't think I will be making his leaving breakfast." Leering at the girl, I ignored Finlayson's look of shock and the laughter from the rest of the men. "Lead on, ladies."

I followed Jade through the crowd of men. A few of them turned to watch Jade and the younger woman tack their way through the tables with interested looks. Admiring the sway of Jade's hips, I ignored any surprised glances thrown my way as I climbed the stairs to the second floor of the gaming house. Women of all ages gazed down from a balcony built over the card table, watching the men as they gambled.

"In here, Mr. Hawk." Jade held open a door, and I followed the girl inside. "This is Mindy. She will be your canvas this evening." I stood still as the young woman walked into the middle of the room. She slowly untied the stays of her silk gown. My mouth went dry as the silk cascaded to the floor and pooled around her ankles. "She is beautiful, is she not, Mr. Hawk?"

Clearing my throat, I replied, "Very lovely." I walked forward and put a finger under the girl's chin and lifted her face up to mine. Her features were delicate, with dark eyes almost black and a small mouth. I brushed my lips over hers, once and pulled back slowly. Mindy's eyes dilated and a flush swept across her cheeks.

"Mindy has not been in the life long," Jade commented as she came to stand beside me. "Please get up on the bed, sit on your knees with your hands clasped behind her back."

I held out a hand, and Mindy used it to leverage herself up on the mattress. She settled herself into the position Jade indicated with her legs spread wide open. Holding onto my senses, I reminded myself I was here to escape only. I didn't need the sex. Charlotte was still my wife. Loyalty was still important to me.

Jade climbed and sat on one side of Mindy. "Shibari, Mr. Hawk, is an art form performed with the rope." She measured a length of the rope she held in her hands and slowly began wrapping it around Mindy's wrists. "If done properly, the person wearing the rope becomes a beautiful sculpture of exotic potential. Jade tightened the rope around Mindy's wrists, and the girl gasped. I watched as Jade's competent fingers ran up and down the girl's arms a few times before tugging the rope down to the girl's ankles. She held them out to me. "Mr. Hawk?"

With a knee planted on the bed, I copied Jade's knots and strokes as I bound Mindy's ankles together. I shortened the rope tied around her wrists and ankles, and her breasts thrust forward. I rubbed hands down her spine to make sure her position was comfortable. Even though I knew Mindy's trust was superficial, the way she let me truss her up, naked and completely at my mercy, unlocked something I had been hiding away all my life. I was eager to continue.

"What's next?" I murmured. Jade took the rope from my hands and began making knots before pressing them into Mindy's skin in a scalloped pattern up her thighs. Concentrating on the knots and the way the rope looked as it pressed into Mindy's delicate skin, I forgot about my problems of the evening. I let Cornelius's murder go, and my marital problems floated away. By the time I reached the last knot, my mind was calm.

Shaking my head to come back to the moment, I admired my handy work.

"Are you sure you have not performed Shibari before, Mr. Hawk," Jade said from across the room.

I looked up to see her seated comfortably in a chair, watching my every move. "No, but I was a sailor once." Running my hands down Mindy's arms, I watched as her chest heaved in large breaths of air. I let my hands cup the breasts I made stand out from her body. "The knots came naturally."

"What else comes naturally?" Jade asked in a challenging tone.

Rubbing a thumb over one of Mindy's nipples, my cock tightened as her breathing increased. Everyone would believe I had sex with her. Why was I so concerned with what everyone downstairs and in Singapore thought? Mindy began to strain against her bonds as she tried to shove her whole breast into the palm of my hand.

Charlotte held me back. She claimed the child was mine, but Cornelius was well aware, as others believed, she was having an affair with Bigham. There were nights when Charlotte worked late, alone with him. Since my return from Calcutta, she had been distant. True she laid the blame on me, but the tension was new. As far as I could tell, Cornelius's murderer was right. She was conspiring against me with some unknown force. I moved my other hand to cup the girl's face. Why shouldn't I take a small slice of pleasure for myself?

I rubbed the girl's lower lip with my thumb while using my other hand to unbutton the front of my trousers. This was a night for new beginnings. The man who had killed Cornelius was either dead or wishing he were. My marriage could not be saved, even with the birth of this child. The East India Company would take its pound of flesh. I needed to move on, and this was the best way forward. Shifting my position, I offered myself to the girl pressing the end of my cock against her lips. "Take it, girl."

As Mindy's lips wrapped around me, I felt pleasure and power surge through my veins. This was something I finally had control over. My head fell back against my shoulder blades, and I let Mindy erase the rest of my evening.

&

Warm breath on my neck startled me awake, and I tried to stay still as I assessed my situation. Cracking one eye open, I looked down to see Mindy's arms and legs entwined with my own on my right side. Her skin retained faint red marks from the knots and ropes last evening, even though Jade and I had rubbed her limbs repeatedly as we undid my handiwork. Turning my head, I looked down at the top of Jade's head. One hand rested on my stomach and the other on my thigh.

"You're awake." Jade's soft voice floated up to me. She moved to get up, but I stopped her.

"A few more minutes," I said, smiling. I closed my eyes as all the erotic things we had done together flooded back. "Or maybe we can continue this morning."

Jade lifted her head from my chest and looked up at me. "Sir Raffles leaves this morning."

With those words, I felt the cold knot of responsibility tight in my belly. Tension rippled through my shoulders, and I let out a long, tortured sigh. "It was such a good morning." I watched Mindy's even breathing and smiled down at her.

"You cannot hide from your responsibilities here, Mr. Hawk." Jade moved closer and licked my nipple.

Groaning, I wrapped my hand in her hair and forced her to look up at me. "Watching Raffles sail back to England is hardly a responsibility."

"What about your wife? She is undoubtedly waiting for you." Jade gave me a sympathetic smile. "We will always be here, waiting for you."

"You'd better be," I said, easing my body away from hers and Mindy's and sitting on the side of the bed. Last night had been better than drinking myself into unconsciousness. It had felt better than the few careful times I had chased the dragon with friends. Even though I could feel my mind shifting back to all my mundane problems, a relaxed core throbbed inside.

Picking up my trousers from the pile of clothing on the floor, I looked at my pocket watch. I swore under my breath, and Jade let out a quiet laugh. "I've missed the damned leaving breakfast. Charlotte would have attended alone."

Jade shook her head, pity in her eyes. "I am sorry for it." Her words sounded genuine. "You have enemies, Mr. Hawk. Men would be very happy to drive a wedge between you and your wife."

"There's already a wedge." The comment was out before I thought to keep the words back. I gave Jade a stern look. "Mr. Hawk, I might be a whore, but I am an honorable one. Your secrets are my secrets."

I nodded at her and decided never to trust her with any of my secrets. Fortunately for me, I was not certain whether I wanted my newfound addiction to be a secret.

Chapter 22
Charlotte

Sipping a cup of tea, I did my best to keep the brittle smile on my face. Not only had Nathaniel not returned home after our argument, but the news of Sarah Buck's son had greeted me this morning. Everyone told me discreetly, of course. They wanted to be the first to tell me how scandalous the whole situation had become. Fresh pots of tea would be made to fill the bellies of the ladies as they talked about my reaction to my rival's happy news.

Many had noted Nathaniel's absence, and I tried to smooth it over by mentioning work commitments and urgent business. I tried to assure anyone who would listen he was only moments away. Unfortunately, as the breakfast wound down and Raffles and Sophia made their final personal goodbyes around the room, there still was so sign of him.

"Still waiting for Mr. Hawk?" Mrs. Meacham's question distracted me from watching the tableau of Raffles tenderly holding his wife's hand as she wiped a tear from her eye.

"He is all business these days," I replied with intentional vagueness. "How is Mr. Meacham?" Women did not mention Mrs. Meacham's husband unless they wanted an earful of bile concerning infidelity. I was willing to risk it if it would distract her from the twin topics of Sarah Buck and Nathaniel.

"Interesting you should mention my husband." Mrs. Meacham began, with a smug little smile on her face. "He said he saw Mr. Hawk last night playing cards." Knowing from gossip the kinds of establishments Mr. Meacham enjoyed frequenting, I could only imagine what Nathaniel had been doing. At least she had not mentioned Sarah Buck.

"I hope Mr. Hawk did not divest Mr. Meacham of too many marks," I replied, bestowing a wan smile. Unlike my brother, Nathaniel was apparently quite lucky at cards. It made me less nervous to hear about him gambling, knowing he normally did well.

"It appears it falls on my frail shoulders to tell you, my dear," Mrs. Meacham began. I held in a groan. She was going to mention Sarah Buck and her new baby. "Mr. Hawk employed the delights of a couple of the girls last night. Usually speaking of this sort of business is below me, but I would want to know what bed Mr. Meacham was crawling out of in the morning."

"You would know, Mrs. Meacham." My smile faltered as I struggled to find an intelligent response. Mrs. Meacham made no secret of the fact she chose and paid for her husband's mistresses. My heart felt like it was breaking in two. How could Nathaniel go whoring after I told him I was carrying his child? Foolish girl! I heard the voice of my mother ringing in my head. It's because you're headstrong, and he doesn't believe the child is his.

"More people should employ the thoroughly modern way we have used to navigate our marriage." Mrs. Meacham's nose rose into the air. "There would be much less crying over tepid cups of tea." She looked me up and down. "I suppose, though, all you young girls still believe in love." When I did not answer, she continued. "Look at what love has gotten Sarah Buck and her ridiculous persistence in chasing after your husband. No one will speak with her. The establishment has closed ranks against her. And for what? To protect the reputation of two stupid girls and one man who cannot keep his front buttons closed."

"Mrs. Meacham, I think you've said enough." I stepped back and shook my head.

"I would like to say far more, but you are a stubborn chit. Everyone knew this was going to happen. Captain Sebastian Hawk was ever chasing after some woman's skirts, and now your husband is following in his philandering footsteps." Drawing herself up to her full height, she continued to pontificate. "Hawk men are incapable of being loyal to one woman. The sooner you realize this, the sooner you can move on." She nodded at her last words and walked off with a false social smile in place.

With unseeing eyes, I scanned the rest of the guests. Nathaniel had been at a brothel whoring last evening, while I sat at home crying and lamenting our argument. I had wanted to take back my cruel words to him when he returned from Calcutta after facing the wrath of the East India Company. There was a part of me that wanted to share my burden with Zheng Jing with him. Last night, it had felt like utter insanity to keep my trouble from him. I resolved to confess everything to him. But then, he had not returned.

Now it was too late. Nathaniel's actions spoke louder than anything else. There was no going back. I was utterly alone. I could not even count on Bigham, as it would put him in danger, either from Zheng Jing and his thugs or the wrath of the East India Company. I felt swamped by utter desolation, and tears welled in my eyes again.

"My dear, it is a sad day, but we shall all reunite in London." Sophia Raffles held out her immaculately gloved hands. I took them in my own and drew a deep breath.

"Singapore will be the less for your absence. Thank you for everything you have done." I hoped my words reflected the sincerity behind them.

"It was my duty, not only as the first lady of Singapore but as a friend." She tucked my hand into her elbow and turned me toward a pair of windows facing the gardens. "I think Singapore will miss my husband much more than me. That is the life of a woman married to a great man." She gave me a sideways look.

"Sir Raffles is a great man, and we will miss him, but your kindness has always been a beacon to me in this faraway place." I tried not to think about how abandoned I felt.

"Whether you choose to accept it or not, you are married to a great man." Sophia waited until I glanced at her. "It's true. Some might say his father was the legend, but I think Nathaniel has the potential to be an even better man than him." Her brows drew together, and she thought through her next words. "I met him, Captain Sebastian Hawk, on a few occasions. He was a fast friend with my Stamford. Everyone thought of him as jovial and devil-may-care." She paused for another moment. "But there was a coldness to him. He was always watching, always waiting for something." She shrugged. "I suppose he found it in the end."

Not knowing what to say, I murmured, "Thank you." I had only ever seen Sebastian Hawk from a distance. I have never had an introduction. He was never still for long. I wondered what it might have been like to have a father like him.

"It is a shame Nathaniel could not get here for breakfast," Sophia lamented.

"He will meet us down at the wharves, I'm sure." Raffles stepped up to his wife, and I withdrew my hand from her elbow, instantly missing the intimacy. "Nathaniel is nothing, if not steadfast."

Sophia gave her husband a brilliant smile, and I was jealous of their happiness. She nodded toward me. "Besides, this separation is not forever. One day we shall all live in London, and when we meet, we shall speak of all our adventures here in the East. To our grandchildren, we will sound like the bravest of folk."

"We will, indeed." Raffles gave his wife an indulgent smile. "Think of all the pirate stories we shall have for the children's bedtime." At the mention of children, Sophia's eyes dimmed. I knew she was thinking of the three little graves she left behind in Bencoolen.

On impulse, I put my hand on her forearm. "It's almost too early to mention, and therefore I will ask you to keep this a secret for now." I waited until Sophia's eyes met mine. "Nathaniel and I are expecting."

A broad smile lit the other woman's face, and she broke away from Raffles to embrace me in a tight hug. "Promise me you will write to me often and tell me how the pregnancy is going! And when the time comes, you will send the child to London to live with us." She paused and swallowed. "You will not make the same mistake."

Wanting nothing more than to comfort her, I nodded. "Of course. Who would not want to live with the famous Sir Raffles and his lovely wife?"

Raffles gave me an affectionate kiss on the cheek. "You and Nathaniel will work through this in time. Marriage is not for the faint of heart, and neither of you are cowards." I nodded, unable to get words past the lump in my throat. "Good girl." Then, glancing at his wife, Sir Raffles announced, "Come, my dear. We have the servants to manage before we leave."

"I will see you down at the wharves," I said to their backs as they randomly made their way across the room, chatting with well-wishers. Watching their departure made my stomach sink because, deep down, I knew we would never meet in London. Whether by the fates or by design, I would never see Raffles and his wife again. Shaking my head, I turned back to the windows overlooking the garden Sir Raffles had carefully nurtured. I was becoming maudlin.

"Charlotte." Nathaniel's voice startled me, and I turned to him. He was wearing the same rumpled clothes as the night before. A light dusting of whiskers covered his face, and he smelled faintly of something floral and exotic. I tried not to choke.

"You're too bloody late." The words meant so much more than him missing the end of the breakfast.

"I know; I'm sorry." His eyes conveyed a real apology, and I looked away, not wanting to face him.

"No point in apologizing to me." I looked around, but Raffles and Sophia had left the room. "You might want to say something to your father's old friend and colleague, but I think he has left."

"I would not have you embarrassed." he began.

"Don't bother to warn me," I said, looking back at him. "All and sundry have told me of your fortuitous news. Sarah has delivered you a son." I smiled to hide the grimace and tears lurking under my social mask. "You are to be congratulated. As for your evening's activities, Mrs. Meacham has already informed me. You spent the evening whoring. Another congratulations are in order. We now have a replica of your parent's marriage."

"We need to come to an understanding," he said quietly. "But this is not the time or place."

"We have an understanding, Nathaniel." There was something different about him. He was angry when he returned from Calcutta and lost after Cornelius's death, but now he looked sure of himself, confident. "There is no need to rehash old wounds."

"There are so many things I want to say." His golden eyes bore into mine, and for a second, I thought we could overcome our differences. Despite my thoughts from only an hour ago, I believed we could be true husband and wife again.

He ran a hand through his already mussed hair. "I will no longer seek to share your bed. You are free to pursue your liaisons after the child is born. I will, of course, recognize the child as my own, despite what I or others may believe."

His rejection made my eyes water. Darkness threatened my vision, and the world swayed in front of me. Nathaniel's hand reached out to grab my arm, steadying me in place. After a couple of breaths, I snatched it back. "How dare you! One night in the arms of some whore, and you release me to do as I please? You come here to say farewell to your friend with the stench of the brothel all over you?" I stepped up to him, unmindful of who might be watching. "I will never forgive you for this," I said each word slowly before stalking to the exit.

Chapter 23
Nathaniel

Charlotte disappeared from the room, and the eyes tracking her angry progress refocused on me. It was evident from the disapproving stares of the matrons and the pitying glances of the men that my evening's activities were well-worn news. A liveried servant approached with a tray of china balanced in one hand.

"Mr. Hawk, Sir Raffles requests your presence in his study, if you please." The man spoke with the soft cadence of a Calcutta accent.

I nodded and departed the room, looking straight ahead. Mr. and Mrs. Meacham stood in the corridor, and I resisted the urge to punch Mr. Meacham in the face. Not only would it ruin Raffles leaving breakfast, but it would also serve no purpose.

The door to Raffles office stood slightly ajar. Hesitating for a moment, I pushed it opened and stepped through. Raffles stood in the empty study, hands clasped behind his back, staring out at his garden.

He did not turn as he spoke. "I thought you might continue to avoid me. It seems you have done nothing but pretend I do not exist these past months." Raffles turned to give me a cold stare. "Cornelius was my friend, too. As was your father."

Guilt washed over me. Raffles had lost friends. He had lost his children and now his position. On his return to London, he would inevitably lose his legacy if the East India Company trustees had any say in the matter. My afternoon with Lord Hastings and McCarr brought home the realities of the cumbersome bureaucracy. It was all politics and trying to save your arse.

"Sir Raffles." I hesitated as the words I needed eluded me. Pushing on in spite of myself, I said, "I'm sorry. I have been so completely absorbed in my misery. There is no excuse, but I have been fighting to keep Thistlewaite and Hawk afloat. Not an easy task when every European ship captain seems wary of dealing with me since father has come under suspicion of treason."

Slashing his hand through the air, Raffles shouted, "You were seen last evening in the company of known Brotherhood members, heading east toward the gypsy encampment! Are you sporting any new tattoos?"

"I am not a member of the Brotherhood," I stated.

"Yet, you shelter them. The Brotherhood is dangerous, Nathaniel. You have no idea the kind of power they can wield." Raffles' voice held a note of warning. "The East India Company has taken a keen interest in them, and it will not be long before the company eradicates them from all East India Company ports."

It was on the tip of my tongue to tell him I was well aware of the company's policy toward the Brotherhood, but something stopped me. There was a reason I no longer came to him with my problems, and it was not only because of his waning power. I couldn't heap any more burdens on him.

"There was some discussion of the Brotherhood in Calcutta," I replied, shrugging. "Mr. Finlayson saved my life, and was a friend long before he joined the Brotherhood."

"Did they find the man who murdered Cornelius?" Raffles asked boldly.

"Yes." There was no point in lying to him.

A weary look passed over Raffles's face. "Did you have your revenge?"

"No.," I replied, disappointment in my voice.

"So the man lives?" Raffles gave me a pointed look.

"I cannot say." Raffles looked like he wanted to ask another question, but I cut him off. "His life was forfeit to another. I gave the courtesy of meeting him before his fate became sealed with the others."

"You believe this man killed Cornelius," Raffles asked quietly, watching my expression.

"In all honesty, I cannot say for sure. The mystery man wouldn't tell me his identity." He had, of course, given me many more concerns than his identity. But I really couldn't share my concerns about Charlotte with Raffles. He was still of the old school. Women always deserved a man's protection because they couldn't fend for themselves. He was incapable of so much as dreaming that Sophia could betray him. I suddenly admired their marriage.

"Why would the Brotherhood involve themselves in your business?" Raffles's voice made the question sound like an accusation.

"I don't know," I said the words carefully. "Mr. Finlayson believes my father would have been a member of the Brotherhood. They have a great respect for him."

Shaking his head, Raffles replied, "Your father would never have joined that group of bandits. They are nothing more than pirates." Raffles stepped forward and placed a fatherly hand on my shoulder. "Promise me you will not get any further involved with them." For the first time, I noticed the bruises under his eyes, the lines around his mouth. "With your father and Cornelius gone, I worry about your safety."

Clenching my jaw stubbornly, I replied, "I'm not a child."

"No, you're not a child. You're not my child, either. But that doesn't mean I don't feel a great responsibility to you." Raffles let his hand drop. "Stay away from the Brotherhood. No good can come of it. Let me help you with the company. But please, do not become beholden to the Brotherhood."

We both knew there was little he could do for me in London, but I wanted to give him something. I owed him. "I will stay away as far as anyone can from the Brotherhood." I knew I was lying and felt not an ounce of remorse for it.

"Good. At least I can sail away now knowing you're safe." Raffles looked around the study as if seeing it for the first time. "I had better find Sophia. She is not taking the move back to London, particularly well."

I held out my hand. "Until we meet again, sir."

"In London. I know Sophia is looking forward to the day you and your wife visit." Raffles took in the state of my attire again. "Fix this thing between the two of you. I know it must feel like I'm pushing you with fatherly advice this morning, but Sarah Buck is hardly worth your marriage. You were both so in love not long ago. It will not take much to find that place again. Before you say it's too hard, remember, I was a cold, lonely widower when I met my Sophia. Now she is the light of my life."

So much for honesty. "Every marriage has a few slipups. I know I can make it up to my wife," unless Charlotte was in league with someone to kill me.

"Good; then we'll see you down at the wharves." Raffles retreated from his former study without a backward glance. It was what I always admired about him. The only times I had seen him not looking straight ahead were the times when grief forced him to contemplate what might have been.

Having discharged my duties this morning, I caught my reflection in the window. I needed a wash, a shave, and a clean set of clothes before I wandered around Singapore any longer. Instead of leaving by the front door, I escaped through the kitchens and out the back. Charlotte and I had provided enough fodder for the gossips this morning. Everyone apparently knew I had been in a brothel all night. There was no need for them actually to see me.

"Creeping out the back, I see." Farquhar sniffed, as I came to the house. He was standing next to a flower bed.

"I could say the same of you," I snapped, as he frowned down at a bush with lush pink flowers. "I'm surprised to see you here."

Using his walking stick to decapitate a couple of flowers before settling his gaze on me, Farquhar replied, "I'm not here to gloat over my victory. In fact, I have come to see you." He looked me up and down a few times. "You have kept me waiting for most of the morning. I was beginning to believe the rumors of a rift between you and Raffles."

"Sir Raffles you mean," I reminded him. "As we did not have an appointment, you can hardly blame me for not cooperating with your plans. What is it you want?" I asked, but I already knew the answer. It was better for him to think I was ignorant.

"You visited the gypsy camp, and I want to know why " Farquhar began without preamble.

I shrugged and said flatly, "You're mistaken."

"Don't lie to me. I have spies all over this island." Farquhar snorted. "I know you went out to the gypsy camp with your Brotherhood friends. Upon return, you entered into an argument with your wife. The argument forced you to a brothel where you spent the rest of the night with not one, but two ladies."

"Would you like me to tell you exactly what I did with them?" I tried not to laugh at the thought of the prudish Farquhar trying to have sex with two women at once.

"You're disgusting. So much like your father." Farquhar said disdainfully.

"I will take that as a compliment." I wondered how much trouble I would be in if I bashed him in the face. The sound of his nose breaking would compensate for any time I spent in the brig.

"Interesting, considering he's a traitor." Farquhar knew where to land the most offensive blows.

"There was and is no evidence against him. I was at the inquiry. They had nothing to base their lies upon." I stepped closer, my temper rising.

"Because you made a deal." Farquhar's words hit close to the truth, and I wondered how much he knew. "Everyone knows you must have had some valuable information to wrest your father's legacy out of the gutter."

"My father was a great man, and I will have words with anyone who says otherwise." My blood was up. "Why do you hate him?"

Farquhar smiled. "I don't hate him. I have a sacred duty to watch out for the interests of the East India Company and the British Empire."

"Captain Sebastian Hawk had the same duty. He risked his life for years in the service of company and Empire. You have much more in common with my father than you believe."

"Is that what you think?" said Farquhar. "You hardly even know the man, if you think he was so charitable. His only duty was to himself."

Stepping away from the other man before I committed another act that would cause Charlotte to be publicly humiliated, I lowered my voice and said, "And you have no idea who you're speaking about."

Just then, from somewhere behind me, I heard the words, "No, he doesn't." I looked over my shoulder to the veranda where a shocked Sophia and Ella stood arm in arm with Raffles. "Major General, I might ask why you're here? And why did you fail to present yourself to the breakfast this morning?"

"Don't be a pompous fool, Raffles." Farquhar spat as he stepped away from the flowerbed he had ruined. The pink flower heads lay strewn across the dirt. "I don't like you, and you don't like me. Why bother playing the charade out to the bitter end."

Sophia's mouth pressed into an angry line, while Ella's mouth opened slightly in shock.

"I will ask you again why you're here?" Raffles appeared more tired than angry.

"Just seeing the work that needs doing in the gardens." Farquhar smiled tightly. "They're in such a state. I'm planning on having them all dug up and replanted."

A widening of the eyes was the only indication that Raffles made to the intended destruction of his beloved gardens. He patted Sophia's arm as she began to breathe rapidly. "Do as you like Major General, but I think you should ask Dr. Crawfurd what he might like done with the gardens of his new home." He nodded at me and led his wife and daughter down the rest of the stairs.

&

I had time to rush home and make myself presentable for the rest of the day. Dutta fussed over me, and it was with relief that I left for the wharves. By the time I reached the foreshore, the residents of Singapore had gathered into small groups to wave the founder of Singapore goodbye. Charlotte had not returned home after our argument, and I searched for the light blue gown she was wearing. I was ready to make some concessions to keep our private spat out of the public realm.

"Mr. Hawk," Hindly shouted at me, and I turned around to face him.

"Mr. Hindly, I'm happy to see you're none the worse for your adventures last evening!" His face searched mine briefly before he nodded.

"And you, too, sir." Suddenly realizing the implications of his statement, his face turned red, and he stared at the ground in embarrassment. "I don't mean anything by it. I meant you look good. Not good, really."

"I perfectly comprehend your meaning." I looked at the rest of the people milling around. "Have you seen my wife this morning?"

Hindly used his stump to point at a group of men. I picked out Bigham among the men since he was easily the tallest. The rest were vaguely familiar, and I realized they were the men we had encountered last night at the gypsy encampment. Before I could ask Hindly for confirmation, one of the men shifted and I spotted Charlotte's skirts. The wind must have caught her bonnet because she moved to stand in a more sheltered spot with one hand on her head. Her face wore a dark frown, and I wondered if she were thinking of me. Bigham bent down and quietly said something to her, and I watched as she pasted a smile back on her face and spoke to the group.

"Are those the men from last night?" Hindly asked. He made no attempt to hide his inspection.

"I was going to ask you the same." Not wanting to draw their attention, I focused my gaze out to sea. "Do you know them? Have you seen them around the docks?"

"Maybe one or two of them." Hindly's eyes narrowed. "I assumed they were part of the Brotherhood last night, and that was how Mr. Finlayson got in with them. But I don't think the two older Chinese men are members. They made their money as mediators during the Junk season. I've seen them working for a few of the European houses."

"Do Carstairs and Son use them?" I should take more of an interest in Charlotte's business dealings. For the first time, I realized what she did at Carstairs and Son could have an impact on Thistlewaite and Hawk.

"Not to my knowledge." Hindly straightened up and looked at me, his inspection of the other group finished. "They used a clerk out of Zheng Jing's firm for the Bugis season."

"Zheng Jing?" I asked, surprised. "Why did they switch to his company?" The whole time I had been back from Calcutta, I was making a discreet study of Zheng Jing. He was elusive and guarded his privacy well. It had been next to impossible to learn anything substantial about him. Now I find out my wife was using his firm for their trading mediation. The words of Cornelius's murderer came back to me, and I turned to glance at Charlotte again.

She must have felt someone watching her because she lifted her eyes up to meet mine. I wanted to crawl inside that beautiful head of hers and find out all her secrets. Her mouth tightened, and she gave her attention to one of the men who was speaking with forceful animation. Charlotte pointedly ignored me.

"Do you know anything else about those men?" I nodded toward Charlotte's group.

Hindly said, "Some say they're smugglers." He shook his head. "But that's only the lads' talk down the tap over a couple of pints. I think some firms are jealous over their success because they're Chinese."

I grunted. Smuggling was a dangerous occupation. Not only was it a hanging offence, but also the men who ran smuggling rings were an unsavory lot. Without the legend of Captain Sebastian Hawk to keep the predators away from the port, we were vulnerable to all manner of criminals. "Does my wife know of their reputation?"

"If she is not aware of the rumors, Mr. Bigham will surely have informed her of them. He is a smart trader and knows his business," he said, nodding.

A ripple passing through the crowd behind me caught my attention, and I turned around. Sir Raffles led Sophia and Ella through the crowd waiting to see them off. They stopped and chatted or touched hands with each group before moving on to the next. Raffles's popularity had declined somewhat in recent years. His policies for a socially and morally clean Singapore were not always popular with men trying to make money. Farquhar's much more liberal view of opium and prostitution had made many men rich.

Raffles spotted me through the crowd and nodded instead of coming over. I understood. We would meet again in London as old friends, as two men who had fought in battles and survived. Not many others could claim to understand the hardships we endured. The trio made their way down the wharf and onto their ship bound for London. Cannons fired out in the harbor marking the raising of the gangplank. With the unfurling of the sails, the ship jerked forward, and Raffles was away.

Something suspiciously like sorrow bubbled up from my gut and settled in the back of my throat. This reminded me of all the times I had waved my father away as a child. I cleared my throat and tamped down the emotion, recalling the power I felt as I made the Shibari knots.

"Not many like him around anymore." Hindly stared at the ship as it tacked its way out of the harbor.

"I don't think there were many like him, to begin with, Mr. Hindly." I turned away from the departing boat with my new sense of calm. Charlotte's eye caught mine again, but she turned abruptly and walked away from me. The thought of being able to convince Charlotte to let me tie her up was a nice one. A lovely dream that would never happen, she was a gently bred lady, no matter the paternity of her child.

"I will see you back at the warehouse, Mr. Hawk." Hindly sighed.

"Yes, I shouldn't be too long." My gaze slid to Bigham, who was finishing his conversation with the group of gentlemen who might be smugglers. He waved to them and walked toward me. "Mr. Bigham, a word if I may." I gave the other man a smile.

"Of course, Mr. Hawk. What is it I can do for you?" Bigham's face showed apprehension. Was it because he had been sleeping with my wife? Or was it due to another reason entirely?

"I was wondering how business has been going? Charlotte has been so busy at work and now with her delicate condition. I would hate to see her working so hard in the future." I watched the other man's expressions. Weariness turned to surprise.

"Delicate condition, Mr. Hawk?" He questioned before a smile lit his features. His eyes then suddenly widened in understanding as he held out his hand. "Congratulations, Mr. Hawk! Charlotte never mentioned it."

There was no artifice in his words. He appeared to be genuinely happy for Charlotte and me. Reaching out, I grasped the man's hand in a firm grip. "Thank you, it's early yet to be making an announcement. I thought it would be a good idea to have a talk with you about her continued duties at Carstairs and Son."

Bigham shook his head. "Your wife is a stubborn woman if you don't mind my saying. We'll probably have to drag her out by her petticoats when the time comes." The happiness on his face disappeared, and he looked lost in thought.

"This is why I asked you how business is going." I needed to be delicate. "Should any emergencies come up, I need to know you or her father can take care of things."

"Yes," Bigham replied quickly, but his mind was somewhere else entirely.

"Those men you were speaking to... I have heard they hold a rather unsavory reputation among us here in Singapore. You aren't planning on doing business with them, are you?"

Bigham's face turned into a careful blank. "They have an unfounded reputation for smuggling, Mr. Hawk. However, I assure you, no one has caught them on the wrong side of the law."

"You haven't answered my question, Mr. Bigham," using the tone I reserved for disobedient clerks.

A worried look crossed Bigham's face for a second. "You should speak to your wife. I realize you are in an awkward position with her running Carstairs and Son, but you cannot expect me to give you insight into our business dealings. Not when you're the sole owner of one of the largest trading houses in Singapore and Calcutta."

"Exactly. The people you and my wife decide to do business with affects my affairs." I gave up the pretense of camaraderie. "If she is doing business with known criminals, I need to know."

"Interesting you choose to interest yourself now in your wife's affairs, especially now that you have an illegitimate son lurking in the wings and a penchant for whoring." Bigham's sneered his last comment.

"What I do with my time is my business." I gave my words a hard edge. "Don't think because you work with my wife means you have some right to her."

Bigham's big frame stiffened. "You had better not be implying I'm sleeping with your wife." He shook his head. "I have known her most of her life. I started working at Carstairs and Son before I had finished at grammar school. She is like a sister."

"Good. Then you will want to protect Mrs. Hawk as much as me." I tried to be reasonable. "Tell me about your plans with those men."

Bigham's eyes grew distant. When he looked back at me, his face hardened into resolved lines. "You're putting me in a damned awkward position."

"I realize you're loyal to her, and I admire you for it." I prodded Bigham a little further.

"At least someone is," Bigham replied shortly.

Holding up my hands, I tried to reason with him. "You're a bachelor and, as you said before, my wife is a stubborn woman." I barely resisted the urge to punch the other man in the face. No need to create another scandal this morning.

"You're right. I'm a bachelor." Bigham words were frustrated. "And I don't know what has happened between the two of you. All I do know is that you need to speak with your wife." He growled out the last words. "When was the last time you looked at her? Spoke with her? Haven't you realized there is something seriously wrong?"

Yes, there was something wrong, a woman was claiming her bastard child as mine, and Charlotte told me she had moved on, but she hadn't. After a pause to try to compose myself, I blurted out, "Stay out of my personal life!"

"This isn't going to work. You are not my boss. I don't have to tell you anything." Bigham stuck his hands into his trouser pockets as if trying to stop himself from throttling me. "Talk to her, dammit." He stalked away down the wharf with his head down. He received a few curious glances and a couple of greetings, but he ignored everyone.

He made it seem as if it was the simplest thing in the world. Talk to Charlotte. It went so well this morning. Now that I knew she was in business with Zheng Jing, I was even more determined to learn what secrets she was keeping from me.

Chapter 24
Charlotte

The look on Nathaniel's face as he stood with Mr. Hindly watching Raffles take his leave of Singapore strongly indicated he wanted to speak with me. I hastily retreated after my business with the Chong brothers was over. It was bad luck they had spotted Mr. Bigham and me down on the wharves. They did not have the best reputation, and if I wanted to keep my pretty neck from the noose, I needed to try to keep a discreet distance from them.

Unfortunately, everyone watched us socialize this morning. I could only hope the news of Sarah Buck's son would captivate the gossips. Shaking my head as I walked through the European Quarter, I fought back an insane urge to laugh. The thought that Sarah Buck's disgrace would save me from answering unwanted questions was laughable.

I needed to retreat, to regroup. Stopping outside my father's house for a minute, I went through my options. If I went home, Nathaniel would find me, and we would have another argument. There was no more to say. He had made his choice, and now the both of us would have to live with it. This would be the next place he looked, but at least the servants and my father could keep him out. Or he might go to Bigham's rooms. The thought that the two of us were having an affair was straining the bonds of reality.

Opening the front gate, I made my choice. The church would never grant us an annulment now that I was pregnant, but perhaps I could gain a divorce. Rubbing a hand over my eyes, I walked up the familiar steps and went through the unlocked front door. Lawyers were expensive. I would need to work even harder this season to make any profit.

"Good morning, Mrs. Hawk." My father's servant bowed to me as I walked down the hall.

"Good morning. Is my father around?" I peeked inside the drawing room I had decorated and presided over. It looked unused and a little sad. On the silk couch, I would sit and dispense with the latest gossip and laugh at the foibles of others. Now I was the subject of the same gossip.

"He's in the dining room having breakfast." The servant used his hand to indicate the familiar door.

"I will join him." Bestowing a tight smile on the servant, I went immediately into the dining room. It was too large for a family breakfast parlor. My father sat at the head of the table with a half-eaten plate of eggs and kippers at his elbow, a daily from London held in his hands. This was going to be a tough conversation. Sometimes the best course of action was to try to breeze my way through hard conversations. "Good morning, father. I hope all is well with you."

Father put down his paper, startled by my interruption. He looked at me with wide eyes as I kissed him lightly on the cheek and settled to pour myself a cup of coffee. "You're visiting early this morning."

"It's not that early. Did you not go down to the wharves to see Raffles away?" I asked, knowing he had been hiding from most social engagements for months. He had found it expedient to allow me to handle probing questions concerning Carstairs' finances. For the first time, I finally understood how hard it must be for him to have his daughter rather than his son run the business.

"All the pomp and circumstance is not my thing." He waved a hand and studied my face. "You know I would rather avoid unpleasant scenes. Raffles and I will have our time together in London, as old men, no doubt sitting in the geographical society arguing over some Eastern discovery."

"You hate the geographical society." I pointed out to him as I enjoyed a sip of the strong coffee.

"I will need something to occupy my time as an old man," he grumbled and looked away.

Wishing I could make things right for him, I placed a hand over his. The last few years had not been easy for him. Mother had succumbed to a fever in Calcutta at the same time Carstairs and Son's profits were beginning to dry up. Last year, we lost the Navarch to pirates, and Frederick had been onboard. Ever since that incident, he had been out of control, bringing us both to despair. Now I was going to tell him I needed his strength to get through the next few months.

"I have some news." I thought about how I wanted to say the next few words as he turned his head. "The business is doing as well as I can manage," I said, assuring him at the outset that there was no immediate worry about money. Without a pause, I continued, "I'm with child."

A smile spread across my father's face and, for the first time in months, I saw he was truly happy. He grabbed my hands and squeezed them. "This is great news, my girl. I am so glad for you. What does Nathaniel think? Shouldn't he be here with you?"

Licking my lips, I broke his hold on my hands. "Father, things have been strained between Nathaniel and me for several months. Since almost the start of our marriage." This was not coming out right. "I am going to petition the courts for a divorce."

Father's eyes narrowed, and he said, "A divorce? It's not possible. No one gets divorced, Charlotte. You will be a ruined woman." I frowned at him and hoped my tears did not spill over.

"Our marriage is a complete farce, Father." I slammed my fist on the table and wished there was more violence behind it. "When I told him of the child, he went out to a brothel. He slept with whores on the night I told him he was going to be a father."

Shaking his head, father reached out to me, but I flinched away. "I'm sorry your marriage has become strained, Charlotte, but surely you see there can be no divorce. Not with a child on the way. There is no court in the land that will grant you one unless Nathaniel also agrees and pays handsomely for it." Father took a deep breath and looked away for a minute. "I wish your mother were here."

"I do, too. My mother would tell you how unfair you're being." I stood up and felt something break inside me. My father had always been my haven. "You will not help me?"

Father smiled up at me, and I knew he was already plotting something. "Let me speak with Nathaniel. He's a reasonable man. With all the trouble he has seen in the last year or so, he will not want to be the focus of more gossip. He only needs reminding of his husbandly duties. Although I daresay the fact you're pregnant makes me believe he has an idea of them already."

I felt my face flush. "No, I'm getting a divorce." As I stood up, the chair I was sitting in scraped against the hardwood floor. It would probably leave a mark, but I didn't care. "Thank you, Father, for your generous offer, but, under the circumstances, I must decline."

I stormed from the room, and it took all my willpower not to burst into a flood of tears. I kept telling myself it was natural for a pregnant woman to go through emotional turmoil. I had heard it happening often enough.

"Charlotte, come back, and we can talk this through," Father shouted from behind me.

I was done talking. "We have nothing further to discuss. You think I'm a silly girl and that talking to Nathaniel will fix my problems." My raised voice had attracted the kitchen maid and the servant who had answered the door. What did I care if all of downstairs Singapore knew my business? Judging by the state of Nathaniel this morning, they were aware of the cracks in my marriage before I was. "Enjoy the rest of your day, Father. I will send the monthly tallies to you." The servant who had welcomed me only minutes before held the door open and bowed me out of the house.

"Be reasonable, Charlotte. Come back!" Father pleaded from the veranda.

Keeping my head held high, I ignored him and tried to think about the problem at hand. I had nowhere to go. I never realized how trapped I was until this moment. Sure, Zheng Jing would probably see me hanging from the nearest tree branch, but I had always had a place to rest my head. After my conversation with Father, I was even more determined not to go back to Nathaniel. I was a businesswoman. There was no reason why I couldn't make a life for myself, and I would use Carstairs and Son to provide that life for my child.

I wouldn't be one of those sad women who went back to their father's after their marriage had broken down. My independence would serve me well now. Walking down to the wharves, I catalogued in my head all the things I needed to do to strike out on my own. Once I secured rooms, it would be easy enough to find someone to move my things for me. By nightfall, I would never have to worry over whether Nathaniel was coming home or not.

The warehouse was empty, save for the man I wanted to meet. He looked up from some paperwork he was studying, relief on his face. "Mrs. Hawk, I need to speak with you urgently."

"Good, because I need to speak with you as well," I said with an efficiency I did not feel.

"You do?" He asked warily before holding up his hands. "Listen, Mrs. Hawk. I put him off as best I could. I told him he had to speak with you."

"Whom are you talking about?" I asked frowning.

"Mr. Hawk, of course." Bigham looked at me as if I had lost my mind. "He was asking a lot of questions about the Chong brothers this morning. I told him I had no right to divulge Carstairs and Son business practices with him. He was not impressed."

Damn. "I was hoping that meeting might have gone unnoticed." A hint of disappointment colored my tone. "If Mr. Hawk took notice, others would have, too."

"I'm surprised we haven't had an inspection, considering their reputation." Bigham shrugged his massive shoulders.

"We will have to do our best to keep the authorities away from our shipments." I wished Zheng Jing at the bottom of the sea with all my heart. "There is nothing to be done about it now. You know who will have his pound of flesh, and I know it will be mine."

Bigham read my face for a minute. He looked as if he wanted to say something but decided against it. "What is it you wanted to speak to me about if not the Chong brothers?"

"Are there rooms available in your boarding house?" I asked quickly.

"Yes. During the off season, the boarding house is usually only half full. Is there a reason why you're asking?" Bigham's brows came together.

"You might as well hear it from me," I said.

"Mr. Hawk told me the news this morning." Bigham's face lit up. "You must be happy."

"I do have a vague sense of relief." I watched his expression. He looked happy. Perhaps I was wrong all these years, and he did have an interest in me. What had Nathanial said? Had he told Bigham he wanted a divorce, too? I suppose I hadn't told him first.

"Another little Carstairs, or should I say Hawk coming into the world." He shook his head.

"He told you I was pregnant?" I shouted. His face turned to shock in a moment.

"Yes, isn't that the news you wanted to share?" Bigham looked confused.

"No." I held my breath for a minute to calm down. "I am pregnant, but I'm getting a divorce. I need a room to stay in, and your boarding house looks good to me."

His shocked expression did not go over very well. It was going to be a very long day.

Chapter 25
Nathaniel

Stacking the papers on my desk into neat piles for the morning, I stretched back. All I wanted was to escape the day's drama by going back to Jade and Mindy's to spend the night tying them up in glorious knots. The thought of decorating Mindy's skin with a rope made anticipation thrum through my veins. I stood up as a short knock sounded on the door.

Dutta pushed through into my office, and I stared at his anxious face. I had rarely seen him away from the house. "Mr. Hawk, you must come home now."

"What has happened?" I asked, thinking of any number of scenarios.

"There are men packing up Mrs. Hawk's belongings. She says she is going to divorce you, and she doesn't care who knows." The words rushed out of Dutta's mouth.

"I don't understand." I didn't. Did Charlotte want a divorce? She hadn't even told me.

"Dutta, I think there has been a mistake. Charlotte would never ask for a divorce. She is with child." I nodded at his look of comprehension. "No court is going to grant her a divorce. Perhaps she is in one of those female states that occur when they are breeding. I'm sure she's only clearing out old things and preparing for the child." She had been terribly angry with him this morning, but she couldn't mean to leave him.

"Sir, you should come home now." Dutta was insistent. A weight pressed down on my shoulders as I thought of not seeing Jade and Mindy this evening.

Letting out a long breath, I moved around the desk. "Come along Dutta, and we shall see what my wife is up to." I didn't bother to try and hide the disappointment in my voice.

"Thank you, sir." Dutta followed me out of the office.

We walked in silence in the thickening night. The sun had only gone down a half hour ago, but twilight did not linger here so close to the equator. Even though it was not quite dark, the windows of the house were glowing with the light from oil lamps. A man was guarding a few boxes. He watched me as I walked up the stairs to the front door. Stepping inside, I could hear Charlotte's voice upstairs as she spoke to someone. A man carrying a large steamer trunk, appearing on the upper landing, struggled down the stairs.

"Where are these trunks going?" I asked as the man set down his burden to rest for a moment.

"The lady wants them delivered to the boardinghouse" The man replied before reaching down to pick up the trunk again.

Anger such as I had never felt before clouded my vision, and I felt my breath come in rapid pants. "Leave the trunk, go and fetch the others inside."

The man shook his head. "The lady was very specific."

"Leave that trunk where it is, or you will have to deal with me," I said stepping forward and crowding the other man. He was taller than I and probably stronger, but at this point, my anger needed an outlet.

"The lady is paying us well for our time." The man shrugged and did not move.

"Dutta, pay this man and make sure my wife's belongings are brought back inside." I walked around the big man and took the stairs two at a time. She was running to her lover. If she thought she could publicly humiliate me in this manner, she was dead wrong.

"You were quick." Charlotte's voice came from inside the room as I approached. "This is the last box. We need to hurry."

"So you don't have a nasty confrontation with your husband?" I asked as I stood in the doorframe.

Charlotte whirled around, shock on her face. There was apprehension there too before she settled into a practiced frown. "You will admit this would be much easier if you had only read the letter I left." She looked over at the vanity where a letter rested against the mirror.

"You're leaving me for your lover, and you decided to tell me in a note?" The words ground out of my mouth. "You're a cold-hearted bitch."

Her back stiffened at my words. "You're never going to believe Mr. Bigham, and I are friends and nothing more. What is there to say? Other than you calling me names."

"There's a lot more to say." I walked into the room and stopped a foot from her. "You are not leaving this house."

"I want a divorce." Charlotte drew herself up to her full height. Her stubborn chin at a right angle. "You will grant me one because you hate this marriage, and it's obvious you hate me."

"What of my child?" My voice had gone cold.

"You don't think it's yours, so what's the problem?" She tried to make me see the logic of her argument, but she was running on emotion.

"Everyone will believe that child in your belly is mine." I pointed to her still flat stomach.

Charlotte laughed up in my face. "You suddenly care about what people say? Since when? Since this morning when you came to Sir Raffles's leaving breakfast in the same clothes you wore last evening with the smell of perfume all over you? I suppose I should be grateful you didn't come home smelling like opium and raving like a lunatic."

"No, I would never do that to you, Charlotte. I left it for your former lover Bishop to humiliate you that way." The words were out before I could recall them. Her face jerked as if I'd slapped her, and she stepped back.

"You forget Mr. Bishop was a friend of yours," Charlotte reminded me primly.

"I'm sorry. I should never have mentioned Bishop." I ran a hand through my hair. "Surely, you see this is madness? No one is going to grant you a divorce while you're carrying a child made by our union."

"Money can buy anything," she persisted stubbornly.

"You're angry, but we can work this out." I tried to be patient.

"Why? If we were separated, you could pursue your pleasures." Charlotte threw up her hands. "You could even marry Sarah Buck."

"I will never marry Sarah Buck," I stated with force. "And we are not getting a divorce. Only death will separate us."

"How convenient," she said under her breath.

Wariness crept over me, replacing the anger. "I asked you last night to trust me with your secret as your husband. I'm asking you again; tell me what has been going on in your life."

Charlotte's eyes widened, and she looked away. She took a long breath before arranging her features again. "There is nothing to tell. You know everything there is to know."

"What of your business? Why are you involved with the Chong brothers? Why are you using Zheng Jing as your mediator?" I asked each of my questions slowly.

"Why did you sleep with whores after I told you I was pregnant?" she asked in return.

Perhaps if I gave her full disclosure she would say what she was involved in; what Cornelius's killer had hinted at last night. "The man who murdered Cornelius was tracked down last night."

A flurry of emotions crossed her features. "Why didn't you tell me? I just thought you were in one of your moods last night." Regret for how the evening had ended up sank into my stomach. "Did you kill him?" she whispered as if she were too afraid to speak the words aloud.

"No," I said firmly.

She looked up at me with surprise. "I wanted to. I wanted to snuff out his life as he had Cornelius's, but he had other debts to pay." I looked her in the eye. "Debts with the Chong brothers. They were both there last night." Charlotte stared up at me in silence. I waited for her to say something, anything.

"It's only business with the Chong brothers," Charlotte said slowly. "I know they have an unsavory reputation, but I've had to take some chances." She took a deep breath. "We did well enough with the sale of the Monarch and the jump in nutmeg prices to pay off most of our debt." Her face crumpled, and I could tell she was trying to hold her tears inside. "Mr. Bigham gave the money to Freddie for the debt to be cleared." She shook her head a few times, and I swallowed down my bile. "But he never got the debt markers back. He thought he could win money on some card game. He lost it all." Her voice cracked, and my heart broke.

Wrapping my arms around her, I said, "When did you find out about this?"

"On the morning of our wedding. I wanted to tell you, but we were happy. Then, you had to travel to Calcutta; then, Cornelius died. There was never a right time. I thought I was protecting you. The Chong brothers gave us the best deals. We had to go with them and try and squeeze out as much profit as we could."

"I'm going to kill your brother," I growled. "How could he do this to you? To your father? What was he thinking?"

"You can't kill Freddie." Charlotte sighed and stepped out of my arms. "It wouldn't solve anything, and you'd likely hang for it. I would hate to see that beautiful neck stretched."

"Charlotte, there must be another way to squeeze your profit margins." I shook my head. Was this all there was to her betrayal? She appeared as if she had completely unburdened herself. Her shoulders sagged, all her aggression gone. It was the first time I had seen her without her shoulders bunched up around her ears in months.

"We have no choice now." She looked at the trunk she had been waiting for the men to take away. "Our contract still has another year on it."

"You could break the contract," I suggested.

"They would only sue us for reparation." Charlotte squared her shoulders. "This is no longer your problem. We are getting a divorce. Our marriage was a mistake."

Had it been a mistake? Cornelius certainly thought our union was doomed. Even though his murderer had paid the price for his crime, I was still no closer to discovering whom he met that night all those weeks ago. "Our joining was in the sight of God and cannot be undone," I said.

"Don't tell me you've decided to become religious now? Does this mean you will forgo the pleasures of the flesh outside this marriage bed?" Charlotte asked with more than a hint of sarcasm.

"Your son will bear my name. Do you want him to grow up and live with the shame of divorce hanging over his head?" Charlotte's eyes widened. Finally, I had something to needle her with. "Give him or her a thought, Charlotte. You're not cruel. I know I haven't been much of a husband, and it probably won't change, but think of the child."

Her voice came out as a squeak. "What do you want from me?" Her eyes lifted, and I saw tears pooling in them. Without thinking, I cupped her face and wiped away the first tears that fell her cheeks.

"Stay here with me. We will raise the child as ours." I took a deep breath and knew I was making a mistake with the next concession, but I could see no way around it. "Unless something changes, your bed will be your own. We were friends before we were lovers. Perhaps we can find somewhere in the middle to meet?"

Charlotte's body shuddered, and I wondered if she truly had feelings for me. Despite everything that had happened to the two of us, I still loved her in my way. I should have known I could never have a traditional marriage after my parent's example.

She looked up at me and nodded her head. I held her in my arms to provide some comfort. Charlotte had lost this battle, and I knew her pride would feel the sting. Now all I needed to do was find her brother. We were going to have a very long talk.

&

"Where is he?" I didn't bother to announce my presence before striding into Charlotte's father's office.

"Who?" Carstairs looked up from a book he was reading by the light of an oil lamp.

"Don't play games with me." I stood in the middle of the study. "Your worthless son. Where is he? It's very unlikely you're unfamiliar with your son's haunts."

Setting his book aside, Carstairs studied me without a hint of urgency. "What makes you think you have the right to come in here and start making demands? Charlotte came to see me today. I believe you're shortly to be on the receiving end of a divorce."

"Why didn't you warn me?" I accused.

"You're very unlikely to grant her request." Carstairs smiled and picked up his drink. "Besides, knowing you were going to squirm has put me in good spirits all day." He took a long drink. "I faced a very unpleasant scene this morning. Surely, you understand that watching a favorite child suffer the kinds of humiliations Charlotte has is upsetting, to say the least."

I sliced a hand through the air. "Anyone could have fathered Sarah Buck's child."

"She not only believes you're the sire of her child. Sarah Buck has made sure everyone knows it, despite the damage it has done to her reputation." Carstairs frowned. "Why would she do so much damage to herself?"

"Sarah Buck has always been a little unstable, and I have no idea why she is pursuing the matter. I will not formally acknowledge the child," I explained stubbornly, even though I wanted to punch the man in the face for questioning my affairs.

"You can understand how this whole affair has hurt my daughter." Carstairs persisted in his inquiry. "Now I hear you have spent the evening with some of Singapore's more colorful residents. I wonder why you bothered to marry my daughter."

"My reasons are my own," I ground out. "And I'm not here to discuss my marriage with Charlotte. I'm here to find out where the son you're protecting is hiding? I have heard he lost a substantial amount of money that did not belong to him."

Carstairs' shoulders deflated, and he finished off the rest of his drink. "Heard about that, did you?"

"You and Charlotte should have confided in me long before now. She has been dealing with the fallout, even going into business with the Chong brothers to try and stretch her profits. No wonder there was a strain on our marriage. Charlotte has not had any time to be a bride and wife."

"I think it's much more reasonable to assume she is using Carstairs and Son as an escape from her marriage with you." Carstairs's assumption held some truth, but I didn't want to talk about Charlotte any longer.

"Where is he? You have no control over him and someone needs to take him firmly in hand." I moved further into the room, standing over Carstairs.

Craning his neck to look up at me, Carstairs grimaced. "You can't kill him. As much as Charlotte is angry with him, she loves her brother."

"He has put you into penury," I stated with heat. "How can you continue to defend him? You might both still end up spending the next several years in the belly of a prison ship."

"I told Charlotte to ask you for the money," Carstairs boldly stated. "The amount would be as nothing to you."

"You want to sell me Carstairs and Son?" I thought for a moment. "It might be the best for both our interests." With complete control over Carstairs and Son, I could not only fire Bigham but also manage Charlotte's activities.

"Why would you bother? It's so far into debt, by the going market rate, I would have to pay you to take it off my hands." Carstairs snorted with laughter and poured another drink. "You need to convince Charlotte the business is no longer viable and let her brother and me pay the consequences."

Shaking my head, I argued, "You know that's never going to happen. You raised a fighter, and she will continue to work for your freedom. Even at the cost of everything else in her life. Besides, the lawyers have not finalized Cornelius's will. I'm not sure if you've paid attention, but I'm not exactly the East India Company's favorite son. Things are tight, and they're likely to remain that way until Lord Hastings either retires or finds someone else's life to ruin."

Carstairs' face turned solemn. "There can be no deviation from the path. It will lead to ruin for all of us, and I worry about the fate of my children." He took a deep breath. "I have heard he spends much of his time at a gambling den called the Red Dot. All manner of men waste their money at this establishment, including my son and his cronies."

"Thank you," I said and stepped back. Now that I looked at Carstairs, I realized he had aged quickly during the past few months. The man in front of me had no youthful glow or even a bit of hope for the future. He appeared to be waiting for death to come knocking. "We're going to find a way to fix this, and Charlotte and I will come around, you'll see."

Carstairs sniffed in response, and I left the study and walked out of the house. I wasn't sure why I comforted him. Charlotte and I were never going to resolve our differences enough to have a genuinely happy marriage. Perhaps now that I knew how it felt to lose all hope, the thought someone else might feel the same way was enough to spur my conscience.

I walked the familiar path across the European Quarter to the drawbridge. The Chinese Campong was still busy this time of night. The trade of opium, cards, and women was always high in Singapore. Turning right as I felt the bridge, I walked through the alleys and unlit streets by memory toward my goal. I had never been to the Red Dot, preferring the card tables where the ship captains drank, but I knew where it was and the reputation that went with it.

Down the street, I saw two burly men standing in front of a black door with a red circle. I nodded to each one. "Good evening, gentlemen." Neither of them gave me a sideways glance as I stepped into the smoke-filled room and surveyed the tables.

Several card games were in progress, while women dressed in shimmering silk kimonos served drinks. A staircase off to the right side led to a second floor and rooms for opium and debauchery.

Spotting my quarry, I smiled. Freddie was sitting at a table with two other men. There were a couple of half-empty bottles sitting on the table. As I watched, Freddie threw down a card, and the other two groaned. Freddie immediately began gathering in the chips strewn across the table.

"I'm feeling dead lucky tonight, boys." Freddie grinned at the other two. "You should tighten your purse strings."

Freddie did not see me until the last second, and by then, it was too late. I hauled him up by the sweaty collar of his shirt with one hand and let my fist smash into his face with the other. "It's my lucky night, too," I hurled out. I felt his nose rupture under my fist, and his squeal of pain fed my desire to annihilate him completely. So much of my life had been out of my control, it felt good to let my anger go. My fist continued to pound into Freddie's face, as his cries became groans and whimpers.

Hands on my body and fingers prying my hand away from Freddie's shirt penetrated into my consciousness.

"You're going to bloody well kill him, Hawk, stop it!" One man shouted, and I shook my head to clear it.

"You're a damned lunatic," another man shouted. I stumbled back as I finally released my hand from the back of Freddie's shirt.

In a haze of bloodlust, I watched as Charlotte's brother fell to his knees and covered his face with his hands. The rest of the room had been still while I pummeled Freddie, and now a frenetic energy took its place. Chairs scraped on the simple wooden flooring as men hastily gathered their belongings. This was a place men went to be forgotten.

A few minutes passed, and my breathing slowed. But instead of feeling more in control, my emotions continued to swirl. I longed for the place I had found when I was with Jade and Mindy the previous evening. Beating Freddie only brought a feeling of darkness and shame.

Freddie looked up at me. His nose squished onto the side of his face. One of his companions was busy trying to press a drink into his hand.

"You know." Freddie's garbled voice held no emotion.

"Yes, I know." The anger that spurred me to come down here started to rise to the surface again, but I ruthlessly held it down. I realized there was no place for it here. In the face of Freddie's stupidity, I had to be calm and calculated.

"I suppose I will not be receiving an invitation to Christmas supper this year." Freddie drawled and rose unsteadily to his feet. The urge to punch him again was strong I had to step back and grab onto the edge of the table behind me.

"Why did you let your sister deal with all of this?" I asked not knowing how to proceed. It was much easier when all I wanted to do was bash his face.

"What does it matter to you?" Freddie sneered and held out the bloodied bandage he had been pressing to his nose. "I heard she was divorcing you."

Shaking my head, I said "Don't be ridiculous. You and I both know a divorce is out of the question. "I'll ask you again, why did you let her deal with the mess you made?"

"She wouldn't let me help," he said petulantly.

Frustration boiled over, and I shoved away from the table only to stop after taking a look at the two burly guards from outside. They stood near the door, ready to throw us both out if I continued to make a scene.

"You need to grow up." I stalked forward and sat down beside Freddie. Grabbing one of the bottles and an empty glass, I filled it up. "Charlotte will never ask for help, even if she's drowning. You have to take some responsibility. Force your way through. Make yourself invaluable. She's pregnant. Soon, she will have no choice, but to give you the responsibility."

"I bankrupted us," he whispered, "She will hand over everything to Bigham."

"Prove you're the only one who can take over. Go home, clean yourself up and show up at Carstairs and Son tomorrow morning ready to work." I encouraged him, not understanding why I was bothering. Forcing Carstairs to sell his business to me was the best way to protect both his children.

He nodded, and his gaze slid away from me. "There's something I need to tell you," he said slowly, looking around to make sure no one stood too close. "You've been searching for the person Cornelius met with the night he died." I nodded, my heart suddenly beating faster. "It was Charlotte. I don't know why, and I'm fairly sure she didn't stab him, but I followed her when I realized she was trying to go into the Chinese Campong. I was too far away to hear their conversation, but that was the last time I saw Cornelius alive."

Cold dread washed over me. Charlotte had seen Cornelius on the night he had died and not said anything. Was Charlotte somehow connected to Cornelius's murder?

Chapter 26
Charlotte

"Father, what a surprise to see you down here this morning," I said as he walked into the warehouse for the first time in months. Several of the men doffed their caps and bade him a good morning.

Bigham stood beside me as he walked over to the small desk in the corner. Neither of us spoke a word until he reached us.

"Good morning, sir." Bigham's voice held genuine affection.

"Good morning, Mr. Bigham. I trust all is well with you," Father said with a nod.

"Indeed," Mr. Bigham replied. There was a moment of silence while we waited to hear what Father had to say. He had made it very clear he was no longer interested in the daily operations of the business.

"I came down to speak with you, daughter." Father looked in my direction, but he stared at Bigham as the other man tried to leave. "However, this concerns you as well, so you had better stay." Bigham turned back to my father and waited. "First, daughter, I am happy to see you have decided to remain under the shelter of your husband." I opened my mouth to protest. "Mr. Bigham was probably well aware of your plans and I, therefore, suffer no qualms in discussing it with you."

Looking uncomfortable, Bigham murmured. "I encouraged your daughter to talk to Mr. Hawk in the hopes there could be reconciliation."

Father smiled for the first time in ages. "I thought you would try and send her back to where she belongs, but she is a stubborn chit who does not know her place. I blame myself entirely for coddling the girl. And I never believed the rumors that the two of you were lovers. The whole idea is preposterous."

"At least someone thinks it's as ridiculous as us," I said under my breath.

"Charlotte, marriages are not easy to navigate. Your mother and I were not always happy, but you must try now for the sake of the child." He took a big breath, and I knew he had something important to tell us. My stomach suddenly felt knotted and twisted. "For us all to move on with our lives, I have decided to sell Carstairs and Son."

Shock hit my system at his words, and I thought I must have heard him incorrectly. "You're going to sell Carstairs and Son?"

"Yes, it has been a millstone around our necks for too long, my dear. Look what it has done to your marriage. It's holding Mr. Bigham back from his real potential and, well, I think the thought of losing the business has warped your brother's mind. We all need a fresh start." Father's face set in grim lines.

A quiet laugh started in my belly, and the more I tried to contain it, the more it fought to be free. The hysterical sound erupted from my throat, and I covered my mouth as Father and Bigham stared at me in varying degrees of shock. Father was the first to find his voice.

"This is no laughing matter, girl," he said, his voice stern as he shook his head.

"I think she has finally cracked," Bigham said as he watched me, brows knitted together in concern.

Taking big breaths of air to calm my nerves, I said, "Father, there is no one in his right mind who would buy this company. We are on the brink of bankruptcy. We could be announcing a foreclosure at any moment. Our creditors are not only circling our decaying carcasses, but they also have full control over what we're doing and how we do it. Any buyer will take one look at our books and run away like any sane person."

"Someone has made an offer," Father stated.

"Who would make such an offer?" Bigham asked curiously. "Zheng Jing has mostly covered up our full financial problems, but it's no secret we struggled after the sinking of the Navarch."

"This potential buyer is well versed in our financial difficulties. If he is willing to take on the company's trouble, then we should be grateful." Turning his full attention onto Bigham, he said, "I will, of course, put in a good word for you, Mr. Bigham. You have been a light in the darkness ever since this whole debacle started."

Shaking his head at the praise, he said, "I was the one who gave Frederick the money." The anguish in his voice was terrible. "If not for my stupidity, we might never have had this problem."

"I'm not going to hold a grudge against you because you believed in one of my children, Mr. Bigham. I would like to think you learned to give people chances from me." Father smiled grimly.

Exasperated at the male shoulder slapping in front of me, I said: "I suppose my hard work has been for nothing because I'm a woman."

"Charlotte, my dear. Once this sale goes through you can concentrate on your marriage and your child. You will have the opportunity to be the woman you were meant to be." Father smiled kindly at me.

Rage boiled inside, and I felt my body shaking. "I have held this business together for months with my sheer will." I shook a finger under my father's nose. Tears sprang to my eyes. "Things have happened because of this whole business with Zheng Jing for which I am responsible. Terrible things that have ruined people's lives." I gasped, trying to hold in my tears. "It was I making things work. I am the reason we still have bread on the table."

"You're going to make yourself ill, Charlotte," Father said in a patient tone. "You must think of what is best for the baby now." I was angry. No coherent thought slipped through my brain. All I wanted to do was hurt my father as much as he was hurting me.

"Who is this mystery buyer?" Bigham asked. The interruption was welcome. "It must be someone close to the family if they know of our circumstances."

Father appeared a little less confident than before. He mulled over his next words. "I would only trust family with the continuation of Carstairs and Son."

I snorted. "Don't tell me you're going to hand everything over to Freddie." I stepped away from father and gathered calm around me. "We all know how giving him any responsibility ended last time."

"It's not your brother. Any money he has is lost on the gambling table or in a pipe." Father said harshly, and for the first time, I saw his real anxiety for his son. He was willing to let his ambitions for his heir go to potentially save his life.

"The only other person is…" Bigham said and stalled. He looked at me expectantly.

Shaking my head, I asked, "Who? They must be either stupid or mad or both to take this company on considering the circumstances."

"I have heard your husband described as both," Father said, watching my expression. For some reason, I was past being shocked. Instead, all I felt was a profound betrayal. Father had already turned his back on me when he would not help me gain a divorce. Now, Nathaniel was doing his best to humiliate me on every front.

"I will fight you." Coldness took over my thoughts.

"There is little you can do, daughter," Father said in a matter of fact tone. "I own all the shares in the company. I have complete and total control. There was talk of me leaving the company to your brother at some point, but never to you."

"After all I have sacrificed," I choked out.

"Yes." Father stepped forward and extended a hand, but I eluded him. "Don't you see this will make sure you never have to sacrifice again? You'll be free."

"This is all I have left; don't take it from me," I pleaded. "Besides, Zheng Jing has already warned me about involving Nathaniel in this mess. If he buys the company, he will buy into the syndicate's black-market plans. Would you do that to him?" I felt better knowing this sale could never go through.

"Your husband already knows of the debt. Mr. Hawk came to see me last night," Father said.

"He knows Frederick lost the money. He has no idea how we are earning our way out of debt. It's dangerous and the more people who know, the bigger chance of being caught." I knew my father was a sharp businessman, but having Nathaniel buy the company now was tantamount to murder. "He will hang with the rest of us."

Father's face paled. "I spent the evening looking over the books. After this Junk season, between the Chong brothers and Zheng Jing, we will have fulfilled most of our debt. We will explain that we cannot go on smuggling for him as it's too dangerous. Besides, he will want to use someone else after the season has ended to avoid speculation."

Bigham spoke up. "It doesn't work that way, Mr. Carstairs. I wish it did. Zheng Jing will continue to use us until we are either caught outright, or the business is so corrupt is doesn't matter anymore." Bigham held out his hands in a pleading gesture. Never had I seen him looking so grim. "We three, along with Frederick, have made our beds, let's not let anyone else fall into it."

"We will stick with my plan." Father's chin rose and for once he looked as if he meant the next words. A glimpse of the former ruthless businessman shone through. "It will take months for a sale to go through. We will keep the deal a secret until the last minute, and Zheng Jing will have no choice but to let us go on our merry way."

"And what of my husband? Shouldn't we at least warn him we are putting him in harm's way?" I asked sarcastically. Nathaniel and I may have come to a cold agreement last night, regarding our marriage, but deep down I still loved him. It's why all of his antics with other women hurt so damn much.

"Hopefully we will never have to tell him," Father said. I was going to ask him if hoping had ever gotten him what he wanted in the past when another familiar voice echoed in the warehouse.

"Good morning, family. Mr. Bigham." Frederick strode into the warehouse. Even from this distance, I could see that he had taken quite a beating.

Bigham was the only one who had not encountered an enraged Nathaniel last evening, so he was the only one to ask. "What the hell happened to you, Mr. Carstairs? Did someone try and take a debt out of your face?"

He smiled and broke open one of the cuts on his bottom lip. Blood seeped out of the wound. Added to his recently reset nose and black eyes, he was in dire shape. It looked as if Frederick had gone several rounds at Gentleman Jackson's, the famous pugilist club in London, with an experienced fighter. I was impressed with Nathaniel's skill; I didn't see a mark on him when he came home last evening. Nor had he said a word about buying Carstairs and Son, but I would have to set that worry aside for now.

"Someone finally put me in my place," Frederick drawled as he joined us.

"And where exactly is this place?" I asked with a horrible premonition of his next words.

"I was given some excellent advice recently, and I have decided instead of being a boy, I am going to follow this advice as a man." Frederick stared into my face. "You had better get accustomed to having me around, sister, because I mean to stay and work. At whatever you give me to do."

An image of me stabbing Nathaniel through the heart blossomed in my head, and I let out a groan.

December 1823
Chapter 27
Nathaniel

"Captain Groot, it's a pleasure to make your acquaintance finally." The ship pitched as I stepped onboard. Happy to be off the rope, I stepped forward to shake the Dutch captain's hand.

"Ja, ja." Captain Groot took hold of my hand and shook. His grip was firm, and his callouses reminded me of how long it had been since I worked onboard a ship. "Maybe nicer if the port agent would let me dock my ships."

"I have filed an injunction with Dr. Crawfurd. Now that Major General Farquhar has left for London, we shouldn't have too many problems getting you through," I said with an easy smile. Captain Groot was the same height as I, with corn-silk yellow hair and sky blue eyes. The wrinkles around his mouth indicated he liked to laugh often.

"Our friend at the East India Company told me this would not be a problem." Captain Groot smiled at my discomfort at the offhand mention of McCarr. He waved a hand in dismissal. "Most of my men do not speak English, and those who do are completely trustworthy."

Having a great instinct for self-preservation, I did not trust any of them. Only a year had passed since a rogue Dutch captain had tried to kill me. "I will have to take your word for it."

"Not all of us are like Captain Collaart." Captain Groot read my mind. "Most of us want to trade and make money without the bother of all this petty rivalry. The Hanseatic League has discussed it at length."

I looked around the ship with a tight smile. "It looks like we will have the chance to make a little profit. Your ship appears to be full to the gunnels."

Captain Groot smiled at my words. "Ja, ja. We will all make a nice profit and set our penance to rest with the company."

For the first time, I wondered how the Dutch ship captain ended up working for his primary rival. I was going to ask when a shout from the boson caught my attention. Someone was asking for permission to come aboard. Looking over the railing, I recognized the figure of Zheng Jing. He saw me immediately and frowned.

Captain Groot nodded to the boson and turned back to me. "I see you didn't inform Mr. Zheng Jing you were also doing business with us."

"No, we are not exactly close." I let the frustration I felt over the situation fill my voice. He denied my attempts to meet at every turn. I even tried to hire one of his mediators for the Junk season to no avail—even risking Carstairs' wrath over the sale of Carstairs and Son. He had wanted to keep the sale of his company a secret, but I started a small, but verifiable rumor that I was interested in purchasing the beleaguered company. I thought since Charlotte used one of Zheng Jing's mediators, he might be willing to meet with me. Nothing.

"He does not look very happy to see you," Captain Groot said as we watched Zheng Jing scramble aboard the ship from the swaying ship ladder. He stepped forward to greet the other man, a social smile in place. I waited for them to become acquainted as I looked around the Dutch fluyt. The crew was quiet and efficient as they went about their tasks on the three-masted ship.

"What are you doing here, Hawk?" Zheng Jing strode across the deck on unsteady legs. It was clear he had never spent much time on a ship.

"I have business with our mutual acquaintance, Captain Groot." My eyes shifted to the captain for a moment. He watched the encounter with an interested gaze.

"How is this possible?" Zheng Jing stared at Captain Groot.

Captain Groot shrugged his shoulders. "The Groot Verzenden line is in the business of making money, Mr. Zheng Jing. Singapore is the only port in the Malacca Straits making much of a turnover at the moment, seeing as how the East India Company has the tea monopoly with China. When you indicated you couldn't accommodate two additional ships with cargo, we sent out a few inquiries. Mr. Hawk here was happy to take on the extra space."

Zheng Jing took a step closer to me. "How is it possible you have enough collateral to expand your fleet by chartering two additional ships? I would have thought the company would have strangled you out of even the Bugis market."

"There are those whose loyalty lay in their good name rather than their loyalty to the East India Company." My chin rose in the air. "Enjoying a good name in the marketplace is valuable, wouldn't you agree?"

"I don't know what you're implying." Zheng Jing appeared to be instantly offended. "And I cannot help but think this is a ploy to get my attention somehow." Zheng Jing's face radiated malice and anger. "I have heard the rumors you're going to buy Carstairs and Son. I hold the debt notes for that sad little enterprise. After the season finishes, there will be nothing left. I will have taken anything of value."

"My wife and her business associate are hard workers, Mr. Zheng Jing. I have tremendous faith in their ability to pay their markers interest on time." I waved a hand out to indicate the entire harbor. "After all, this is going to be Singapore's most profitable season yet."

"Stay out of my way." The look on Zheng Jing's face might have meant to be threatening, but I wasn't in the mood to take him seriously.

"Or what, Mr. Zheng Jing? I hardly think you have the power to do anything to me." My voice held the contempt I felt. "I welcome any challenge from you."

Captain Groot cleared his throat. "Gentlemen, if you do not mind me interrupting your discussion." Zheng Jing and I both looked reluctantly away from one another. He pointed and said, "I believe that's the harbor master coming out in a pilot boat. We might see the shore after all."

The harbor master, Briggs, stepped onboard the ship and looked around the deck with annoyance. Several men came onboard behind him, armed as if they were going into battle.

"Captain Groot." The wireman's voice was raspy. "We have come to do an inspection of your ships. You understand this is procedure."

"I understand no such thing." Captain Groot held his ground. "This is a free port. All who wish to trade here are welcome. You are obligated to extend the hand of hospitality to my men and me."

"Listen here, you Dutch bastard. The war may be over, but memories are long. I have friends who died in battle against your kind. Don't think we're going to welcome you to Singapore." The harbor master turned and looked at Zheng Jing. "You, I cannot understand. The damned Chinese would betray their mothers if they thought they could make a shilling off them. But you." He pointed a gnarled finger in my direction. "Your father is rolling in his grave, boy."

"He's probably doing the backstroke," I interjected. The harbor master was technically the most powerful man in port. He granted permission to ships for their wharves to unload their cargoes and seek new trades. I knew that Singapore's harbor master, despite his feelings against the Dutch, would have to let Captain Groot into port; otherwise, McCarr's plan would fail.

An incredulous look passed over the harbor master's face and his eyes bugged out of his head. "Why you ungrateful little sod. I served with your father and let me tell you how disappointed he would be to see you colluding with the enemy."

"Not to worry, Mr. Briggs, my father told me on a number of occasions of his disappointment." I didn't bother to repress the smile spreading across my face.

"Damned puppies." Mr. Briggs swore under his breath before turning his attention back to Captain Groot. "I want to see the cargo manifests for each one of your ships. Not until I have confirmed everything about your cargo is legitimate will I allow you anywhere near my port." He turned back to face Zheng Jing and me. "I don't care what Calcutta says or if we sign a hundred treaties with the Dutch. You two should be ashamed of yourselves."

Captain Groot, Mr. Briggs, and the boson began opening ledgers on a table hastily set up on deck. With nothing to do, I walked around the deck of the fluyt a few times. I noticed the crew avoided me as much as Zheng Jing. Either my father's bloodthirsty reputation was holding them at bay, or they were waiting for a chance to spring into action and slit my throat.

After a few minutes, the boson led Mr. Briggs down a set of stairs, and the harbor master disappeared from view. Captain Groot shook his head as he approached. "This might take some time. The harbor master has assured me of his intense dislike. Apparently, my head is where my ass should be."

"He is not normally so aggressive or thorough," I sighed, thinking about the wasted afternoon.

"I for one will be writing a letter to the officials in Calcutta and London." Zheng Jing had approached Captain Groot and me. "Is this how we treat Britain's allies?"

Shrugging, I said, "It is if we had only stopped killing one another a few months ago. Commerce makes strange bedfellows." I watched a couple of the harbor master's men climb onboard and follow their boss down the stairs.

"There is no reason why I cannot trade with you, Captain Groot. Let me assure you." Zheng Jing looked me up and down, and by the look on his face, I was left wanting. "On the other hand, Mr. Hawk may have some patriotic ties to the East India Company. Why don't you let me take the cargo on those additional two ships? It might be tight, but I'm sure I could find a load for them."

"You little thief." My blood was up again as Zheng Jing tried to steal my cargo out from under me. "I'm standing right here, you charlatan. Have some bloody respect."

"For you, never," Zheng Jing vowed. "You ride on the greatness of your father and your mentor, but you have yet to prove yourself." He turned back to Captain Groot. "Please let us do each other a mutual favor and cut out Mr. Hawk entirely."

A part of me wondered what Captain Groot would do. Would he try to take on Zheng Jing alone, or would he play the safe option and follow the East India Company's instructions?

"It seems that Mr. Hawk could have very few patriotic ties to a country and a company that seeks his demise at every turn." Captain Groot shook his head. "Many times in the Hanseatic League we have discussed the prowess of his father, Captain Hawk. Now that he is dead, some are happy as he murdered many of my countrymen, but there is respect for an old fallen foe. I think Mr. Hawk has a right to be angry when the country his father defended so diligently has made his memory an enemy."

Surprise lit my features. "Thank you, Captain Groot."

"We are allies now. We must form the bonds of cooperation." Captain Groot sighed. "Besides, I have a legal contract with Mr. Hawk, to provide two ships worth of cargo for this season as well as cargo space for the journey back to Amsterdam. It would look very weak if I backed out of our deal now."

Zheng Jing bowed, but his eyes snapped with anger.

"I would like to invite you both to supper this evening here on my ship." Captain Groot waved his arms to indicate the deck. "We will have good Dutch food and drink."

The look of pure horror on Zheng Jing's face was worth all the time wasted by the harbor master.

Chapter 28
Charlotte

"I will be out this evening." Nathaniel crossed to the mirror hanging beside the door to the hallway.

"Thank you for telling me." I rested my feet on a stool in front of the couch. Normally, he wouldn't bother to say anything or even come home. He spent his evenings at the whorehouse with the rest of the estranged husbands.

He turned to me and surveyed my face. "You were unwell today?"

Taking a deep breath, I looked up at him. "Yes, the doctor told me rest would help."

"Good." He nodded, and I knew he wanted to say more. Instead, he walked over to the liquor cabinet and rummaged through the bottles. He pulled one out from the back. The label was peeling off, and it looked like it had been around for a while. Nathaniel held it up. "For my new friend, Captain Groot."

"The Dutchman." My voice was flat. "It would have been nice to have been warned that you were going to set Singapore's gossips' tongues wagging. I've hardly had any rest since they arrived."

"It's business." Nathaniel's eyes narrowed as he looked at me.

"Just as your stealing my father's company is only business," I retorted, sinking back into the familiar argument.

"Charlotte, you know it's for the best. Today's incident proves you need to rest and be in a comfortable environment for the baby." He gave me a patronizing smile.

Looking away from him, I did my best to hold my temper. The doctor told me I needed to stay calm for the sake of the child. If only he knew how hard that was living with my husband. I glanced back at Nathaniel, who now wore a frown on his handsome features. "Have a good evening, Nathaniel."

He stood there watching me for another moment. "A good evening to you, Charlotte."

Thus has been the extent of our conversations since we made our bargain in October. The only other topic we discussed concerned his presumption at buying Carstairs and Son. I tried to dissuade him, using all manner of arguments, but he was immovable. Sighing, I looked at the pile of ledgers a runner had brought around this afternoon. The first of the Chinese Junks and European vessels had arrived in port. The work was piling up on Bigham. Unfortunately, I could hardly rummage up enough enthusiasm to get out of bed in the morning. The monotony of life was wearing thin.

A movement by the door caught my attention. "Yes, Dutta. It will be dinner for one this evening. Please, something small. I will eat in here."

Dutta cleared his throat, and I looked over at him. "Yes, madam. There is another matter, however; a boy has a message for you."

I sat up expectantly. "What is it, Dutta? Something from the wharves?"

"He says he must give it to you himself." Dutta's voice rose in agitation.

"Bring him through." I was weary. Perhaps I would forego supper and go to bed early. I rubbed my eyes.

As soon as the urchin crossed the threshold, I knew who sent the message. The boy gave Dutta a dirty look before holding out his hand. In his palm, just as before, lay a coin with two hands shaking. With care, I rose to my feet and tried to stop my hand from quivering as I took the coin. Zheng Jing had promised not to contact me, and this was the second time. Furious knocking on the door grabbed my attention, and I looked at Dutta. "Whoever it is, Dutta, send them away." He bowed and walked out of the room. A second later, I heard a shrill feminine voice erupting in the front hall.

"Charlotte, I know you don't want to see me, but I'm desperate." Sarah Buck bullied her way into the study. I'm sure my face expressed the shock I was feeling on the inside. "Please, give me a few minutes of your time."

Standing up from my seat on the sofa, I hoped she ignored the urchin standing incongruously in my study. "What are you doing here?" I finally managed to get some words out. "You must understand we can have nothing to say to one another."

Sarah Buck's eyes filled with tears. It had been months since I had seen her at Cornelius's dinner where she informed me she was carrying Nathaniel's child. The old hurt rose up and choked me.

"Please, I wouldn't have come if I had any other choice," Sarah Buck pleaded. There were lines around her eyes now that hadn't been there before.

"Why have you come here?" My husband is not at home." I hoped she would go away once she realized Nathaniel was not here.

"I know. I waited for Nathaniel to leave for the evening. I wanted to speak with you. Mother to mother." She nodded her head at my stomach.

"You have heard the news." I wearily sat back on the couch, aware that I needed to get rid of her as soon as possible to meet Zheng Jing.

Sarah Buck fell to her knees and grabbed my hand. Fat tears ran down her cheeks ruining her beautiful face. "I am undone, Charlotte. No one will speak to me. It has been months since I had an invitation in society. "You must help me."

Tugging my hand out of the other woman's grasp, I wiped her tears from my fingers on my dress. "Sarah you knew this would happen if you continued to pursue my husband after we were married. What did you expect?"

"Show me some kindness." Sarah lifted her face to mine.

"What can I do?" I asked sharply, rising to my feet and stepping away from the other woman. "You have brought this trouble on yourself. Is the child my husband's?"

"How can you doubt it? You saw us that day." Sarah Buck slowly rose to her feet. A red tinge appeared on her cheeks, and I wondered if she was embarrassed.

"I've heard the rumors like everyone else," I tossed back. The urchin was slowly backing out of the study door, but not before Sarah Buck got a good look at him. She frowned.

"Who is that?" Her attention snapped back to me. "I'm surprised you put much stock in rumors, considering the tattle making the rounds about you."

Letting my pride take a hit, at the expense of hers, I said, "Unfortunately, it is much more accurate than I would like. If that is all you have to say to me, you may go. Even if I were inclined to help you gain entry back into polite society, not even a gaggle of nuns could resurrect your reputation."

"You could go out with me in public," Sarah Buck announced.

"There is no way I will ever do you any favors, Sarah. Get out of my house." I pointed toward the door. "And do not think to come back here asking for any more favors. You will not receive any Christian charity from me." I set my jaw as she began crying in earnest.

"You have turned into a very cruel woman," Sarah Buck huffed as she turned to the door.

"You and life have taught me to be cruel, Sarah. Do not seek to erase history. You have brought this on yourself," I called out as she walked into the hall. Dutta disappeared to make sure the other woman left the house. I waited for the sense of satisfaction to come. Before I was married, I might have reveled in the other lady's social demise. The revenge I had wished for finally occurred, but I only felt more tired and worried. A light twinge in my stomach reminded me that there was more at stake here than Sarah Buck's pride. I had a child too, and I needed to protect him or her as much as I could.

"Take me to your master." I looked over at Dutta. "I will need a light wrap."

A few minutes later I was following the urchin through the darkening European Quarter. I wore the shawl over my head and tried to hide my features as best I could. Instead of continuing west toward the other side of the Singapore River, the urchin ducked down into the warren of alleys and streets surrounding the warehouses.

We approached a tap called The Yard, surrounded by sailors and laborers drinking ale. I might be able to hide my identity, but my skirts gave me away as a woman. I ignored the catcalls and rude suggestions thrown my way and entered the tap. It was full to bursting with revelers for the evening, and the thick pipe smoke burned my eyes. The urchin gestured to a set of stairs set into the wall on the left side.

I climbed them, hoping Zheng Jing would be standing at the top and not Nathaniel. Or even one of his workers. Mr. Finlayson was always hanging around, watching. I got the impression he was waiting for something.

The urchin knocked on the door then opened it after a shout from the inside.

"Mrs. Hawk, a pleasure to see you this evening." Zheng Jing's voice rang out over the crowd below. The door closed behind me and shut out most of the noise. "I would ask you to have a seat, but you will not be staying very long."

"You said we would never meet," I replied stiffly.

"Your husband is getting in my way. Fix it." Zheng Jing stood up.

"I had no idea about the Dutch." I shook my head. "Surely you realize by now. Our marriage is in name only. He would not confide in me if I were the last woman in Singapore. You might try his whores; it's possible he speaks to them." A terrible feeling of betrayal swamped my stomach as I thought of Nathaniel's other women.

"Perhaps I will," Zheng Jing said cryptically. "Are you ready for the shipments of goods to Portsmouth?" He asked changing the subject.

"Yes, the captain of the Regal Lady knows he must make a delivery in Cornwall before he continues to Portsmouth."

"Good. You know what will happen if you do not cooperate with me. And having your husband buy out Carstairs and Son will not help you. I own you, Charlotte, and when Mr. Hawk becomes entangled in your lies, I will own him, too." Zheng Jing's grin turned calculating.

A large man standing by the window said something in Chinese, and Zheng Jing strode across the room. He looked out the window briefly to where the man was pointing. "Come here, Mrs. Hawk." I hesitated. "I assure you, I am not going to push you out the window."

"No you will stab me in the back like you did Cornelius Thistlewaite." I came forward and stood to the side of the window.

"Careful, Mrs. Hawk. A lesser man than I might think you were insulting," he said before pointing down into the crowd of drunken men. "Do you know that woman?"

Sarah Buck looked up at the pub. "No, I have never seen her before in my life." The large man beside me spoke in rapid Chinese, and Zheng Jing shook his head.

"Mrs. Hawk, you should choose your lies better. That is Sarah Buck, one of your husband's mistresses. My men tell me she followed you here," he said before looking away from the crowd to stare at me.

I didn't bother to correct him. Sarah Buck was no longer Nathaniel's mistress, but what did it matter? "She is only looking for a little revenge on me. Let me handle it."

"No." Zheng Jing's arm shot out, and he grabbed onto my wrist. His grip was tight and painful. "She is jeopardizing a deal that has been years in the making and could see all of us hanged. We will deal with her."

My blood ran cold. "Mrs. Buck knows nothing of my business. I pray you will let her leave in ignorance." Here I was pleading for Sarah Buck's life after telling her I didn't care if she remained ruined.

"You will leave out the back. The boy will show you." Zheng Jing nodded his head at me. "I assure you, she will leave here in ignorance."

His words did not reassure me, but I had little choice but to follow the urchin back out into the hall. Zheng Jing held all the trump cards in this game.

Chapter 29
Nathaniel

"Captain," I shouted from the wharf. Captain Groot leaned over the side of his ship and waved me onboard. Using the gangplank, I stepped onboard the ship and held out the bottle of rum. "A gift to our continuing friendship." I had decided that McCarr had done me a great favor in aligning me with Captain Groot. His family owned a large fleet of vessels that plied the waters all over the world. With Thistlewaite and Hawk's contacts, we could be a powerful combined force.

"Thank you." Captain Groot's accent was thicker than usual this morning, and his cheeks were red. "Let us have a good season," he said and turned to a boy who had stepped up beside him. He had two small crystal glasses on a silver tray. "Please." Captain Groot indicated the glasses, and we each took one. "This is Jenever for our health," he said and downed his in one gulp.

I held up my glass and saluted each man before downing it in one. The alcohol was strong, and I had to force down a cough rising in my throat. It had the distinct flavor of juniper berries since it was the Dutch version of gin.

Looking Captain Groot in the eye, I replaced the glass on the tray. "Very nice," I lied. I looked back to shore. Faint lights moved around the jungle. "Mr. Zheng Jing is not here?"

"Not yet." Captain Groot's eyes tightened. "I have to wait and see what he tries to smuggle onboard. What comes off the ship is of little concern to me."

"This might be a good time to discuss the future," I hedged as the cabin boy refilled our glasses. Holding down my acute discomfort, I drank the fiery liquid in a gulp again. It was going to be a long night.

"What future?" he asked cautiously. Captain Groot might appear to have imbibed too much Jenever, but he was still sharp and lucid. "My orders are for this season only."

I shrugged and tried to appear unconcerned. "You have ships that need filling, and you were right this morning. There is nothing coming out of Malacca. Java has run out of resources to trade. Singapore is the future. I have contacts here and in China, we can both expand and make a tidy profit."

"You have been hit hard by the East India Company and their attitude toward your father." Captain Groot's gaze was steady. He was reading my every movement, cataloguing all of my words, spoken and unspoken. Should I lie or tell the truth? I'm sure the company would not like me to discuss their business with outsiders, especially the Dutch, but what had occurred was technically part of the public record.

"Yes." I decided, to be honest. "I am tainted by association. A few months ago, my business partner Cornelius Thistlewaite met an untimely end and rumors are circulating that I killed him to control the whole company." My voice was thick with bitterness, but I could not change it. The insinuations people had made burned into my consciousness.

"Did you?" Captain Groot asked. His gaze never wavered.

"No, of course not." I huffed out a strangled breath. "In some ways, Cornelius Thistlewaite was more of a father to me than my own." I had no idea why I was telling him this. Just months ago, the only way I would have spoken to Captain Groot was with a loaded cannon. There was something about the ship captain that made him easy to approach.

Captain Groot nodded to the boy to refill the glasses before looking out at the Singaporean shoreline. "My father was also a hard man." He saluted me with his full glass before drinking. I followed his actions. "He was a high-ranking member of the Hanseatic League, so everything had to be done in a certain way when he was home." He looked back at me and continued, "Thankfully, it was not often." Captain Groot was silent.

"Is your father still a member?" I asked. The Hanseatic League had been legendary only a hundred years ago, but now its power was dwindling. It was as much a victim of progress as the East India Company in India.

"He was murdered by political rivals. Much like your father." Captain Groot's attention fixed on someone coming down the wharf. It could only be Zheng Jing.

"My father was murdered by the ghost ship." My voice held no emotion.

"Who do you think captains the ghost ship?" Captain Groot asked. I thought of the man I had seen on the deck of the ship. "Interesting that it hasn't been around this season; it must have succeeded in its mission."

Zheng Jing called for permission to come aboard. Captain Groot waved an impatient hand. "You are late, Mr. Zheng Jing."

"It is the middle of the busiest time in port," Zheng Jing groused as he came to stand with us.

"Evening," I said at the other man. He only nodded in return.

Captain Groot presented the silver tray of glasses full of Jenever once again. This time, a third glass had appeared. "It is customary in my country to celebrate a new friendship with a glass or two of Jenever." Zheng Jing peered down at his glass like it was a snake. "You do not drink Mr. Zheng Jing?"

"Life is short. Sometimes we need to celebrate." Zheng Jing looked up from his glass and stared at me while he drank the strong alcohol. He coughed a few times but did not break eye contact.

"To life," Captain Groot said, downing his glass.

I wondered for a minute what Zheng Jing meant? He seemed to be giving me a warning. Perhaps he was still trying to undermine me. I knew he would not succeed with Captain Groot, but Singapore was a small port. Zheng Jing, along with his Brotherhood, could make life tough for me, even if Finlayson said they wanted to help the son of Captain Sebastian Hawk.

"What's for supper?" I asked, changing the mood of the evening from serious to light in an instant. "I have no idea what Dutch food entails."

"My cook makes an excellent hutspot with rookworst; my wife Anne Mieke smokes it for me before I leave Amsterdam."

"That sounds delightful." I noticed the look of revulsion on Zheng Jing's face before we turned toward the stairs leading into the ship's interior. "My wife is pregnant at the moment, and she craves boiled cabbage. I think this is similar to your hutspot."

"This is your first child?" Groot asked, watching me intently from under white bleached brows.

"Yes, it is our first child." Strictly, it was not a lie. I pushed aside thoughts of the other nameless boy.

"I remember my first," Groot said with a smile as he stared into the distance for a minute. "Now I have seven!"

"Congratulations," I said, knowing there would only be the one child from Charlotte. The distance between us grew every day. I tried to push the thoughts aside.

"If I get her pregnant before I leave port every time, I know there is no trouble. Simple." Groot laughed at his genius, and I tried to join the mirth. "Tonight, you will have the best rookworst. My wife is splendid with sausage."

Zheng Jing's back stiffened, and I laughed more at his discomfort than Captain Groot's joke. It might be an entertaining evening.

&

The light hit my face, and I tried to turn away from the persistent irritation. I hid my head under a pillow and tried not to vomit at the sudden movement. Taking several deep breaths, the events of the night washed over me. We must have consumed a barrel of Jenever before opening the bottle of rum I brought. I hardly remembered how it tasted. I do remember Zheng Jing hanging off the side of ship feeding the fish.

I lifted the corner of the pillow and opened one eye. The charming décor of the spare room at home met my gaze. So I had wandered home last night after the supper. Perhaps I knew the dangers to be had in the Chinese Campong at night too well.

Shouting from the foyer downstairs caught my attention, and I sat up. My head swirled, and I was perilously close to heaving up my stomach contents. Boots stomping and scraping the floor continued to ring through the house. I got up and was thankful I had fallen into bed fully clothed.

Yanking the door open, I saw Charlotte emerge from the main bedroom as she tied a wrap around her middle. She looked as confused as I as she walked forward.

Dutta's angry voice came from below, and I looked over the railing. Dr. Crawfurd stood there with a soldier dressed in a full military uniform. He looked up the stairs, relief on his face. "Mr. Hawk, Dr. Crawfurd and Major Randall are here to see you."

"To what do I owe the pleasure at this early hour of the morning?" I asked as I solicitously held out a hand for Charlotte to take.

"It might be best if you came down here first." Dr. Crawfurd looked weary. His soft brogue was lyrical. The older man watched us descend the stairs.

"Dutta, coffee, if you please, and pastries if you have them," Charlotte directed as she looked at the two men. I felt her hand shake, and I covered it with my own. Did she know why they were here? We might not be on the best of terms, but I would see her through this. Only for the sake of the child, I tried to convince myself.

"The study is pleasant this time of the morning." I held out a hand indicating the door on the right. Charlotte led the way followed by Crawfurd and the unsmiling Major Randall. Dr. Crawfurd took a seat opposite the sofa where I settled Charlotte and sat next to her. I wished I could study her expression, but I needed to appear the doting husband. Major Randall stood beside Dr. Crawfurd's chair.

"This will be disturbing news for the both of you to hear," Dr. Crawfurd began, and I felt Charlotte tense. I grabbed her hand and once again held it in mine. "This morning the body of Sarah Buck was found in the wash of the Singapore River."

My mind went blank. "I beg your pardon? I don't think I heard you correctly," Charlotte gasped beside me.

"Mrs. Sarah Buck's body was found in the river this morning." Dr. Crawfurd repeated. I had felt the gazes of the two men on me before Charlotte gasped. Her hand tightened around mine for a second. I looked at her. She was pale and looked terrified.

"We have some questions to ask. Considering the circumstances." Dr. Crawfurd. "Some say Sarah Buck is your mistress, Mr. Hawk."

I shook my head. "Sarah Buck was never my mistress." I briefly glanced beside me and admitted something I had kept to myself for many months. "We did share a bed once. My wife is aware of it."

"So the child she bore could have been yours." Dr. Crawfurd nodded.

"It is not outside the realms of possibility," I acknowledged.

"You were upset when she started saying you were the father," Major Randall interjected. Dr. Crawfurd frowned at the other man for interrupting him.

"I do not believe that is a question," I said stiffly.

"Were you upset by her claims that you're the father of her child?" Major Randall rephrased his question.

"Any number of men could have been the father of Sarah Buck's child," Charlotte spoke in a thin voice. "Including her husband. We were both greatly aggrieved she would single my husband out."

"Mrs. Hawk." Dr. Crawfurd's intent gaze settled on Charlotte. "Several people have said they saw Mrs. Buck visit you yesterday evening."

Charlotte's hand tightened in mine, but she did not look away from Dr. Crawfurd. "Sarah Buck did come to see me yesterday. The visit was short as I was not feeling well."

"Why did she come to see you?" Dr. Crawfurd asked. "Did you send for her?"

"No." Charlotte frowned. "I had not spoken to Sarah Buck since before the Bugis trading season. We were both guests at a supper hosted by Cornelius Thistlewaite. My husband was in Calcutta."

"You did not warn her to stay away from your husband?" Dr. Crawfurd pressed gently.

"There was no need to warn her to stay away," Charlotte explained. "They shared a brief encounter after her husband's death. She was never his mistress." The last word came out in a huff.

"You did not argue with the woman who claimed she bore your husband a bastard?" Major Randall snorted derisively. "I find it very suspicious the two of you would enjoy a cup of tea together and speak of old times. You are lying, Mrs. Hawk."

"I never said we didn't argue." Charlotte shook her head, and I knew her temper was rising. "She came to ask me to help her gain re-entry into polite society. I refused. She left. That was the whole and the end of it."

"Do you know where she was going after she saw you?" Dr. Crawfurd interjected.

"No, as I said we are not friends. She came to request a favor, and I refused." Charlotte's voice evened out.

"Did you leave the house last evening, Mrs. Hawk?" Dr. Crawfurd.

Charlotte hesitated for a second. "No, as I said. I was not feeling well last evening, and the doctor told me to rest."

Silence followed Charlotte's answer. I made to stand up. "If those are all your questions for this morning, you will understand if I rush you out. It's a busy time of the year."

"Mrs. Sarah Buck was murdered in precisely the same manner as Mr. Cornelius Thistlewaite." Major Randall's pronouncement pushed me back into my seat. "A single thrust of a knife under the ribs and into the heart."

My mind reeled with this new information. Could the Brotherhood have let the man they believed killed Cornelius go after I had confronted him at the gypsy camp? Impossible. The Chong brothers were not known for their mercy. The man who claimed he had killed Cornelius would be dead by now, rotting in an unmarked grave somewhere in the jungle.

"How is this possible?" I muttered.

"It appears more than likely the same individual who murdered Mr. Cornelius Thistlewaite also killed Sarah Buck." Major Randall spoke with conviction. "We never caught Mr. Thistlewaite's murderer, and so it is highly likely the same person committed both murders."

I bit back my retort that it was not possible.

"Mrs. Hawk, several people claim you were seen in the Chinese Campong the evening Cornelius Thistlewaite died." Major Randall's blue eyes bored into Charlotte. Even though Frederick told me Charlotte had met with Cornelius the night he died, I never questioned her about it. By that time our relationship was strained, and I never believed she was the one who killed him. "Did you meet with Mr. Thistlewaite that night?"

"Of course not." Charlotte's back stiffened. "Why would I meet with Mr. Thistlewaite in the Chinese Campong at night, when I could leave a card at his house and meet him there during the day? Or speak with him down at his warehouse during operating hours."

"I don't know, Mrs. Hawk. Why were you in the Chinese Campong the evening Mr. Thistlewaite died?" Major Randall pressed forward.

Charlotte shook her head. "I don't know who said I was down there that evening, but I assure you they're mistaken. No business would have brought me to the other side of the river at night, especially alone. It's dangerous."

"Yet you have business there during the day." Dr. Crawfurd had been watching the exchange.

"It's no secret Carstairs and Son changed the mediator we use with the Bugis and the Chinese. We are making a much greater profit. The Chong brothers have helped us get access to some of the better ships coming into port." Charlotte shrugged one delicate shoulder, but the movement looked forced.

"You're aware that Mr. Zheng Jing and his associates the Chong brothers are affiliated with a group named the Brotherhood." Dr. Crawfurd spoke in a quiet voice.

"I've heard the rumors like everyone else," Charlotte replied cryptically.

"You have not been very helpful, Mrs. Hawk." Dr. Crawfurd sat back in his chair as Dutta brought in the coffee tray. No one made a move toward it. "I would have thought you would be more concerned over finding who killed not only a member of your social circle but the mother of a now orphaned baby."

"My wife and I are very concerned about Sarah Buck's death. She was not only a member of our circle but the widow of a childhood friend." I looked at Charlotte and saw her relief at my taking over the conversation. "Now, as she has said before, the doctor has ordered her to rest." I stood up and indicated Charlotte should remain seated.

"A couple of dock workers said they saw you go into The Yard tap yesterday evening." Major Randall looked at Charlotte, his brows coming together. "These same men claim Mrs. Buck asked several of the men if they had seen you."

"Ridiculous," I said and motioned toward the door. "My wife has already told you both she was here last evening resting. Whatever those men thought they saw or heard is nothing more than slander, and I will have words with any man who spreads such lies about my wife."

Dr. Crawfurd rose from his chair. "Those are all the questions we have for this morning."

"You will inform us of any new developments?" I asked as I followed the two men into the hallway. Major Randall snorted, and I wished I could break his nose. "As I said, my wife and my relationship with Sarah Buck became strained over the last year, but she was an acquaintance."

Before either of the men could respond, Charlotte's voice sounded from behind me. "What of the child? What will happen to her son?"

"Sarah Buck has a father who still lives in Calcutta. I will write to him today and see if he is willing to take the child." Dr. Crawfurd cleared his throat. "It is my understanding, given the nature of the child's parentage; the late Captain Buck's family is unwilling to take on the burden of the child."

"We must hope for the child's sake that Sarah Buck's father has some measure of Christian charity," I said, trying to rush the two men out the door. I had my questions for my wife.

"She hated her father," Charlotte's quiet voice rang in the entry as the two men left. I shut the door behind them.

"There's nothing we can do for the child." I walked past her and back into the study. Pouring a cup of the coffee, I took my time and selected a pastry. I felt her presence behind me. "Why didn't you tell me you had seen Cornelius the night he died?"

"I didn't." She turned back to the door.

"Frederick saw you," I spoke over a mouthful of buttercream.

Her shoulders slumped, and she came back into the room. Sitting down, she poured a cup of coffee but did not drink it. Despite the warmth of the chamber, she cradled the porcelain in her hands like she was trying to warm them.

"It was a mistake." Charlotte stared out the window. "All of this has been a terrible mistake."

"You were seen with the victims of a murder the night they died." I shook my head. "There's more than a mistake in this or mere coincidence. I believe your story about Sarah Buck, but what of Cornelius? You hated one another. Why would you meet him? I cannot protect you and the child when you continue to lie to me."

She finally turned away from the window, a haunted look in her eyes. It made her seem younger and more fragile than I had ever seen her. "If I asked you to stay out of this and forget your assumptions and let me handle it, would you?"

Letting out a long sigh, I said her name. "Charlotte," as I set my coffee back on the tray and sat next to her on the sofa. "This is much bigger than you can handle alone. Why can't you trust me to help you? I promise, all I ever wanted was to make you happy."

She snorted with laughter, and I took the coffee cup away before she buried her face in her hands and began to sob in earnest. "Is this happiness?" She choked out between sobs.

I wrapped my arms around her shoulders, and for one blissful moment, she accepted my comfort. Charlotte pressed into me and gave way to her tears, before pushing back and rubbing her eyes dry with the sleeves of her dressing gown.

Taking her shaking hands in my own, I said, "I know you didn't kill Cornelius and Sarah." I tried to smile. "There were days when I'm sure you could have thought about murdering them, but whoever did this is experienced. I've killed men and I know the stab wound Cornelius and Sarah died of must have been precise."

Charlotte's voice sounded reedy. "I had nothing to do with their deaths."

My hands rested on her shoulders, and I squeezed them. "Whether Major Randall's assumptions over your guilt are correct or not, he makes a valid point. You are the common thread between Cornelius and Sarah. It was you they saw the night they died." I took a deep breath. "Tell me about the trouble you have hidden from me all these months."

"It is a coincidence. Nothing more." Charlotte tried to twist out of my grasp, but I held firmly. I knew my fingers were digging into her flesh painfully, but I didn't care. This whole charade would end now.

"You've plotted my demise for months. Since before we were married. Am I next on the list of victims?" I ground out. Charlotte's face went white with terror.

"Let go of me. You're hurting me." Fresh tears poured down her cheeks as she continued to fight my grip.

"Charlotte, you are not going anywhere until you tell me what trouble you're in," I said firmly. "You are going to get yourself killed."

"It's too late for me," she moaned and collapsed back on the sofa. I let go of her, and she fell. Once her back hit the cushions, she sprang up with surprising speed. "Leave it alone, Nathaniel. You may not believe this, but I'm protecting you." She stepped toward the door with her dressing gown pulled away from her ankles.

"Come back here and speak to me like an adult. I'm done with the games, Charlotte," I shouted after her as I stood up. There was no way she was going to get away from me now. She tried to move faster up the steps, and her foot slipped. I watched as she let go of the hem of her dressing gown to catch the railing, but even as she twisted, I knew she would never make it.

She screamed out as I shouted her name. She fell with a sickening thud and slid down a couple of steps before she halted in a heap. I ran up the stairs two at a time and picked her up. Charlotte looked up at me with glazed eyes as I felt sticky wetness on my arms. We looked at each other and realized the dreadful truth.

Chapter 30
Charlotte

"Charlotte, my dear, this is what I was worried might happen if you continued to work." Father stood at the side of my bed and reached for my hand. The urge to pull it away from the smug expression on his face was nearly overwhelming, but I was too tired. "Now you can see the sale to your husband is the best for everyone. When you're up on your feet again, you can start fresh and try again for another baby."

I nodded and gave him a small smile. Except we wouldn't try again, because our marriage was a sham to protect the child I had lost. My eyes hurt, but all the tears I had to give were gone. I had cried for three endless days, Nathaniel hardly leaving my side. It was as if he loved me.

"Would you like a glass of water, love?" Nathaniel spoke from the doorway of the bedroom. He was giving Father a hard look. He wanted him to shut up about more children because he didn't want to make them with me. "Mr. Carstairs, I think it's important for Charlotte to have rest and calm while she recovers."

"You have been such a good husband to her. I cannot understand why she would have ever wanted to divorce you," Father huffed, looking over the tea tray Dutta had brought up earlier.

Nathaniel looked straight at me as he walked in and poured a glass of water. "She had some very valid reasons."

Surprise flooded my system. I was waiting for some banal comment about women's issues. Instead, Nathaniel handed me the glass, an apology in his eyes. "Thank you." I murmured and took the proffered glass.

"Still, young ladies of breeding do not go around shouting to all and sundry about how they want a divorce." Father had become very pompous in the last few weeks. A terrible time for him to come back to the world of the living, the pending sale of Carstairs and Son had given him a new lease on life.

"A shame indeed," Nathaniel said and took the glass back from me after I had taken a few sips. "There are some married couples who would benefit greatly from the reprieve a divorce would grant."

"Your parents are the exception. How unhappy they must have been." Father chose a small cake and popped it into his mouth. Over his chewing, he continued. "The rumors when we lived in Calcutta were salacious, to say the least."

Nathaniel did not appear to be offended. "You should hear some of the rumors circulating about my mother when I left London last year." He indicated the clock on the mantelpiece. "It's getting late, and the doctor said Charlotte was to rest and not have too many visitors."

"I am not a visitor. I am family." Father puffed out his chest and took a deep breath. "However, I suppose she does look rather pale. You should be eating more liver, my dear. My doctor has recommended I consume the organ at least three times a week. I am already enjoying the benefits of good health."

"Thank you for coming to see me," I said and let him squeeze my hand. "I will think over the liver." The thought of eating liver was revolting. I had to hold in a gag.

"You can see yourself out." Nathaniel turned his back on father and looked at my face. Once he knew we were alone, he reached out and pushed a strand of hair away from my face. "You look tired."

"I wish I could have told him to leave." I huffed a little and sank back into the pillows.

"I agree." Nathaniel sat on the edge of the bed. "When did he become so pompous?"

"When you decided it would be a good idea to bail out his business." I knew my reply was tart, but I didn't care. "He was perfectly beaten down and manageable before that."

Nathaniel stared at me for a moment with an unreadable expression before throwing his head back and laughing. When was the last time I had heard him laugh? Our wedding? The mirth on his face made him look younger, and for the first time, I realized we had become an old couple with worries far beyond the norm in the past few months. I wished we had had a chance to be like any other newly married couple.

"What are you thinking right now?" Nathaniel asked the question quickly.

"Why do you sleep with the women down in the whorehouses?" The question was out of my mouth before I could think. The last thing I wanted was an argument. "I'm sorry. I don't know why I asked that." I turned my head away.

Taking up the hand my father had abandoned, he said: "Look at me, Charlotte." I hesitated, while I gathered my courage. He squeezed my hand, and I looked at him. "It's not about the act of sex." He stopped for a second, and a flush went over his features. "It is, but it isn't."

I shook my head. "Please, you don't have to explain yourself. We have an arrangement."

"Maybe I want to change the agreement." I stared into the golden depths of his eyes. "So much of my life is out of control, Charlotte. My father, Cornelius, the business, the East India Company; even you. I needed something to give me back my peace. When I spend my night down at the Red Door, I am practicing a form of rope bondage." He stopped again, and a pained expression crossed his face. I let go of his hand and reached out to stroke his face.

"It's fine. Whatever you say cannot be worse than I have imagined a thousand times over." My voice sounded soft.

"I tie women up in ropes." Nathaniel's words came out in a rush, and it was my turn to laugh. After I had caught my breath, he smiled. "That did not come out right."

"Thank you for telling me." I wondered what he meant, and I was little curious. "Why don't you tie me up?"

"You are a proper young lady, Charlotte." Nathaniel ran a hand through his hair. "You should not be subjected to my baser needs."

"My father told me just now that I did not act like a proper young lady." I took a deep breath and fortified my courage. "Show me this rope tying."

Nathaniel studied my face before leaning down and placing a chaste kiss on my forehead. "When you are better, we will discuss it." I was unaccountably disappointed. He chuckled. "I give you my word we will discuss it." His words warmed me. "I have to get back to the docks. A few of our ships are leaving in the morning, and I want to go over their manifests. Is there anything you need from Mr. Bigham?" He didn't show a hint of hesitation or disgust at Bigham's name.

"Father has given Mr. Bigham strict instructions that I am not to be disturbed during my recovery." I let out a long sigh. "At first I did not mind, but now…" I waved a hand around. "It's boring, and I know I have books to read, but I'm accustomed to being useful."

"Charlotte, you are useful. You're healing." I opened my mouth to retort, but he stopped me with his next words. "I will stop and speak to Mr. Bigham on my way home. After all, once I buy Carstairs and Son, you will have full control over the company." It took a minute for his words to sink in, but when they did, I threw my arms around his neck.

"Thank you, Nathaniel," I said on a choked sob.

"Concentrate on getting better." He disentangled my arms from his neck and stepped away. "I will check on you this evening." He turned and walked away without a backwards glance.

He meant to let me have control of Carstairs and Son. My father would have a fit if he knew. I would have to keep this secret.

"Mrs. Hawk." Dutta bowed quickly at the door before coming in to clear away the tea tray. "Did you have a nice visit with your father?"

It occurred to me that Dutta saw rather a lot and still he managed to keep his mouth shut. "He was a boorish ox, as always."

Dutta turned to me, and I saw his eyes were grave. "There is something of great importance I must bring to your attention."

"What is it, Dutta? You know you can speak to me of anything." I wondered if he was going to ask me about the urchin and the Brotherhood. What could I tell him without putting him in harm's way? After Sarah Buck's murder, I knew one thing. I was walking a very narrow line between life and death. Zheng Jing would not hesitate to eliminate anyone he saw as a threat.

"The orphan of Sarah Buck," Dutta began, watching my reaction closely. I tried to do my best not to think of my small baby. Born far too early. "Dr. Crawfurd has decided to leave the child in the care of Sarah Buck's maid at their cottage." He stopped.

"Go on Dutta. It does not hurt me to hear of him." But it did a little. It hurt to know he was thriving while my child lay dead in the little plot beside the church reserved for stillborn babies and unbelievers.

"She is not taking proper care of the child. She has men over, and she drinks and smokes opium with the money Dr. Crawfurd gave her. He is too busy to see to the child's welfare." He took a deep breath. "He might die, Mrs. Hawk. Babies need proper care. This I know."

I understood what he was asking. No one else wanted anything to do with the poor child. His mother was a whore, and the man she claimed was the father had disavowed him. "Fetch me hot water Dutta. We're going out."

"Mrs. Hawk, you do not need to go yourself. I can take care of this," Dutta explained. "I only need your authority."

New vigor pumped through my limbs. "You do not have my authority. I wish to see the child's circumstances for myself."

Several minutes later, I dressed and slowly left the house. It had taken much longer than normal to get ready as my body was still healing. Several people nodded their heads at me but did not approach as I followed Dutta to Sarah Buck's cottage. He pounded on the door for several minutes with no answer. I could hear a baby crying from somewhere inside. I reached around him and tried the handle of the door. It gave way, and I shrugged at Dutta. He shook his head and went inside first, evidently believing there might be some danger lurking in the corners.

Peeking into the living room, I saw a young woman laid out on a couch, an opium pipe next to her. The child's cries from upstairs started again, and the woman opened one of her eyes. She let out a soundless, panicked scream before finally finding her voice.

"Who in the bloody hell are you?" The woman spoke with a strong northern English accent.

"I'm the woman who is firing you. Pack your things and go." I looked around the small drawing-room, and it was easy to tell she had been selling Sarah Buck's possessions. "Dutta here will watch you pack up and do not think to take anything that does not belong to you."

"Listen here, miss. I'm taking care of the poor orphan boy." The woman rose unsteadily to her feet.

"Not anymore." I turned on my heel and went up the stairs as I listened to the maid argue with a very determined Dutta. I went down the hall to the source of the crying. Pushing open the door, I walked over and stood over the crib. Immediately the crying stopped, and a pair of golden eyes stared up at me. Leaning down, I took the child in my arms and held back my tears. "We're going home, little one. Whether your father wants you there or not."

Chapter 31
Nathaniel

"Have you found anything?" I asked as I stepped aboard Captain Groot's ship.

He jerked his head, and I followed him across the deck of the fluyt and through the narrow passage leading to his captain's quarters. "That will be all, boy." Captain Groot waved his cabin boy away and shut the door behind him. The wooden portal would only give a modicum of privacy. The closing door was symbolic. "Nothing. Not one damned tea leaf." Captain Groot said something under his breath. I imagined it was uncomplimentary.

"Maybe McCarr has it wrong," I said and waved away the offer of a glass of Jenever.

"I think Zheng Jing knows." Captain Groot narrowed his eyes and looked out the darkened windows in the rear of his cabin. "McCarr overplayed the game sending you in, too."

"Or underplayed." I sighed and sat down in one of the two chairs facing the captain's desk. "Zheng Jing and I have never been friends. On our very first meeting, I had the impression he disliked me. At first, I thought it was because of my ties with the East India Company. If that were the case, then we should be fast friends now. I believe that it must be personal."

Captain Groot grunted before slamming his empty glass down. "I cannot get away from McCarr unless I bring him evidence of Zheng Jing's smuggling."

"You aren't the only one." I realized for the first time the plan might fail. What else would McCarr have me do to protect my father's reputation?

"We have to find the ship he's sending the tea on." Captain Groot nodded his head. He turned and stared at me. "I like the idea of us becoming partners in the future, but I must help McCarr in every way possible or face ruination."

"It must be one of his mediator clients," I muttered as I thought. "He is connected with a wealth of dangerous men."

"Zheng Jing is smart. This I know. Whoever is smuggling his tea into Europe will be above suspicion." Captain Groot's voice held a note of certainty.

"He has many honest clients," I said thinking of Charlotte. She was using the Chong brother's as her mediators through Zheng Jing. "I will make some inquiries."

"I would speak to other ship captains." Captain Groot waved a hand in the air vaguely.

"None of them will speak to you for fear they're aiding the enemy," I said with a tight smile. "All we have to do is bring in the highest profit, and suddenly, everyone will want to befriend you."

"Ja, ja." Captain Groot looked older than he had the previous evening. "For now, we all have our parts to play."

Standing up, I held out a hand. "I will let you know if I find anything."

He took my offered hand in a biting grip. "Do not seek to undermine me with McCarr. The Dutch may be fading in Java and Malacca, but we still have bite."

"Noted." I increased my grip on his hand. "I am my father's son, so do not forget it." I released his hand and walked out of the captain' cabin. On deck, I nearly collided with Zheng Jing.

"Evening, Mr. Hawk. Are you here on final business?" Zheng Jing asked nosily. I had a feeling he was only onboard to catch Captain Groot and me colluding.

"My business does not concern you." I stepped around the other man. "I'd wish you a good evening, but I wouldn't want to lie."

Zheng Jing stopped. "Most men would be afraid of me and what I can do."

The air between us grew thick with anticipation. We might finally have the fight I had been dreaming about for months. "What can you do that should frighten me?"

The other man smiled like a man who believed he held all the cards. "I am going to tell you something, Mr. Hawk. Something very few people know, but many have speculated over." He cleared his throat and paused for effect. "The Brotherhood exists, and I have spies everywhere. I know what happens in this port before everyone else."

"I'm not afraid of you or the Brotherhood," I murmured. "You work in secrets and lies. Eventually, you will be found out as a villain."

"You know nothing." Zheng Jing's eyes narrowed. "If you knew what I'm capable of, you would not still be standing here taunting me."

"Mr. Zheng Jing." Captain Groot's voice sounded from behind me. "What a surprise."

"Not as unexpected as I would like." Zheng Jing sniffed and stepped around me. Our sleeves brushed in the confined space. "One day I will teach you to know your betters," he threw over his shoulder. My hands clenched at his words, and it took all my willpower not to turn and punch the other man in the back of the head. I did not fight fair. My father taught me to win a fight, not to pander to some outdated notion of chivalry.

Without thinking, I left the ship under the watchful eye of the Dutch crew. I wondered what most of them thought about being here in an enemy port.

"Mr. Hawk," a familiar and unwelcome voice rang out on the wharf once I stepped onto the wooden planks.

"Mr. Meacham." I had not forgiven him or his wife for causing problems between Charlotte and me. Logically, I knew the blame was my own for letting my inner desires become public, but I could still hate inveterate gossips.

"Damned unpatriotic of you to trade with the Dutch." Mr. Meacham's voice carried in the semi-darkness.

"So I have been told by numerous individuals." I did not stop to address Meacham formally. Instead, I continued toward the shore. He rushed to catch up.

"What would your father think?" he asked boldly.

"Again, I have been asked that same question." I thought seriously about what my father might think. Too many people had told me that I didn't know him. "I have no idea. He was not a businessman, so I don't suppose he would understand."

"Using the Dutch instead of honest Englishmen to transport your goods to and from Europe will never work." Meacham shook his head as we reached the shore. "The Dutch will cheat you at every turn."

"You must look forward to my demise with relish." I turned toward the Thistlewaite and Hawk warehouse. "A good evening to you."

"No good can come of any this, Mr. Hawk." He called out after me. "The company is watching." The company was watching; the Brotherhood was watching. I felt like the most watched man in Singapore.

"Nathaniel, you're out late this evening." Finlayson stood at the door to the warehouse.

"I'm out late most evenings, Finlayson. What has you guarding the doors?" I asked, looking past him. Had he been spying on me since our escape from Collaart last year? Or had he only taken up his orders in Calcutta?

"We have finished loading the Dutch ship's cargo, and they're preparing to sail in the morning." Finlayson nodded toward the wharf. I stood beside him. "But you must know this already. I'm waiting for the final manifests."

I grunted in response and stepped away from him. Turning back after a few feet, I said, "How could you ever think I would join an organization that was run by that mad man?"

Finlayson turned around and stared at me, his expression going blank. "I don't know what you mean."

"Zheng Jing is a liability if you have plans for the Brotherhood." I watched as his face relaxed.

"He's not the leader of the Brotherhood." Finlayson shook his head.

"Someone had better remind him of it, and they had better tell him I'm not one to play games." Turning, I spotted Hindly at the top of the stairs. "Hindly, I need some information." Workers moved around the boxes of cargo, and I watched them as they finished their jobs for the evening. Who else was feeding Zheng Jing his information?

"Yes, sir." Hindly came up in front of me.

"I need to know everyone the Chong brothers are working with this season." He looked like he wanted to protest. "I realize this is the busiest time of the year for you, but it's a matter of grave importance."

"Yes, Mr. Hawk." Hindly rubbed his face. "I have some contacts with the other lads. I believe I can find out something tonight down the tap."

"Good lad." I slapped him on the shoulder and watched as he returned to his duties.

"Why don't you come out and say it?" Finlayson's voice was grave behind me.

"The man you claimed killed Cornelius Thistlewaite could not have done the job." I had my suspicions on the night, but I refused to say anything. Looking at Finlayson now, I felt stupid and betrayed.

"I assure you the Chong brothers were quite insistent," Finlayson argued back; tightness around his eyes the only sign he might be in distress.

"This is not public knowledge, but footpads did not murder Sarah Buck." Suspicion was still on Charlotte's involvement in the killings. I knew her. Deep down in my gut, I knew her better than myself. She would never cause anyone harm, even her enemies. "The killing wound was the same as the one Cornelius suffered. A bit too much of a coincidence for my liking."

"Some are saying your wife had her killed." Finlayson's voice was flat.

"There are those who still believe the earth is flat." My voice grew hard. "I consider us friends. You saved my life once, and I have put up with this Brotherhood nonsense from you since Calcutta." My features grew harder, my stance readying for battle. "You have to make a choice. You can either stay loyal to me, or you can stay loyal to the Brotherhood. Despite all your assurances that the Brotherhood is some goodwill group only looking for the betterment of their members, all I see is a bunch of men with tattoos on their arms working for men like Zheng Jing. If you're not here in the morning, I know what choice you made."

Finlayson only stared at me as I walked away. I felt his eyes on my back. There was a time I would have trusted him with my life, but the past few months had proven people change. Their loyalties move to other people. I thought I could sway him from the Brotherhood, but he only appeared to make his connections stronger.

With quick steps, I watched the ships moored in the harbor turn with the current, waiting for their berths. It would be a bigger season than last year. The profits made from this port were bottomless. Next year, there would be more traders and ships. The deal I made with Captain Groot was smart. It was far better to keep expanding, and why not do that with someone I knew was not be a member of the Brotherhood.

The sign for Carstairs and Son loomed ahead, and I nodded to the familiar guard at the door before going inside. Bigham stood staring at a stack of boxes that reached high above his head. He held an unlit pipe in his hands.

"I've got some rather fine tobacco," I called out as I approached. The other man jumped and turned at the same time. His face changed from startled to weary when he recognized me.

"Mr. Hawk, I wasn't expecting you this evening." He paused for a second. "Is Mrs. Hawk…" he let his question hang in the air between us.

"She is supposed to be resting under the doctor's orders, but we both know it will not last much longer." I smiled thinking I couldn't keep Charlotte from what she wanted to do for long. I reached into my pants pocket and pulled out a small package of tobacco I had delivered from Virginia not long ago.

"Charlotte was excited to be having the child." Bigham's voice was hesitant. "I'm sorry for your loss." He accepted the small package and sniffed the contents in appreciation. Without hesitation, he stuffed his pipe.

I was sorry too, for so many things. "In the past, there have been misunderstandings between us." I hesitated for a second. As soon as Charlotte had looked me in the eyes that day and told me she was losing our child, I knew. The baby could never have been Bigham's. Charlotte had remained faithful to me, and I had hardly done the same for her. "I hope we can put the past behind us." I pulled out my pipe as he handed the pouch back to me.

"We all need to get through this trading season." He cleared his throat before setting a taper he had lit to the end of his pipe. Bigham coughed a few times as he enjoyed the smoke. "I assume you will want to keep as much of the business out of Charlotte's hands while she recovers."

"On the contrary." I took the taper and lit my pipe. Letting the relaxing smells of vanilla and cognac fill the air around me. "She needs the distraction, and it's true: I am buying Carstairs and Son to keep an eye on the business. Not because I don't think she can handle her affairs, but because it's the only way I can be sure she's safe." Nodding to Bigham, I said, "I'll rely on you to keep her on an even keel. There's more to the story of Frederick losing the debt money than either of you are telling me. Waiting for her to trust me is placing us all in danger." After a short pause, I added, "Soon you will have no choice as my employee. You will have to divulge everything, you know."

"You're going to keep me on?" Bigham looked at me with surprise; the grip on the pipe he was holding slackened.

"I won't lie." For the first time, I felt no animosity toward him. "The first thing I was planning on doing when I officially took over was to get rid of you. Even though I know you're a damn fine trader and have been propping up Carstairs for years." Shrugging my shoulders, I added, "But I have seen the error of my ways."

Bigham went back to smoking his pipe. "I was looking for new positions. It was impossible to leave Mrs. Hawk, under the circumstances this past year, but with you taking over, I thought she would be..." He thought over his next words for a minute. "Retiring early."

"She'll be free to run the business as she sees fit," I said and tapped the ash out of the bottom of the hot pipe. "As long as I'm kept apprised of everything that's happening."

"You should know we have Frederick down here every day." Perhaps my talk with him had gotten through his thick skull. "Mrs. Hawk and I agreed to keep him out of the office, but he hauls goods and does grunt work with the rest of the sailors. I think he's trying to prove something."

"He's proving he can be a man," I said thinking of Frederick. All he needed was the proper motivation. "Is there anything I need to pass on to Mrs. Hawk? That's the real reason I stopped here this evening."

"Tell her the first ships are full and heading back to Europe." Bigham let a grin stretch across his face. "We did well, but not as well as the bloke who got in with the Dutch. Bloody mastermind, he is."

"You don't condemn me?" I asked bringing my brows together. "You must know most of Singapore thinks I'm a traitor."

"The other half of Singapore is saluting you." Bigham thought for a moment. "Quietly, of course. The rest are only jealous. The East India Company has kept their monopolies for too long."

"Good luck getting any tea trade out of the Chinese; the company has them under their complete control." A shadow passed over Bigham's face. It was fleeting, but I watched as he put a smile on his face. "They can't keep it all to themselves."

"One day. Good evening, Mr. Bigham." I turned and walked toward the door.

"Good evening, Mr. Hawk," he called out after me.

Somehow Zheng Jing had maneuvered Charlotte into smuggling the tea into England. I knew it as surely as I knew Cornelius was dead. It was time she confided in me. I thought of all the ways I could convince her to give up her secrets. Perhaps the best way to loosen her tongue was to loosen mine. I had not told her of the deal I made with McCarr because I thought I was protecting her. But I was only protecting myself; I didn't trust her enough with the secret. It was time to put my faith to the test. She would either betray me or give me the information I needed to rid myself of Zheng Jing and McCarr.

Walking through the European Quarter, I hoped she was still awake. None of the people I knew acknowledged me as I passed; they were too afraid of what might happen to them should they be seen with the traitor. All the lights in the upper rooms of the house were lit up. I wondered for a brief second if she was leaving me again. Perhaps all her words from a few hours ago were for nothing, and she still wanted a divorce. I wouldn't think this way. Instead, I would speak with her and tell her she was never leaving me.

It only took a minute to rush into the house. I could hear Charlotte's voice. She was singing. I stood at the bottom of the steps and listened to her for a minute. Curious, I went up the stairs, following her lyrical voice. She was standing in the spare room. Her body turned away from me. She slowly rocked back and forth, keeping her voice steady. She had finally gone mad under the pressure of running Carstairs and Son and losing the baby.

A baby's gurgling broke into my thoughts, and I stood in the doorway stunned. Charlotte must have noticed my presence because she turned around and looked at me, a guilty look crossing her face.

"Nathaniel, would you like to hold your son?" she asked and held the baby up.

"We lost our son, Charlotte," I said suspiciously, certain I would not like the answer to my next question. "Where did this baby come from?"

Charlotte sighed and looked at me for another second before she cooed down in the child's face. "He's your son by Sarah Buck. I had to take him away from the woman who was supposed to be taking care of him." She looked back at me with pleading eyes. They begged me to understand why she had committed this unbelievable social misstep. "The maid was smoking opium when I arrived, and he was screaming up in his room alone. Surely, you can understand he needs better care."

"We can find somewhere else for him to stay," I said stubbornly, looking at the squirming bundle. "But you must understand why we cannot keep him. Everyone will say you're raising the child of my mistress. Besides, we will never know if he's mine or not."

"He's yours, Nathaniel," Charlotte stated with conviction and nodded her head when I opened my mouth. "He has your eyes, Nathaniel. Unless your father also shared a bed with Sarah, he is yours. The resemblance is astonishing."

"We can send him to England to be raised by a real family until he can go to school." I worked it out in my mind. There were always couples around who wanted children but have none. I could give them a tidy sum of money to raise the child. "Charlotte, we need a fresh start. This child will only continue to put a wedge between us. How will we ever move on if he is here as a constant reminder of my past indiscretions?"

"Perhaps I would have seen him as such in the past. But now..." She stopped for a minute to adjust the bundle in her arms. I knew she was thinking of her perfect little boy, born far too early to survive in this hard world. "I believe he is an extension of you. He's perfect and innocent, and we must shelter and love him. Who else knows better how cruel the world can be?"

"Charlotte, we can make sure he has a good life from afar," I argued, and her chin grew stubborn.

"I don't want to fight with you over him." She clutched him to her chest for a couple of breaths. "Hold him. Hold your son and look into his eyes and then tell me you want to send him away." She held out the bundle in her hands.

"This is a terrible idea. Do not force me," I said as she took a step closer. A tiny face peered out of the blankets, staring at me with a look of curiosity. Charlotte thrust the bundle at me, and I had to grab him before she let go. I peered down into the pink face. His eyes caught my own, and I exhaled slowly. Up until this moment, I never believed he was mine, but those eyes could not lie. He was a Hawk.

Looking up, I saw Charlotte smile. "He is perfect. Dutta has already found a wet nurse for him. We can do this."

"What if Sarah Buck's father decides he wants the child?" I glanced down at the baby whose golden eyes had begun to shut lazily.

"We will tell him that option is no longer available. The child is ours now." Charlotte's voice held a note of triumph. She smiled for the first time in months. The sight warmed my heart, and I found myself rocking back and forth with the child in my arms.

"This is not permanent, Charlotte. I will write to a few people I know back in England. We will find him a loving home, and we will try again for our child." I made my words firm.

Charlotte smiled and kissed me. The natural affection surprised me, but I did not pull away. Instead, I leaned into the kiss, wanting more, taking everything she had to offer. Only the child in my arms stopped me from pulling Charlotte's gown off and making love to her on the empty bed.

She ended the kiss and carefully took the sleeping baby out of my arms. Without missing a step, she turned and placed the infant in a wooden crib that was standing near the end of the bed. She pulled the mosquito netting over the top. "Thank you." She wrapped her arms around me and placed her head on my chest.

A feeling of contentment filled my gut, and I put my arms around her, resting my chin on the top of her head. I wanted to spin this moment out longer, but I was out of time.

I had to tell her of the deal I made with McCarr and my haphazard pursuit of Zheng Jing. If I wanted her honesty, then I must start with my own. We were partners once. It was time to be partners again.

Chapter 32
Charlotte

Nathaniel took my hand in his and led me down the hall to the master bedroom. He kissed each of my hands before closing the door. Instead of turning and motioning toward the bed, he went straight to the large winged chair set in the corner of the room and sat down. He undid the top buttons of his shirt and ran a hand through his hair.

I followed him to the small nook and sat in the chair opposite. Only a small table rested between us, and I took my time arranging my skirts before I looked back up at him again. Apprehension made my heart pound furiously as I waited for him to speak.

"In Calcutta, I made a deal with a man named McCarr." Nathaniel exhaled and waved a hand in the air. "He is a lord of something or other, but he wishes to be known as Mr. Salcombe." Nathaniel frowned. "I am making a hash of this."

"No." I reached out and touched his arm. He did not pull away as I expected. Instead, he smiled at me. "Just tell me as best you can."

"Lord Hastings is on his way out they say. He needed a reason to lay blame for the loss of the Diligence and some other accounting discrepancies on father." Nathaniel took a deep breath. "The problem was that if Hastings discredited him outright, all the work my father did might come under speculation, especially all the fighting he did against the enemies of England and the company."

"They wanted to discredit him, without actually making any accusation," I said, trying to understand.

"Yes." Nathaniel's shoulder slumped. "McCarr told me he would have the company look elsewhere to lay blame if I did a service for the company." My gut grew cold as I thought of what kind of service the company might need. "They asked me to find evidence of a tea smuggling ring here in Singapore." I gasped involuntarily, and Nathaniel stared at me. "They're already investigating Zheng Jing and the Brotherhood. All I need to do is provide the proof they needed."

"The Dutch," I asked in a choked whisper.

Nathaniel appeared to make up his mind about something. "Captain Groot is working for McCarr, as well." He smiled for the first time this evening. "Not that I'm not making a tidy profit off him. Mutually beneficial spying, I suppose."

"Does the company have any leads as to whom Zheng Jing is using to ship the tea?" I asked cautiously.

"I have no idea." Nathaniel sat back in his chair and squeezed his eyes shut. "McCarr told me I was responsible for finding the name of the smuggling ships, but for all I know, he could have other men doing the same thing or know the names already." Nathaniel opened his eyes. "I have been honest with you in the hopes you'll be frank with me. There is more to the story of Frederick losing the debt money. I want you to trust me."

Right in front of me was the rest of our lives written out. What I said in the next moment would sculpt the people we would become. I had to lie. Not only to protect me but to protect Nathaniel. The company already knew Zheng Jing was the tea smuggler. Tomorrow my ships would leave port with a belly full of contraband. If anyone else knew but me, they would hang right beside me. I cursed my fate and my brother, as I yearned to have a future with the man sitting in front of me.

"I want to trust you," I said, thinking of Cornelius and Sarah Buck. They had both found out my secret, and now they were both dead. "I owe money to the Chinese lenders. They have made certain threats if I'm unable to come up with the payments." So far not an outright lie, I was merely bending the truth. "Father wanted to beg the money from you." I shook my head, and real tears of frustration came to my eyes. "But I couldn't. I didn't want our marriage to begin with me needing something from you. Mr. Bigham and I have worked over the past few months to keep up with the payments, but the interest is crippling." I took a deep breath realizing for the first time how much of a burden I was carrying. "We were made to use to the Chong brothers as our intermediaries, even though everyone knows they're crooks." I buried my face in my hands.

Nathaniel's arms came around me, and I melted into his embrace. "My love, I'm sorry you thought you had to hide this burden from me. I know the past few months have been hard, but we can get through the rest of our lives if only we trust each other. Let me try and fix the problem with the moneylenders. Is that why you didn't want your father to sell me Carstairs and Son?"

With his gentle coaxing, I let my hands fall away from my face. "Yes. I didn't want to see you burdened with the same worries. My father would have happily sold you the company with the debt still attached."

"What of your brother?" Nathaniel asked seriously.

I shook my head. "He knows we're in big trouble, but he has become surprisingly noble in the past few weeks. I suspect I have you to thank for his showing up at the warehouse every morning, sober and ready for work."

"We might have had a small discussion on his responsibilities." Nathaniel used his thumbs to wipe my tears away. "I wouldn't trust him with anything more important than a mop and bucket."

Laughing shakily at the thought of my brother swabbing the floors, I said, "Not to worry, Mr. Bigham has learned his lesson and so have I."

Nathaniel kissed me. It was a sweet brushing of his lips against mine before he pulled away. A soft knock on the door stopped him from leaning down again.

"What is it?" Frustration made his tone guttural.

"There is a messenger downstairs. He says the message is urgent." Dutta's voice floated through the portal.

Swearing under his breath, Nathaniel looked at me with regret filling his eyes. "I have to go. This might be the information I need to end Zheng Jing."

I nodded, doing my best to keep the frown from my face. "You go. I will be here when you get back."

He took my chin in between his thumb and forefinger and kissed me soundly. "Let me take care of your worries for a little while, Charlotte. Get some rest." Nathaniel gave me a lopsided grin. "We have a baby in the house now." He stood up and walked out of the door, closing it behind him.

Looking around the familiar room, it hadn't taken me long to feel at home in the bachelor space. My gowns hung in the wardrobe beside Nathanial's clothes, and my perfumes sat next to his shaving kit on the washstand. Even though we had been living separate lives all these months, we still lived together. I sat back in my chair and tried to think of my options.

Nathaniel knew far more about Zheng Jing's business than I ever imagined. How long would it take for him to find out the truth? I took a long, shaky breath. He could be off to find out right now. Sitting back in the chair, I cursed myself for the hundredth time. My husband might be walking into a trap because I was too stubborn to tell him of my connection with Zheng Jing. Unfortunately, if he knew all my business, he could hang.

Slipping from the chair, I hurried over to the wardrobe and pulled out a black shawl. Tying it around my head and shoulders to obscure my features, I opened the door to the hallway. Low voices reached me from the back of the house. Doing my best not to make a sound, I swiftly went down the stairs and crept out the door. Calming my breath, I went out the front gate and stood in the shadows of a large tree.

From here, I had a clear view of the house. When Nathaniel emerged, I would follow him on his errand and make sure he was safe. At least I could warn him if someone was trying to attack him from behind.

It had felt like an hour before Nathaniel emerged following a young boy. I waited until they had turned down the street, then followed them, hoping neither one of them would notice me. It was always busy on the streets of Singapore during the Junk season. Sailors, merchants, and traders from countries all over the world were in port to soak up some of the exotic atmosphere. I had not forgotten my warning about how vulnerable I was as a woman, so tried to stay out of the men's way.

Instead of turning left toward the wharves and the big warehouses, Nathaniel and his guide continued to head for the drawbridge over the river. My stomach clenched with nerves. Should I follow him over the bridge into the Chinese Campong? As far as I knew, Zheng Jing controlled most of the port through his connections in the Brotherhood, but he had ultimate power on the other side of the river. If I crossed the bridge, he would know immediately. Unfortunately, he would also know that Nathaniel had passed over, too.

With a mind to rush and catch up with Nathaniel, to tell him of the danger he was in once and for all, I pushed my legs to move faster. He was too far ahead of me, and I lost him in the crush of people, carts and bullocks trying to negotiate the bridge this evening. Before I could even shout his name, he was halfway across, listening intently to something the boy was saying.

A nervous frenzy suddenly gripped me, and I twisted and turned trying to get through the crowd to my husband. It was imperative that I speak to Nathaniel. The dread I had been carrying inside me since Cornelius's death, which had been immeasurably amplified by Sarah Buck's death, pounded in an uneven rhythm in my chest. In my heart, I knew if I did not speak to him right away, something terrible would happen.

My slippers crunched in the dirt on the opposite side of the river, and I searched left and right for any sign of my husband. I watched as Nathaniel's back disappeared around the corner of a building not too far ahead of me. Dodging around men and carts, I picked up my pace to catch him. The thought of Nathaniel and me living the rest of our lives together thrummed through me. All I needed to do was keep him safe tonight. I turned down the same street he had disappeared on and watched as he stayed just out of my reach.

We twisted through alleys and streets until I became completely muddled. I broke into a run to try and catch him, panic giving my feet wings until I recklessly threw my body around a corner and hit a solid wall. Except this wall had two arms and they both went around me. For a second, relief flooded through me. I thought perhaps Nathaniel had realized someone was following him in a haphazard fashion, and chosen to investigate. Looking up, I was disappointed, but recognition flashed across my brain.

"Mr. Finlayson." I tried to catch my breath. "Will you beg my pardon? I am on some urgent business."

"I know, Charlotte." His voice held a deep note of sympathy. I looked into his eyes, and for the first time, I felt strangely afraid of the young man who had saved Nathaniel's life last year. He shook his head and grimaced. "I really cannot allow you to complete your business. I wished to God you hadn't left your house this evening."

Opening my mouth to ask him what he meant, I was cut off by a searing pain in my chest. Looking down, I watched perversely as the knife slid into my dress, blood already staining the front. My eyes flew to Finlayson's face. Terrible regret marred his features, and I felt his arms take my slackening weight from my legs.

"It's done now, lovely Charlotte." He laid me on the ground, but I could not yell or speak. All my breath came in short, painful stabs. "I will take care of Nathaniel, I promise." Finlayson's voice sounded very far away, and I wanted to scream.

Chapter 33
Nathaniel

"Boy!" I shouted at the urchin who had been taking me in circles through the Chinese Campong for the last few minutes. "Stop!" He jogged back to me. "Do you know where you're going or have you been paid to mislead me deliberately?" The big dark eyes of the child widened, and I cursed under my breath. "I suppose you cannot reveal the name of the person who paid you?"

"No, uncle," the boy said solemnly. Whoever had targeted me chose their errand boy with care. They knew I would not harm a child.

"I'm going home." I walked back the way I had come. The urchin raced to stand in front of me.

"Uncle, you cannot go back. You must go with me." He stepped in front of me when I tried to go around him.

"You admitted we're not going anywhere." Exasperation colored my voice, and I reached a hand out to shove the boy out of my way.

"This job is of very great importance." The boy grasped my sleeve and tried to pull me in the opposite direction.

Reaching into my pocket, I pulled out a small coin and held it out. "Here, so you don't feel cheated when your master doesn't pay you for a job well done."

The boy shook his head. "This is more important than money."

"I'm not playing the game with you any longer." I reached out and grabbed the boy by his shoulders and forced him from my path. Here I was, waylaid by an urchin. I needed to get home to Charlotte. Before I left the house, I sensed I was finally getting through to her. For the first time in months, I had finally made some progress. By the look on her face, Zheng Jing had been using Carstairs and Son to smuggle his tea. If I was right, I could maybe shield her from the worst of the company's wrath.

Listening to the boy's determined steps as I trudged my way back through the darkened alleys and streets, I wondered why anyone would want me wandering around the port at night. Ahead, a lantern from inside a shanty spilled a column of light onto the ground. A pile of refuse caught my eye until I noticed a pair of slippers. Surging forward toward the slippers and petticoats, I thought of the vulnerable women who could not get employment at the gaming hells or whorehouses.

The sight that met my eyes had me stumbling forward onto my knees. Charlotte's beloved face was stark white. Her beautiful violet eyes stared into the night, unseeing. A guttural cry erupted into the air near me as I lifted her precious head and held it to my shoulder. A thousand thoughts screamed across my brain. I looked down into her empty face and slackened jaw, hoping I had been wrong.

Looking down, I noticed the red stain on her dress, and I held a hand over it. The handle of a knife protruded from a wound in her chest. The incision would have struck into her heart, giving her only a few moments of life before she bled out. Even if I had been standing next to her, I couldn't save her.

I cradled her in my arms and let my tears fall into her hair. It smelled of jasmine, and I choked at the thought of never seeing it pulled by the wind again. Why was she down here? Had she followed me? If so, why?

"My darling Charlotte, I am so sorry. I wish I could have been better for you, but I was afraid. Always fear kept us apart." I sobbed out my anguish. A shadow fell across my face, but I ignored it. If I stayed like this, then the reality of Charlotte's death would not be real. I would not have to live my life without her, which suddenly seemed long and endlessly alone.

"Nathaniel." A voice I recognized spoke with urgency. "You must come with me now."

"Finlayson." My voice croaked out. "It's Charlotte. This is Charlotte."

"I know." He sighed and did not move. "You must come with me now, Nathaniel. There is no way to hold back the tide now."

Angrily I looked up and stared into the barrel of a primed pistol. "What are you about, Finlayson? She's my wife. I'm hardly going to leave her body in a stinking alley."

"I'm very sorry for your loss, Nathaniel." Finlayson brought another pistol around. "But I really must insist you come with me at once."

"Why are you here?" I asked as I eased Charlotte's body to the ground. The handle of the knife rubbed against my chest, and I stopped for a breath. Lifting the knife from her body, I slipped it into my sleeve and let the blade press into my skin. Laying Charlotte down on the filthy ground of the street, I smoothed the hair away from her face.

"Don't worry, Nathaniel, the boy will make sure nothing defiles her body." Finlayson used one of the pistols to motion for me to stand. "Come, now. I don't want to have to harm you."

I stood up hoping he would not see the knife. Charlotte's blood covered me, and I hoped it was all the other man could see. "Would you kill me, Finlayson? I believed we were friends."

"We are friends." Finlayson sighed. "So much of this could have been avoided if you had only joined the Brotherhood back in Calcutta."

"I would never do the bidding of your master Zheng Jing." I held my arms out to my sides and meant my next words. "You had better shoot me now."

"There is so much for you to learn." Finlayson sighed and motioned to the end of the alley. "Mr. Zheng Jing is not my master."

"Who is your master?" I spat out ready to take the lead from Finlayson's pistol rather than leave Charlotte behind.

Finlayson blinked once and nodded. I felt two sets of hands grapple with my arms. Not willing to give up, I wrestled and shouted until I felt an explosion of pain in the back of skull. Stars and darkness filled my vision, and my knees went limp.

"Where are we going?" My voice was sluggish and sounded very far away as the men dragged me in the direction Finlayson indicated to the two men.

"You'll know soon enough." Finlayson's voice floated from behind me. My feet shuffled underneath me, but the two big men kept up a quick pace. The Chinese Campong might be a Brotherhood stronghold, but it appeared Finlayson did not want to be caught dragging a half-unconscious man around the streets.

The path we walked along led away from the shanties, and I could see the shoreline ahead. A skiff, pulled up on shore, waited for us, and the men pushed me into the bottom of the boat. I looked up and recognized the two sailors who had rowed us out to the gypsy camp. Neither of them acknowledged me as I stopped in front of the boat.

"I suppose our direction is no surprise." Finlayson prodded me in the back with one of the pistols.

"Are you even a member of the Brotherhood?" I sat on the backbench. Finlayson sat stiffly beside me. Once the sailors had pushed the skiff away from the shore, he relaxed and tucked his pistols away inside his coat."

"In your position, I would have had many more questions." Finlayson turned his head to stare at me. We jerked forward as the oars pulled us through the water, the current high at this time of night.

"Perhaps I am silenced by your betrayal," I returned.

Finlayson laughed. "Knowing you as I do, Hawk, you're contemplating making an audacious escape." He shook his head, serious once again. "I wouldn't attempt it. There is nowhere for you to run." His brows drew together. "Nor is there any reason for you to do so." He appeared so damned sincere. Wherever he was taking me, and whomever I was meeting had convinced him, I was safe.

The sailors continued to row, and I caught sight of the lights in the gypsy camp once again. I remained silent as thoughts turned over in my head. If I wanted to escape from the gypsy camp, I would have to make my way through the jungle at night back to Singapore. There was no way I could handle this size skiff on my own.

I followed Finlayson out of the skiff, and we splashed in the knee high surf until we reached the sandy beach. The two sailors labored to pull our dinghy onto the beach next to another boat of similar size. Finlayson looked over the other craft and inhaled deeply.

"It looks like everyone is here," he said cryptically and motioned with his hand to the same trail through the jungle. Finlayson did not take out his pistols. "There are at least a dozen eyes on us, Nathaniel. If you try to run, I cannot vouch for your safety."

Taking care to watch my steps, I tried to search through the dense undergrowth of the jungle. It would be very easy to hide among the lush ferns and foliage. My best bet was to keep moving once an opportunity arose.

We walked into the same village where I last saw the man the Brotherhood had told me killed Cornelius. Whoever he was and wherever he went, he was not the killer. Not after hearing of Sarah Buck's wound and seeing Charlotte's with my own eyes. Charlotte. She was long gone from this world, and yet, I could hardly believe it. I spent too much time fighting with her. Now, I could never make it up to her.

A fire had burned at the end of the village. I looked left and right, but there was no chance of a clean escape. It looked as though I had no choice but to meet with this unknown person As we approached, I saw a man throw something into the fire.

"You little liar," I said under my breath. "I don't know why I'm not surprised. You've been working for Zheng Jing this entire time." Before Finlayson could respond, Zheng Jing looked up from the flames.

"Hawk," he said with a bite in his voice. "I might have known this was your doing."

"I think we both know who the ringleader of this fiasco is." I rushed forward. "Did you have my wife killed, you bastard?" I shouted as a pair of muscular arms came around my middle. Another pair grabbed onto one of my arms. "I am going to kill you with my bare hands."

"In fact, I don't think either of you know why you're truly here." A man stepped out of the shadows and into the light. The glare from the fire blinded me, and I thought I saw my father standing only feet away from me.

"Father?" My voice was a hushed whisper. The man chuckled and came into view.

"No," he said as he stood with his hands on hips. "The resemblance can be striking, and I have to say I was curious to know if you thought I was your father last year."

"You're the captain of the ghost ship." I gasped. "You killed my friends. Did you kill my father?"

"I was one of the captains of the ghost ship." The man nodded without any embarrassment. "But I don't think we should discuss family matters in front of outsiders." He looked pointedly at Zheng Jing.

"You have no idea who you're dealing with," Zheng Jing said in clipped tone. "I'm a very important man. You had better release me before my men come to find me."

"Mr. Zheng Jing," the other man began. "You were a very important man; however, you have now become troublesome. The Brotherhood does not like trouble. Nor do they like to be cheated." Zheng Jing's face grew pale. "Yes, we know of your little scheme. You have been making money on the side with tea stolen from us." The man shook his head. "You should never steal from a thief, Zheng Jing; we have terrible ways of demanding our pound of flesh."

The expression on Zheng Jing's face became stark "Who are you?"

"I am the man who has ordered your death," the man said with a nod to Finlayson. Without hesitation, Finlayson removed one of the pistols from its hiding place and shot Zheng Jing between the eyes. Zheng Jing didn't even have time to blink before his body crumpled to the ground.

After living on my father's ship and the time I spent fighting Captain Collaart last year, I had seen many dead bodies in my life. Some in the heat of battle and others through sickness, but for some reason, the cool efficiency of Zheng Jing's dispatch sent a chill down my spine. I looked at the unknown man. He was familiar in many ways, and yet so cold and calculating.

"Who the hell are you?" I felt the hidden blade in my sleeve. He might kill me, but I would take either him or Finlayson with me.

The man finished his inspection of Zheng Jing's body and gave me a broad smile. "I have been waiting many years for this introduction." He stepped forward. "I'm your half-brother. Henry Cornwall." He held out his hand, and I stared at it dumbly.

Shaking my head a few times, I took the proffered hand automatically. The other man's callused fingers gripped mine tightly. "I suppose I shouldn't be shocked. Father was..." I realized I was about to make his mother sound like a whore and stopped.

He let go of my hand and chuckled. "No need to spare my feelings, little brother. I am well aware of our father's proclivities."

"Little brother?" I asked, still trying to absorb everything.

"Yes," he snorted. "My mother is a member of the upper crust back in England. She and Father fell in love, but before they could be married, he sailed away. She was pregnant with me." Cornwall gave me a self-deprecating smile. "Her family was appalled, and after I was born, I was sent away to live with a well-to-do merchant family while she married into another noble family willing to look past her moral lapse."

"Where is our father?" I stumbled on the word 'our.'"

The smile fell away from Cornwall's face. "I'm sorry if you were hoping to have a reunion with Father. I know of your strained relationship with him for many years." His face grew pensive, and he looked into the distance.

"We were not always on the best of terms," I said.

There was a moment of silence before he continued. "He's dead. It was always his plan to scuttle the Diligence. Unfortunately, the rest of his plan lacked imagination. He needed me to take it forward."

"You killed Sebastian Hawk?" I choked out.

He was silent.

"Did you kill Cornelius Thistlewaite? My wife?" There was nothing I could do to stop the hysterical note in my voice. My vision was starting to narrow, and I felt rage bubbling up inside me.

"Not by my hands." Cornwall glanced at Finlayson. Cold betrayal infused my chest, and I could hardly swallow the bile rising in my throat. "I have men to do that for me."

"Charlotte. That's why you were in the alley. You killed my wife!" I shouted and lunged for Finlayson. He quickly sidestepped me, and I was grabbed around the waist and hauled back.

"Your wife was an unfortunate victim of our brethren." Cornwall waved his hand to indicate Zheng Jing's corpse. "As you can see, I have seen your wife avenged."

I strained against the pair of arms that held me back. "You're a damned assassin! Why did you bother to save my life last year?" I railed at Finlayson.

He looked at Cornwall for approval before turning his attention back to me. "Your father wanted to protect you. He knew things would get out of hand in Singapore once the Diligence went down." He shook his head. "Although he thought he would still be alive." Finlayson shot Cornwall a look of anger. "He knew Raffles and Farquhar would never keep the peace. Your father entrusted me with your safety before he died."

"So you killed everyone around me?" I asked incredulously. "How is that protecting me?"

"Cornelius had stumbled upon Charlotte's secret." Cornwall took up the story. "And young Charlotte had a change of heart. She wanted to warn you of Zheng Jing. Unfortunately, they were loose ends the Brotherhood does not like to have, especially with non-members." A sheepish grin split Cornwall's face. "I must also admit to being jealous of your loyalty to them. We are family. You owe me the devotion you once heaped upon their unworthy heads."

"I begged you to join us." Finlayson's eyes held remorse. "Had you acceded to the Brotherhood, we would have protected Cornelius and Charlotte as proxy members. As it was, they could have ruined all our plans and sent good men to the gallows because of the greed of the East India Company."

"Let go of me." I stopped struggling, and the two men who had been holding my arms let go. "I will never forgive either of you for what has happened." I pointed the finger at Finlayson. "I will make sure you feel half the pain I do before I cut you like you did my wife."

"There is no need to make threats, Nathaniel." Cornwall appeared utterly unruffled by the evening's confessions. His eyes remained cold and distant. "Father had great plans for you. Now is your time to join us and stand with me. The Brotherhood and the two of us are his legacies, Nathaniel. Together there is nothing to stop us from taking on the corrupt power of the East India Company and winning."

"You're mad," I said, drawing a deep breath. "You can never win against the company. Don't you understand? They are England." I swiped a hand through the air. "I would never dishonor my wife's memory by cooperating with her murderer. You should kill me now."

"Why do you think father called his ultimate revenge against the East India Company the Brotherhood? It was for us." Cornwall's cold eyes lit up with fire. "He knew we could break the company and take the spoils."

"You sound like a pirate. Father fought against piracy his whole life." The blade hidden under the sleeve of my shirt gave me some comfort as I made my threats.

"He might have at the beginning before politics and bureaucracy threatened to ruin him and his men. Old Seb started the Brotherhood to protect men from the company. We continue that legacy." Cornwall's voice took on the edge of pompous severity.

"The only thing the Brotherhood is interested in is power. You killed our father for it, brother." I spat the last word out. "You might dress your intentions up in a noble cause, but at the end of it all, you're a pirate and a murderer. Nothing more than the captain of a rogue ship."

"I have hundreds of ships at my disposal, Nathaniel. You would do well to remember that as much as the East India Company believes they control the waves, I control the men on those waves." He took a couple of steps forward. "I would hate to kill one of my half-brothers. Especially you, Nathaniel, when I know you only need to see reason to join the cause. Father always said you were stubborn."

With a shake of my wrist, I palmed the handle of the knife that had killed my wife as I stared at the man who had ordered her death. Beyond the fire was the darkness of jungle, my best chance was to run and hope to find Singapore in the dark.

Taking a deep breath, I lashed out at Cornwall's face; hoping surprise was on my side. "I will never join the man who murdered my father and wife. I will hunt you down and kill you if it's my last act on this earth." Cornwall jumped back and held a hand to his bleeding face. I was disappointed the slash had not taken at least an eye. Unfortunately, I had no time to wallow in my disappointment. Jumping away from the fire, I ran into the jungle. I could hear Cornwall screaming at me and ordering his men and Finlayson to follow me.

Shots fired into the air, and I hit the ground with a thud. I tried to control my breathing as I looked around. Finlayson had said there were eyes watching everywhere and I believed him. Crouching down, I was thankful moist debris covered the ground.

"Nathaniel, there is nowhere for you to run." Cornwall's voice was close to the edge of the trees. "I own Singapore. Even if you make it back there, no one will help you," he shouted. "You have no choice, but to join me or die."

I resisted the urge to yell back and crawled on my hands and knees further into the undergrowth. I needed to try and get back to the water's edge and use the shore to make my way back to Singapore. Thrusting aside the worry of what I would do once I reached civilization, I stood up and began to run.

My lungs burned, and I tripped over debris on the jungle floor as I tried to get to the shoreline. My flight was less than stealthy, and I had to believe my brother and Finlayson were not far behind. This would be my only chance to run for freedom, and I was not going to give up. After interminable minutes I saw the flames flicker through the trees; the torches lit on the beach where we left the skiff. I could hear angry voices shouting. Looking to the west, I was preparing to move away from the landing beach when a hand clasped my shoulder.

"For the love of God, don't shout!" I recognized Hindly's voice.

"What the hell are you doing here?" My breath was raspy from trying to catch my breath.

"It's a long story, boss." He nodded toward a clump of trees, and I could make out the figures of several men. "When I started asking questions about the Chong brothers, Major Randall had me pulled into his office. While I was there, the man who was sent to watch your movements sent a message you were wandering around the Chinese Campong." Hindly shook his head. "I'm sorry about Mrs. Hawk."

Unable to comment on the loss, I looked around me. "Has Major Randall brought the whole garrison?" I asked. A loud report from the water made me cover my ears. It was a signal for the men in the jungle to begin their attack on the men on the beach. I started forward, but Hindly held me back.

"Wait, you don't want to get caught in the crossfire," Hindly said as men in red coats poured onto the beach. I stood up and watched. I saw Cornwall scramble and jump into a skiff while firing pistols back at the advancing soldiers. Finlayson was not far behind him. The boat fought against the tide, but with the help of a couple of burly sailors, it was soon pulling away.

I ran out onto the beach and watched my quarry row away. I swore under my breath and did not move until the little craft was out of sight.

"Mr. Hawk." Major Randall approached me. "I have a few questions for you."

Epilogue

"Singapore will be the less for your departure, Mr. Hawk." Dr. Crawfurd held out his hand.

"It's time for a fresh start," I said, thinking of the graves I had visited this morning. My gaze shifted to my infant son, swaddled in the arms of his nurse. Dutta hovered nervously behind her on the docks, while Hindly watched the workers load the rest of the cargo onto the ship bound for England. I took the other man's hand in a firm grip.

"You will always be welcome in Singapore." Dr. Crawfurd nodded his head and let go.

"The East holds no appeal for me any longer. My wife would have wanted our son raised in the safety of England. The climate is far better for the constitution of children." I gave the man a small smile.

"I understand," Dr. Crawfurd acknowledged. "Until we meet again."

"Indeed." I watched the other man walk down the wharf. The only way I would ever see Dr. Crawfurd again was if he came to England. I had no intentions of ever traveling to the East again. In many ways, my leaving was as bitter as Raffles's had been only months before. With my loved ones buried here, Singapore would never be far from my thoughts, but revenge against the man who took them from me took precedence. I knew the only way to track him down, was to hunt for him in the one place he would have trouble controlling. England was the heart of the East India Company and my new base for hunting down my brother.

Historical Note

Several Chinese friends have pointed out that they spell Campong with a K in reference to the Chinese Campong section of Singapore. I have chosen to use spelling used on maps commissioned by the British, as seen on Lieutenant Philip Jackson's 'Plan Town of Singapore', which is readily available on several internet sources.

www.ingramcontent.com/pod-product-compliance
Lightning Source LLC
Chambersburg PA
CBHW020922090426
42736CB00010B/998